Children's Literature in Translation

Texts and Contexts

Translation, Interpreting and Transfer

2

"Translation, Interpreting and Transfer" takes as its basis an inclusive view of translation and translation studies. It covers research and scholarly reflection, theoretical and methodological, on all aspects of the core activities of translation and interpreting, but also similar rewriting and recontextualization practices such as adaptation, localization, transcreation and transediting, keeping Roman Jakobson's inclusive view on interlingual, intralingual and intersemiotic translation in mind. The title of the series, which includes the more encompassing concept of transfer, reflects this broad conceptualization of translation matters.

Series editors
Luc van Doorslaer (KU Leuven / University of Tartu)
Haidee Kotze (Utrecht University)

Editorial board
Lieven D'hulst (KU Leuven)
Daniel Gile (University Paris 3, Sorbonne Nouvelle)
Sara Ramos Pinto (University of Leeds)

Advisory board
Pieter Boulogne (KU Leuven)
Elke Brems (KU Leuven)
Leo Tak-hung Chan (Lingnan University, Hong Kong)
Dirk Delabastita (University of Namur)
Dilek Dizdar (University of Mainz)
Yves Gambier (University of Turku)
Arnt Lykke Jakobsen (Copenhagen Business School)
Reine Meylaerts (KU Leuven)
Franz Pöchhacker (University of Vienna)
Heidi Salaets (KU Leuven)
Christina Schäffner (Aston University, Birmingham)

Children's Literature in Translation

Texts and Contexts

Edited by
Jan Van Coillie & Jack McMartin

LEUVEN UNIVERSITY PRESS

This book was published with the support of

KU Leuven Fund for Fair Open Access

and

Ceres – Centre for Reception Studies

Published in 2020 by Leuven University Press / Presses Universitaires de Louvain / Universitaire Pers Leuven. Minderbroedersstraat 4, B-3000 Leuven (Belgium).

Selection and editorial matter © Jan Van Coillie and Jack McMartin, 2020
Individual chapters © The respective authors, 2020

This book is published under a Creative Commons Attribution Non-Commercial Non-Derivative 4.0 Licence.

Further details about Creative Commons licences are available at
http://creativecommons.org/licenses/
Attribution should include the following information:
Jan Van Coillie and Jack McMartin (eds), *Children's Literature in Translation: Texts and Contexts*. Leuven, Leuven University Press. (CC BY-NC-ND 4.0)

ISBN 978 94 6270 222 6 (Paperback)
ISBN 978 94 6166 320 7 (ePDF)
ISBN 978 94 6166 326 9 (ePUB)
https://doi.org/10.11116/9789461663207
D/2020/1869/43
NUR: 617

Cover: Daniel Benneworth-Gray
Typesetting: Crius Group

Table of Contents

Contributors   7

Introduction: Studying texts and contexts in translated children's literature   11
Jan Van Coillie & Jack McMartin

Part 1   Context » Text

"Only English books": The mediation of translated children's literature in a resistant economy   41
Gillian Lathey

Two languages, two children's literatures: Translation in Ireland today   55
Emer O'Sullivan

Cultural translation and the recruitment of translated texts to induce social change: The case of the *Haskalah*   73
Zohar Shavit

Associative practices and translations in children's book publishing: Co-editions in France and Spain   93
Delia Guijarro Arribas

Translation and the formation of a Brazilian children's literature   111
Lia A. Miranda de Lima & Germana H. Pereira

Said, spoke, spluttered, spouted: The role of text editors in stylistic shifts in translated children's literature   125
Marija Zlatnar Moe & Tanja Žigon

Diversity can change the world: Children's literature, translation and images of childhood   141
Jan Van Coillie

Part 2 Text » Context

The creative reinventions of nonsense and domesticating the
implied child reader in Hungarian translations of *Alice's Adventures
in Wonderland*   159
Anna Kérchy

"Better watch it, mate" and "Listen 'ere, lads": The cultural
specificity of the English translation of Janusz Korczak's classic *Król
Maciuś Pierwszy*   179
Michał Borodo

Brazilian rewritings of Perrault's short stories: Nineteenth- and
twentieth-century versus twenty-first-century retellings and
consequences for the moral message   197
Anna Olga Prudente de Oliveira

Translating crossover picture books: The Italian translations of
Bear Hunt by Anthony Browne   215
Annalisa Sezzi

Pettson and Findus go glocal: Recontextualization of images
and multimodal analysis of simultaneous action in Dutch and
French translations   231
Sara Van Meerbergen & Charlotte Lindgren

Translating violence in children's picture books: A view from the
former Yugoslavia   249
Marija Todorova

Defying norms through unprovoked violence: The translation and
reception of two Swedish young adult novels in France   263
Valérie Alfvén

Index   277

Contributors

Valérie Alfvén is Assistant Lecturer in translation studies at the Institute for Interpreting and Translation Studies at Stockholm University. She has a PhD in French from Stockholm University (2016). Her dissertation explored the translation and reception of Swedish young adult novels in France. She is especially interested in the translation of sensitive topics in children's and young adult literature and the circulation of these translated novels from Sweden to other countries.

Michał Borodo is Assistant Professor in the Department of English Linguistics at the Kazimierz Wielki University in Bydgoszcz, Poland. His main research interests include the translation of children's literature, the translation of comics, non-professional/volunteer translation, translation and globalization, and translator training. His recent book publications include *Translation, Globalization and Younger Audiences: The Situation in Poland* (2017) and *English Translations of Korczak's Children's Fiction: A Linguistic Perspective* (2020).

Delia Guijarro Arribas is a specialist in the sociology of culture and in children's book publishing in France and Spain. She holds a PhD in sociology from EHESS (École des Hautes Études en Sciences Sociales) in Paris. She currently lectures on the book industry at the University Paris-Nanterre. She is also a research associate at CESSP (Centre européen de sociologie et de science politique), a research center of EHESS.

Anna Kérchy is Associate Professor of English literature at the University of Szeged, in Hungary. She is interested in Victorian and postmodern fantastic imagination and transmedial, material, and corporeal narratological dimensions of children's and young adult literature. She authored the monographs *Alice in Transmedia Wonderland* (2016), *Body-Texts in the Novels of Angela Carter* (2008), *Essays on Feminist Aesthetics, Narratology, and Body Studies* (in Hungarian, 2018), and (co-)edited *Postmodern Reinterpretations of Fairy Tales* (2011), *The Fairy-Tale Vanguard* (2019), and *Transmediating and Translating Children's Literature* (forthcoming).

Gillian Lathey is Honorary Senior Research Fellow at the University of Roehampton, and co-founder and member of the judging panel of the Marsh Award for Children's Literature in Translation. Publications include *The Translation of Children's Literature: A Reader* (2006), *The Role of Translators in Children's Literature: Invisible Storytellers* (2010), and *Translating Children's Literature: Translation Practices Explained* (2016).

Lia A. Miranda de Lima holds a PhD in literature (2020) and a master's degree in translation studies (2015) from the University of Brasília (UnB). She is the author of the book *Traduções para a primeira infância: O livro ilustrado traduzido no Brasil* [Translations for Early Childhood: Picture Books Translated in Brazil] and guest editor of a special issue on children's literature and translation in the journal *Belas Infiéis* (2019).

Charlotte Lindgren is Senior Lecturer in French at Dalarna University, in Sweden. She obtained her doctoral degree in French language studies at Uppsala University in 2005. Since 2006 she has worked on the translation of modern Swedish children's books into French, particularly studying representations of children, translation of spoken language, translation of sensitive themes, and systemic functional grammar in text and image and in translation (so-called multimodal text and its translation).

Jack McMartin is Assistant Professor in the Translation Studies Research Unit at KU Leuven, in Belgium. His current work investigates the production and reception of Dutch literature in translation, focusing on the people, institutions, and spaces that shape the global book market. He has also published on the life and work of the American-Dutch translator, translation scholar and poet James Stratton Holmes. Jack is vice-director of the Centre for Reception Studies (CERES) and a research member of the Centre for Translation Studies (CETRA) at KU Leuven.

Anna Olga Prudente de Oliveira is a postdoctoral research fellow at the Federal University of Paraná (UFPR) with the project *A Feminist Perspective to Fairy Tales: The Work of Angela Carter in the Brazilian Literary System*. She holds a PhD and a master's degree in language studies from the Pontifical Catholic University of Rio de Janeiro (PUC-Rio) and bachelor's degrees in letters from PUC-Rio and in performing arts from the Federal University of the State of Rio de Janeiro (UNIRIO). Her doctoral dissertation examined the rewritings of the work of Charles Perrault in Brazil and was voted the best dissertation of 2019 at the Centre of Theology and Human Sciences at PUC-Rio. It will be published in book form in 2020.

Emer O'Sullivan is Professor of English literature at Leuphana Universität Lüneburg, in Germany. She has published widely in German and English on image studies, children's literature, and translation. *Kinderliterarische Komparatistik* won the IRSCL Award for outstanding research in 2001, and *Comparative Children's Literature* the ChLA 2007 Book Award. *Imagining Sameness and Difference in Children's Literature*, co-edited with Andrea Immel, was issued in 2017. She is currently updating and expanding her *Historical Dictionary of Children's Literature*.

Germana H. Pereira has been Associate Professor in the Department of Foreign Languages and Translation at the University of Brasília since 1992. She coordinated the master's program in translation studies from 2011 to 2012 and from 2015 to 2016. She currently leads the Studies in History of Translation and Literary Translation (Nethlit/UnB) research cell and has been the director of UnB Publishing House since 2016.

Annalisa Sezzi holds a master's degree in literary translation (English to Italian) from the Catholic University of Milan where she also completed her undergraduate studies in foreign languages and literatures. She received her PhD in comparative language and cultural studies from the University of Modena and Reggio Emilia with a dissertation on the translation of picture books. Her research interests include translation, translation of children's literature, and popularization for children.

Zohar Shavit, incumbent of the Porter Chair of Semiotics and Culture Research, is Full Professor Emerita in the School for Cultural Studies at Tel Aviv University where she established the master's degree program in Research of Child and Youth Culture. Shavit is an internationally renowned authority on the history of Israeli culture, child and youth culture, and Hebrew and Jewish cultures, especially in the context of their relations with various European cultures.

Marija Todorova is a postdoctoral fellow at the Hong Kong Polytechnic University where she is a member of the Research Centre for Professional Communication in English. She has served on the Executive Council of the International Association for Translation and Intercultural Studies (IATIS) and is the Chair of the IATIS Outreach and Social Media Committee. She is an awarded literary translator and has published on translation for children and multimodal translation, among other topics.

Jan Van Coillie is Emeritus Professor affiliated with the Faculty of Arts, KU Leuven, Belgium, where he taught applied linguistics and children's literature (in translation). From 1999 to 2006 he was acting chairman of the Belgian National Centre for Children's Literature. He has published widely on children's literature in translation, children's poetry, fairy tales, and children's literature generally. He is also active as a critic, author and anthologist.

Sara Van Meerbergen is Senior Lecturer in Dutch at Stockholm University. She obtained her doctoral degree in 2010 with a thesis about multimodal translation analysis of picture books, focusing on Dutch and Flemish picture books in Swedish translation. Her research interests include multimodal studies, social semiotics, translation studies, children's literature and media for children, multimodal depictions of children and childhood, globalization, and spatial discourse analysis.

Tanja Žigon is Associate Professor at the Faculty of Arts, Department of Translation, University of Ljubljana, in Slovenia. She holds a PhD in literary studies (2008) and a master's degree in modern German literature (2003). She is the lead researcher of the Slovenian national research program Intercultural Literary Studies and was the project coordinator for Slovenia for the EU project "TransStar: Raising Transcultural, Digital and Multitranslational Competences" (2013–2015). Her research is mainly focused on literary translation and Slovenian–German intercultural relations. She translates from German into Slovene and vice versa.

Marija Zlatnar Moe is Assistant Professor at the Faculty of Arts, University of Ljubljana, in Slovenia. She works in the Department of Translation where she teaches general translation courses from English into Slovene at the BA level, and literary translation and translation for arts and humanities at the MA level. Her research is focused mainly on literary translation with a focus on translation between peripheral/minor languages, drama translation, the ideological issues of translation, translation of sacred texts, and translation didactics. She also translates literature and text for humanities from English and Norwegian into Slovene.

Introduction

Studying texts and contexts in translated children's literature

Jan Van Coillie & Jack McMartin

Be it explicit or implicit, all translators have some awareness of context when translating a text. Rodica Dimitriu calls context a key notion in translation studies and one that allows for "complex analyses of the translator's activities and decisions, of translation processes and, ultimately, of what accounts for the meaning(s) of a translated text" (Dimitriu 2005, 5). However, there is no settled conceptualization of context among translation studies scholars, nor of the relation between context and text. As a subject of academic research, translated children's literature provides fertile ground for examining this relation, precisely because its defining characteristics – the asymmetric relationship between the adult author/translator and the child reader; the heightened cultural, political and economic preoccupations that tend to accompany children's books as they cross linguistic borders; the multimodal interplay between image and text that must be renegotiated when a children's book is translated for a new audience – defy any straightforward conceptualization of context and its relation to text. In this introduction, we retrace three decades of scholarship at the intersection of translation studies and children's literature studies, using the text/context conceptual pairing as our frame. This overview is meant to foreground the studies collected in this volume, which build on the work discussed below. While each chapter has its own theoretical and empirical signature, all had their impetus at the "Translation Studies and Children's Literature: Current Topics and Future Perspectives" international conference held in Brussels and Antwerp in October 2017.[1]

In translation practice, context is often understood as referring to the text-internal, linguistic context surrounding a given textual feature: the words, sentences and ultimately the text as a whole in which the textual feature being

---

1 This conference was occasioned by the emeritus celebration of Jan Van Coillie. On behalf of the many colleagues, students and readers who have been inspired by his work, his co-author respectfully wishes to acknowledge a career well spent.

studied is situated. As early as the 1960s, Eugene A. Nida (1964) emphasized the importance of this particular understanding of context. He gives the example of the word 'run,' whose meaning only becomes clear within the syntactic context, in combination with other words. At the same time, Nida also emphasized the need to be attentive to the context *outside* the text. He calls on the translator to take into account the wider culture, previous translations and the commissioning client when interpreting a text's meaning (Nida 2001, 9). This concept of context was expanded in the 1980s within the pragmatics tradition of linguistics, which understands translation as a form of communication by which meaning is transmitted to and from participants. The interconnectedness and interdependency of text and context is even more central to discourse analysis, which uses the wider communication context to explain shifts in meaning in translations, with a particular emphasis on power relations. This focus is also at the explanatory heart of critical discourse analysis and linguistic criticism, which focus mostly on ideological concerns. Research in pragmatics and critical discourse analysis assume that syntactic and semantic choices reflect the values and beliefs of the author and the social group(s) to which s/he belongs.

Clearly influenced by these ideas, Juliane House defines translation as "recontextualization," which she characterizes as "taking a text out of its original frame and context and placing it within a new set of relationships and culturally conditioned expectations" (House 2006, 356). House makes a distinction between what she calls 'overt' and 'covert' translation:

> In overt translation the original's context is reactivated alongside the target context, such that two different discourse worlds are juxtaposed in the medium of the target language; covert translation concentrates exclusively on the target context, employing a cultural filter to take account of the new addressees' context-derived communicative norms. Covert translation is thus more directly affected by contextual and cultural differences. (*ibid.*)

As a linguist, House focuses on translation practice, in which a translator is constantly drawing connections between the contexts of the source and target cultures. In this sense, House approaches context as something static, invariable and relatively fixed in time. Mona Baker (2006) also studies context from a translation practice perspective. However, she emphasizes precisely the dynamic nature of context. She sees translation as a variable and interactive process of contextualization determined by a diverse set of contextual factors that affect the choices made by a translator.

While context as a heuristic concept slowly gained analytical robustness among scholars of translation, linguistics-inspired theories continued to dominate the academic discourse throughout the 1970s. Emphasis remained squarely on translation practice and on the linguistic (text-internal) context of the translated text. It was not until the arrival of Itamar Even-Zohar's polysystem theory in 1979 that translation studies scholars turned their attention to the text-external context, simultaneously shifting from a prescriptive to a descriptive mode, and from the source text to the target text. Even-Zohar's theory enabled the diachronic study of a literary system in its totality, including the position of translated literature and children's literature within it. He defines a polysystem as "a multiple system, a system of various systems which intersect with each other and partly overlap, using currently different options, yet functioning as a structured whole, whose members are interdependent" (Even-Zohar 1979, 290). Polysystem theory opened the way for research into the contexts and systems beyond texts, enabling analyses of how literary texts functioned in a complex whole of contexts and how literary texts were both influenced by and exerted influence upon these contexts. Working in the same tradition, Gideon Toury combined linguistic comparison of source and target texts with an analysis of the cultural context of the target text in order to explain translation shifts. Central to this method was the identification of the culturally and historically specific norms that determine dominant translation strategies in a given target culture. Toury defines norms as "the translation of general values or ideas shared by a group – as to what is conventionally right and wrong, adequate and inadequate – into performance instructions appropriate for and applicable to particular situations" (Toury 1999, 15). Since Toury, norms have become a key concept in the study of context and translation. His notions of 'adequate' translation (where the norms of the source culture prevail) and 'acceptable' translation (where the norms of the target culture prevail) continue to be tremendously influential.

Taking cues from linguistic-oriented studies, literature-oriented studies in translation appearing in the 1980s and 1990s tended to take a functionalist tack. One particularly dominant line of research was Skopos theory, developed by Katharina Reiss and Hans J. Vermeer (1984). They understood translation primarily as a purpose-driven language act and studied the role of the various participants (client, source and target publishers, receiver) involved in the commissioning and carrying out of a translation. For them, translation strategies were driven by a translation's purpose (as defined by the commissioning client). A particularly well-elaborated model using Skopos theory was that of Christiane Nord (1991), who combined a textual analysis of the translation with a treatment of the intended text functions (which are inseparable from the target culture) as well as an analysis of the context in which the translation under study came to be and the various people involved (initiators or commissioners, authors, translators). For Nord, translations are located in what she calls 'linguacultures' (Nord 1997). Translation thus always constitutes an act of intercultural communication.

Indeed, in translation studies the term 'culture' has increasingly come to be used in relation to context. Susan Bassnett and André Lefevere (1990) announced a "cultural turn" in 1990, signaling a trend to situate source and target texts within the source and target 'culture.' Researchers in this tradition focus mainly on the study of literature in translation and explore the place of literary translations within a wider cultural context. They investigate the manner in which sociocultural factors like poetics, ideology, politics, power, ethics, colonization, and ethnic and gender identity influence translations and the role of translators as cultural intermediaries. Translations are seen "as a cultural political practice that might be strategic in bringing about social change" (Venuti 2012, 276). Lawrence Venuti's concepts of 'foreignization' and 'domestication' are particularly inspiring for this line of research. Foreignization usually refers to a translation method which takes the reader to the foreign text, preserving significant stylistic and cultural features of the source text, whereas domestication assimilates the text to target cultural and linguistic norms and values. Venuti rejects domestication as an "ethnocentric reduction of the foreign text to the target-language cultural values" (Venuti 1995, 20) and advocates foreignization because it "challenges the dominant aesthetics" and signals "the linguistic and cultural differences of the foreign text" (Venuti 1995, 309).

Translation studies has also borrowed from neighboring disciplines to augment its understanding of context. Advocating for a fusion between translation studies and cultural studies, David Katan's *Translating Cultures* emphasizes the importance of cultural context in translation practice. For Katan, the translator must be aware of both text and context, which is to say both the words s/he is translating and the text's 'implied frames,' its ideological and culture-linked presuppositions. As he has it, "the context of culture is an important frame from within which we perceive, interpret and communicate" (Katan 2004, 167).

Perhaps the most conspicuous cross-disciplinary fusion since the 1990s has been with sociology. Sociological approaches understand translation as a form of 'social practice.' More so than with cultural studies, sociologists of translation place the analytical focus on people and their social behavior. This enlarges the conceptual boundaries of context to include the entire (professional and social-cultural) sphere in which translation takes place. Michaela Wolf (2010, 337) identifies a number of possible research domains at the nexus of translation studies and sociology: training institutions, working conditions, professional institutions and their social role, questions of ethics in translation, (auto)biographies of translators, translation in the global book market and sociopolitical aspects of translation. Alongside examining culturally determined norms that help explain individual translation choices, sociologists of translation have also explored the various individuals (literary agents, publishers, editors, marketers, critics) and institutions (publishing houses, prizes, government agencies) that play a role in the production and circulation of translated texts.

Many translation studies researchers found inspiration in the work of the French sociologist Pierre Bourdieu. His concepts of field, habitus and the various forms of capital have been fundamental to the development of a sociology of translation. Theo Hermans (1999) analyzes the manner in which agents take up positions of power in the literary field and the role of economic factors, publishers, marketers and book clubs in this process. André Lefevere (1998) works with Bourdieu's notion of 'cultural capital' to reveal translations as important vectors for the dissemination of cultural capital within and between cultures and human networks. Several researchers have applied Bourdieu's ideas to the study of translation flows in the world market for book translations and the production and distribution of translated books. This focus has shifted the attention even further away from the (translated) texts themselves and placed it squarely on the context of production and cross-border circulation. Michael Cronin (2003), for example, has studied how translators are influenced by global changes such as machine translation and the internet. Johan Heilbron (1999) analyzes translation flows between core and peripheral languages, while Gisèle Sapiro (2010) traces translation flows between the US and France, emphasizing the political, economic and social factors that shape the worldwide exchange of books.

Perhaps the most central concept shared among these sociological approaches to translation is power. Inherent in Bourdieu's notions of capital and field is the assumption that literary, symbolic and economic resources are not equally distributed among the people and institutions involved in the coming-into-being and circulation of translated texts. In fact, the fields in which these practices are carried out are defined by the opposition between the haves and the have-nots: some languages are more dominant than others; some publishers are perceived to be more prestigious than others; some roles in the translation process are more decisive for the creation, production and reception of translations than others. It is precisely the study of power relations that helped train scholars' analyses on the context(s) of translation (Fischer and Jensen 2012). This brings us to research on the *contexts of translation of children's literature*. Power takes on an additional guise here through the inherent power inequity between adult and child.

The first studies of children's literature in translation, which date from the 1960s, reflect an idealized belief typical for the immediate postwar era that a peaceful future could be guaranteed by the (proper upbringing of) the younger generation. Because translations transcend borders between cultures, translations were seen as a way to advance international understanding. This was the stated aim of a 1962 volume of essays on translated children's literature edited by Lisa Christina Persson. Among its contributors was the American librarian Virginia Haviland, who argued passionately that books from other countries were a significant enrichment for young readers in the US. Another contributor, the British editor and translator Monica Burnes, nominally endorsed the volume's cross-cultural ethos but also argued frankly that "children's books must be tailored to their new country" (Persson 1962, 78). This prompted the following response from Reinbert Tabbert:

> Rarely will target-language oriented scholars find a less disguised plea for the subjection of translations to conventions, in this case the shared belief, initiated by Rousseau, that children have to be protected against anything culturally unfamiliar or morally unbecoming. This leaves little room for vicarious experience of foreignness. (Tabbert 2002, 308)

The tone was set for a decade of debate for and against the domestication of translated children's literature.

A leading voice in this debate was Richard Bamberger (1963), who emphasized the importance of high-quality translations for the development of one's own national (in his case German) children's literature. Like Persson, he situated translated children's books in a discourse of international understanding:

> We can now rightly speak of a genuine world literature for children which can do much to further international understanding. Children all over the world are now growing up enjoying the same pleasures in reading, and cherishing similar ideals, aims and hopes. (Bamberger 1978, 21)

This perspective has a long tradition. The French comparatist Paul Hazard considered each translated children's book to be "a messenger that goes beyond mountains and rivers, beyond the seas, to the very ends of the world in search of new friendships" (Hazard and Mitchell 1944, 146).

Idealized notions of translated children's literature were not called into question until the end of the 1970s, with Göte Klingberg's prescriptive study which argued that a translated children's book should have the same 'degree of adaptation' as the source text. By adaptations he meant the changes made on account of the child reader, which for him followed as a necessary result of the knowledge and experience gap between the adult author and the young reader. As it happens, the notion of context was central to Klingberg's argument. He introduced the term 'context adaptation' (1978, further developed in 1986 under the term 'cultural context adaptation'), which he considered a central difficulty in (the study of) translation:

> The problem of context adaptation is that on the one hand it is necessary in translations of children's books if one wants to retain the same degree of adaptation of the source text, but, that one of the aims of translating children's books must be to further the international outlook and the international understanding of the young readers. (Klingberg 1978, 86)

He rejected ubiquitous forms of context adaptation: modernization, purification, abridgements and 'localization,' or the transposing of the entire text into the culture of the target readership. Since Klingberg's study, the term 'cultural context adaptation' has appeared regularly in research on children's literature in translation. Cecilia Alvstad calls it "one of the most frequently quoted characteristics of children's literature in translation" (Alvstad 2010, 22).

The resulting stream of studies on the adaptation of culture-specific items in translated children's books gradually gained in scientific rigor, particularly thanks to polysystem theory and cultural studies (see *infra*). Zohar Shavit (1986) was among the first to apply polysystem theory to children's literature. She argues that manipulations and adaptations are often motivated by the ideology or the stylistic norms of the target culture and are typical for (translated) children's literature. In various studies, she examines the mediation between the pedagogic and literary system and the impact translation has on it, emphasizing the complex position of children's literature in this polysystem. According to Shavit, "children's literature, more than any other literary system, results from a conglomerate of relationships between several systems of culture" (Shavit 1994, 4). The insights of Gideon Toury also had a major impact on the study of children's literature in translation. Jeremy Munday (among others) popularized Toury's model in his study of the Spanish and Italian translations of J. K. Rowling's *Harry Potter and the Philosopher's Stone*, which appeared in his handbook *Introducing Translation Studies: Theories and Applications* (2001, 121-125). Echoing Toury's method, Munday places the target texts in their cultural context/system, compares segments of the source and target texts, and draws general conclusions about the translation strategies used and the norms upon which they are based.

Isabelle Desmidt (2006) offers an interesting addition to Toury: her model calls out norms specific to children's literature. Like Shavit, she underlines the complexity of the norms that shape the specific communication process involved in children's literature. She distinguishes between source text-related norms, literary aesthetic norms, business norms, didactic norms, pedagogical norms and technical norms. The first two categories correspond with Toury's basic initial norm, addressing adequacy and acceptability. Business norms relate to the context of editing, publishing and distribution. Didactic and pedagogic norms are linked to two functions unique to children's literature: that children's books must educate children (didactic norms) and that they must be adapted in such a way as to be understandable to children (pedagogic norms). Finally, technical norms determine (among other things) the layout, including the relationship between text and image characteristic of (translated) children's literature.

The influence of cultural studies is particularly apparent in research on translated fairy tales, a line of research that emerged in the 1990s and has since blossomed into a sub-discipline in its own right. One of the more remarkable studies to emerge out of this line is Cay Dollerup's book on the international reception of the Grimm tales, which is presented as an illustration of "aspects of translation as cross-cultural communication" (Dollerup 1999, ix). Karen Seago's work on the translations of *Sleeping Beauty* in the 1990s is another example of research that places cultural context at the center of the analysis. She examines not only the intentional changes in target texts made for "didactic and moral reasons" but also "the unconscious shifts in meaning as an expression of the social and political environment which has shaped the translation" (Seago 2006, 179). She finds that fairy tales actively contribute to "the articulation of domestic ideology" (*ibid.*, 188) while at the same time exposing latent tensions in society. The title of a recent volume on one of the most widely translated fairy tales illustrates the centrality of cultural studies to this line of research: *Cinderella across Cultures*. The first section is titled "Contextualising Cinderella" and explores the circulation of the fairy tale "in numerous different contexts" (De La Rochère, Lathey and Wozniak 2016, 2).

In the 1980s and 1990s, researchers working within Skopos theory also turned their attention to children's literature in translation. Like the polysystem researchers, they zeroed in on the tendency among producers of translated children's books to change the text, often drastically. Katharina Reiss (1982) distinguishes three factors that lead to a divergent (adaptation-rich) translation: the imperfect linguistic competence of the young reader, his/her limited knowledge of the world, and taboos. Christiane Nord (1995) focuses on the specificity of translated children's books when she adds a fourth function, the phatic function, to Reiss's three (informative, expressive, and operative or appellative). The phatic function refers to the relation between sender and receiver, for instance in forms of address like 'dear children.' Nord (2003) also studied the translation of names in children's books, one of the most researched types of cultural context adaptation.

Two influential studies on the translation of children's literature were published at the turn of the century, both of which placed context at the center of the analysis. The first is Emer O'Sullivan's (2000) impressive synthesis arguing for a comparative approach to the study of children's literature. She focuses particularly on the culturally specific status of children's literature, its international circulation, the influence of norms on the transfer of children's literature across linguistic and cultural boundaries, and the relation between word and image in translated children's books. As O'Sullivan writes in the introduction to the English-language edition: "Comparative Children's Literature, like mainstream comparative literature, must consider those phenomena that cross the borders of a particular literature in order to see them in their respective linguistic, cultural, social and literary contexts" (2005, 11). In another seminal book, *Translating for Children,* Riitta Oittinen (2000) places the child front and center as the primary reader of translated children's books. For her, adaptation and domestication are part and parcel of translation, particularly translations for children. She takes up a prescriptive position: "Translators of children's literature should reach out to the children of their own culture" (Oittinen 2000, 168). Drawing on insights from Mikhail Bakhtin and Christiane Nord, Oittinen furthermore considers translation to be a goal-oriented dialogue that the translator undertakes with the text, author and reader. This dialogical situation encompasses both text and context: "Throughout my book, I have understood the situation as involving not just the texts (in words and pictures) and their different creators and readers, but also the text's contexts, including the child images that mirror our cultures and societies" (*ibid.,* 159). Oittinen's work inspired a new flurry of research on child images (the ideas adults have about children, how they are and how they should be) and the relation between text and image in translated children's literature.

In 2006, Gillian Lathey published a reader surveying research on translated children's literature up to that time. The titles of the book's main sections give an idea of its thematic range: "Narrative Communication and the Child Reader," "Translating the Visual" and "The Travels of Children's Books and Cross-Cultural Influences." The notion of (cultural) context is particularly central in this last section, where various authors address the "ideological differences between the contexts from which national children's literatures emerge, of which didacticism and censorship are just two aspects" (Lathey 2006, 7). In her more recent work, Lathey continues to emphasize the specific contexts in which translated children's literature is produced and received. In *The Role of the Translator in Children's Literature*, she examines the 'voice' of the translator as expressed explicitly in forewords and implicitly in translation changes. She argues that "translators of children's literature are mediators not just of unfamiliar social and cultural contexts, but also of the values and expectations of childhood encoded in the source text" (Lathey 2010, 196). Lathey's *Translating Children's Literature* (2015) is practice-oriented and research-informed and pays special attention to the translation of culture-specific elements.

Since the 1990s, another buzzword in research on translated children's literature has been ideology. Gaby Thomson-Wohlgemuth (2009), for instance, studies the effects of ideology on the translation of children's books from English in the former German Democratic Republic (GDR). Grounding her research in André Lefevere's theories on patronage and rewriting, she focuses especially on extratextual factors, including an extensive treatment of the GDR's censorship apparatus. Ideology is also of central concern in studies on retranslations, when a book that has already been translated into a language is translated again at a later date. Myriam Du Nour (1995) shows how retranslations expose changing societal norms. In his study on the English retranslations of Jules Verne's *Tour du monde en quatre-vingt jours*, Kieran O'Driscoll (2011) seeks out what he calls "the web of causation" to explain translation shifts. He combines a comparative study of source and target texts with a thorough study of the context in which translators work and the personal and professional circumstances surrounding a translation. Inspired by Toury, he also considers the social and cultural norms that shape translation strategies. Virginie Douglas explores how the socioeconomic context and ideology shape the specific communication situation characteristic of (translated) children's literature:

> The fact that a children's book, translated or not, appears in a world of adults, and therefore that contextual factors cannot be ignored, explains why [researchers] place a strong emphasis on retranslation and the ways in which a particular retranslation is inscribed in the socio-economic sphere – elements that are at the core of the strongly ideological dimension of children's literature. (Douglas and Cabaret 2014, 327; our translation)[2]

---

2   In the French original: "Le fait qu'un livre pour la jeunesse, traduit ou non, voit le jour dans un monde d'adultes et que les facteurs contextuels ne peuvent donc pas être ignorés explique que les [chercheurs] insistent beaucoup sur ces instances extérieures, sur l'inscription de la démarche de retraduction dans la sphère socio-économique, éléments qui sont au cœur de la forte dimension idéologique de la littérature pour la jeunesse."

Ideology is also emphasized in studies on canon formation and the influence of translations and adaptations on the canonization process. Sylvie Geerts and Sara Van den Bossche make explicit the link between ideology and adaptation in translated children's literature: "This observation, that stories are adapted to correspond with a new context, points to the ideological implications of the process" (Geerts and Van den Bossche 2014, 5). They draw inspiration particularly from John Stephens' *Language and Ideology in Children's Fiction* (1992). Writing in 1998, Stephens and co-author Robyn McCallum showed how retellings lay bare dominant ideologies:

> Any particular retelling may purport to transmit elements of a culture's formative traditions and even its sustaining beliefs and assumptions, but what it always discloses is some aspect of the attitudes and ideologies pertaining at the cultural moment in which the translation is produced. (Stephens and McCallum 1998, ix)

Bettina Kümmerling-Meibauer and Anja Müller (2017) make clear how research on canon formation is determined by how researchers understand the relation between text and context. Some limit the analysis to the textual criteria that lead to a text's being included in the canon. For these researchers, adherence to standards of aesthetic quality is what determines whether a work makes its way into the canon. For others, market mechanisms and extratextual factors are decisive in determining which books are canonized. The latter group tends to focus on the sociocultural context and emphasizes the role of the canon in society (as a tool for nation-building, for instance). This line of research has become dominant in recent years and can be seen as part of the wider embrace of sociological approaches in translation studies: "Research into the canon thus not only pays attention to texts but to the entire literary field: production, market, publication, education, criticism, readership, etc." (Kümmerling-Meibauer and Müller 2017, 3). It is also important to note the link between canon formation and translation of children's literature: canonized works in the source culture stand a better chance of being translated, which increases their chances of entering the international canon, which in turn increases the prestige of the work in the source culture.

Researchers working within linguistics have also focused attention on ideology. In their comparative discourse analysis of translations of English children's books into Greek, German, Korean, Spanish and Arabic, Kaniklidou and House (2017) call out many examples of 'massive cultural filtering.' They find that translators as well as editors and publishers "openly manipulate original texts, thus changing the relationship that addressees can establish with STs and source cultures" (*ibid.*, 243). According to them, such manipulations can often be traced back to financial and marketing factors. Kaniklidou and House also call attention to the (ethical) responsibilities of adult actors vis-à-vis their dominant position in the power relation between adult and child: "Children cannot guard against shifts imposed on translated texts they read or listen to. They are only permitted to experience another culture through translated products" (*ibid.*, 243), which are always already mediated by adults. Haidee Kruger draws a connection between cultural adaptations and "the asymmetrical power relationships involved in the production of children's literature" (Kruger 2011b, 122), by which adults determine what children can handle and what is valuable to them. Her study, based on original survey data from South African translators of children's literature, shows that translators' opinions also "provide insight into the ways in which ideology influences perceptions of translation in particular contexts" (*ibid.*, 131).

Taken together, the perspectives on text and context distilled from the research discussed above reveal three main characteristics that typify translated children's literature: (1) the *asymmetric communication*, resulting from the differences in knowledge and experience between the adult translator (straddling source and target cultures with specific conceptions of the function of a given title and of its intended reader) and the child reader (often with limited preconceptions of the source culture); (2) the *dual audience*, which includes both children in their roles as readers and listeners, and adults in their roles as consumers, critics, mediators, marketers and readers (aloud); and (3) the *multimodal character* of children's literature, the translation of which requires consideration of the interplay between text and image. Let us now briefly elaborate each of these three characteristics.

The asymmetrical relationship affects not only the translator, but all adults involved in the production, distribution and reception of children's literature: authors, publishers, parents, teachers and so on.[3] As soon as adults attempt to bridge that asymmetry, they have adapted the text to the young audience in some way.

In the case of translated children's books, adaptations are often of a cultural sort, where translators remove or replace culture-specific elements because they judge them to be too difficult for, or simply unsuited to, their young target audience. In doing so, they (consciously or not) express a specific child image, which is informed by both their personal, situational context and the wider cultural context; that is, from both their own childhood and

---

3   For a more detailed conceptualization of the narrative communication process in translated children's literature see O'Sullivan (2003) and Kruger (2011a).

life experiences with children and the norms and values that their society or social group seeks to pass on to the younger generation.

The situational context of the translator is shaped by other participants involved in the production process as well: publishers, editors and marketing specialists. They too take part in the asymmetric relation of power with the youth audience and are often also responsible for adaptations. These adaptations are inevitably informed by book producers' ideas about what children – and adults – are able to appreciate. Publishers, editors and marketing staff thus allow their decisions to be led not only by their image of young readers but, consciously or not, also by that of the adult intermediaries that bring books to children: parents, teachers, librarians and the adult critics or prize juries that evaluate and publicize them. This 'dual audience' also forms an important part of the context of the translator and therefore also partially steers his/her translation strategies. Furthermore, when an adult reads a book to a child, this occurs in a very specific context whereby the auditive elements of the text also play a role in the communication process. The translator may take this aspect into account in his/her decision-making as well.

Finally, the interaction between text and context can also be colored (figuratively and literally) by the multimodal character of many children's books, where the 'text' consists of both words and images. This brings the illustrator and graphic designer into the situational context. Images are regularly adapted in the course of translation, or they may influence or even necessitate textual changes. Alternatively, illustrations may also depict culture-specific items, which make their adaptation in the written text redundant. Often due to commercial considerations, source text illustrations are also regularly changed out for new illustrations by an illustrator from the target culture.

All of this may give the impression of a lopsided relationship, where context tends to determine text. However, the opposite also occurs. One of the most interesting areas of research in the area of translated children's literature today is the study of texts that bring about changes in the context of the target culture in which they are translated. Translations can have an impact on the literature of the target culture (Ghesquiere 2006), and can help shape views, norms and values in the wider society (see Zohar Shavit's chapter in this volume, and Xu 2013). In the case of translated children's literature, this has most often been studied in relation to pedagogy. However, the power of translated children's literature to transform societies surely reaches far beyond the classroom – a promising direction for future interdisciplinary research.

Despite the range and diversity of the contributions compiled in this volume, all have one aim in common: to better understand the complex interaction between text and context. Each contributor has woven this thread into the analysis in a different way – precisely the added value of a volume with such a broad methodological, historical, linguistic and geographic scope.

The text/context relationship is complex and co-implicated, and no single analytical framework can fully account for it. We can, however, glean two main analytical orientations in the contributions collected here and have organized this book accordingly. The first part, "**Context » Text**," entails a mode of analysis oriented towards understanding the national and linguistic spheres in which the production and reception of translated children's books take place: How is the marketplace for translated children's literature structured? What were the historical conditions under which this market developed? It also seeks to understand the practices of the people occupying these spheres: publishers, editors, translators, illustrators and others. What roles do these various agents take up in the communication process? What social factors explain how a children's book comes to be produced and received as it is? The answers proposed by our contributors highlight the complex and unequal relations that hold between the various contexts and people that shape the translation process. These relations are the result of historical developments over time and, while they are embedded in national and language-specific contexts, they are very often transnational in scope. This is no surprise, as translation necessarily involves interactions across multiple linguistic, economic and sociocultural contexts. Some agents enjoy dominance or influence in their respective contexts. Others are obliged to develop strategies to coexist alongside more powerful players in a game whose rules are weighted against them.

Part 1 opens with two contributions that examine translated children's books in the UK and Ireland. Both zero in on the selection processes and strategies of a number of small, independent publishers who have successfully introduced translated children's books, despite the market's notorious resistance to translations and the overwhelming dominance of conglomerate publishers. In "'Only English books': The mediation of translated children's literature in a resistant economy," **Gillian Lathey** traces this resistance back to anti-French sentiment at the beginning of the nineteenth century, when prominent voices protested "that torrent of infidelity and immorality (…) from the continent through the channel of French books" (Lathey quoting Trimmer 1803, 406). With few exceptions, the wariness towards books from 'the continent' has persisted to the present day. This, combined with the dominance of English-language children's literature internationally, has led to an oversaturation of the British market, leaving little room for translations. Indeed, only 2 percent of publications for children produced in the UK each year are translations. Lathey goes on to examine translation strategies. She qualifies Venuti's call to always maintain the foreignness of a translated text, arguing instead for a more nuanced mix of domestication and foreignization – a "subtle linguistic and cultural negotiation" necessary for ensuring that "translations are read at all." She then surveys the publishing landscape in the UK, singling out the importance of small-scale publishers of translations, government and charitable organizations, and prizes like the biennial Marsh Award for Children's Literature in Translation. She closes with an expression of hope that these actors will continue their efforts to "maintain links with Europe and to overcome the echoing clarion call for 'only English books'" in post-Brexit UK.

That effort reverberates in **Emer O'Sullivan**'s contribution, "Two languages, two children's literatures: Translation in Ireland today." O'Sullivan traces dual traditions of children's literature in Ireland, each with its own specific history and set of conditions relating to translations. While Irish-language publications, including translations, have been heavily subsidized by the Irish state since Irish independence in 1922, those published in English by Irish publishers have had to compete on the open market with the publishing conglomerates on the neighboring island. Official measures making Irish compulsory in schools increased demand for Irish-language children books, further shifting the publishing landscape inward. Nonetheless, as with modern Hebrew, translated literature played an important role in reviving and fostering the Irish language. Today, a number of small, innovative independent Irish-language presses produce a steady stream of children's books for the small minority of children who are either Irish native speakers or attend an Irish-medium school. Among these books are a fair number of translations.

The source language from which these works are selected, however, can be a contentious issue indeed – and here is where Ireland's two traditions intersect. For decades, books from English were adamantly resisted by the Irish government and were not eligible for translation subsidies. The result: while some books were arriving into Irish from the USSR and former Eastern Bloc countries, virtually none were being translated from English. It was not until the turn of the century, when the Irish state changed its position on English in the wake of the Good Friday Agreement, that children's books from English began to be translated into Irish, the first popular title being *Harry Potter*. Many children's books from English quickly followed – to the extent that the Irish-language writers' association protested and petitioned (successfully) to limit incoming translations. Nonetheless, O'Sullivan credits the influx of translations from English with motivating young readers to read in Irish and raising the perceived status of the Irish language.

O'Sullivan concludes her chapter with a look at Irish children's literature in English. Until the 1980s, almost all English-language books for children in Ireland (including those by Irish writers) were imported from the UK. Faced with such extreme intralingual power asymmetries, Irish publishers generally refrained from publishing books for children in English. After a boom in the mid-1990s, which saw seven Irish publishers regularly publish books for children in English, "the economics of publishers surviving in a small market" caught up (O'Sullivan quoting Coghlan 2004, 1099). Only two remained by 2007. However, the few Irish publishers working in English today continue to issue translations from various languages and express an openness to diverse titles from around the world. O'Sullivan attributes the survival of both Irish-language and English-language publishing for children in Ireland to two factors: the courage and creativity of passionate independent publishers, and generous state subsidies.

In "Cultural translation and the recruitment of translated texts to induce social change: The case of the *Haskalah*," **Zohar Shavit** challenges the common usage of the term 'cultural translation.' She argues for a narrow definition reserved for "cases where translations play an active role in the dynamics of a given society, for instance when translations function as agents of change and serve as a vehicle for presenting and exhibiting a desired social change." Shavit holds up the *Haskalah* movement (the Jewish Enlightenment movement), as one such case, showing how translated texts were intentionally used to disseminate bourgeois societal values and a modern habitus throughout German-speaking Jewish communities in late-eighteenth-century Europe. She focuses especially on translated texts intended to provide Jewish children and young adults with guidelines for everyday practices, such as how to interact with others and how to maintain proper personal hygiene. These seemingly mundane texts served a central aim of the *Haskalah* movement: to assure Jews' integration into non-Jewish bourgeois society, a development resisted by the insular, traditional Ashkenazi religious elite that dominated Jewish cultural life at the time. Following Toury and Even-Zohar, Shavit shows how translations of texts borrowed from other systems (in her case, educational texts inspired by German Philanthropinism) provided the raw materials for the importation of new cultural and social models, which were then molded to suit the needs and demands of the target system. She goes on to contemplate the effectiveness of this large-scale translation effort, concluding that the *Haskalah* translations "opened the door to the creation of a modern Jewish society."

Delia Guijarro Arribas examines contexts of transnational publishing in her chapter entitled "Associative practices and translations in children's book publishing: Co-editions in France and Spain." Drawing on insights from the sociology of translation, she concentrates on co-editions, an increasingly common tool used by publishers of children's literature to reach readers beyond their borders. Arribas traces the history of co-editions (where a publisher secures rights buyers abroad prior to publishing a book and then prints multiple language-specific editions of that book simultaneously), situating them alongside other cooperative forms of publishing. She goes on to analyze the various strategic uses co-edition schemes offer children's book publishers. These depend on a publisher's position in the field: dominant publishers often use co-edition schemes as a means to 'conquer' new language markets, whereas dominated publishers use them as a way to make new book projects viable and to affiliate themselves with more prestigious counterparts in other languages. Furthermore, co-edition strategies are subject to the prestige possessed by each respective language, nation and publishing house involved in a given rights negotiation. Comparing the French and Spanish subfields, Arribas finds that French publishers who publish co-editions look outward, leveraging their historical dominance, stores of know-how and prestige while Spanish publishers look inward, using co-editions to capitalize on a multilingual publishing field that includes the co-official state languages of Spain's five autonomous communities. Several (Catalonia in particular) have developed flourishing publishing industries in post-Franco Spain. Nonetheless, they remain subordinated to Spanish-language publishers: publication timelines must be managed carefully to prevent the Spanish translation of any given title from swallowing up their version, a function of the fact that all those who read Catalan, Galician, Basque or Valencian also read Spanish. Arribas' contribution highlights the need to take into account national, linguistic and international contexts simultaneously when explaining cooperation among publishers.

Lia Miranda de Lima and **Germana Pereira** describe the gradual formation of Brazilian children's literature over the course of two centuries, linking periods of aesthetic innovation and stagnation with political developments in the country. Their chapter, "Translation and the formation of a Brazilian children's literature," takes inspiration from Even-Zohar's polysystem theory and a similar framework developed by the Brazilian scholar and critic Antonio Candido to trace the historical role of translations in the constitution of Brazil's national literary system. They sketch five periods that were pivotal to the formation of Brazilian children's literature: (1) the last decades of the eighteenth century, on either side of the proclamation of the Republic in 1889, during which localized adaptations of European classics for children were translated into Portuguese in the service of constituting a Brazilian national identity in the Romantic ilk; (2) the emergence of an innovative system of literary production for children starting in the 1930s pioneered by the editor, translator and author Monteiro Lobato (1882–1948), who combined characters from European and North American fairy tales with Brazilian folklore figures; (3) children's authors' resistance to state-sponsored narratives of national progress, culminating in a regime change to democracy (1945-1964); (4) a period of political repression and censorship (1964–1979) following the military coup; and (5) a flourishing of politically engaged books for children following gradual re-democratization after 1979. This last period encapsulates the "Brazilian children's literature boom," which saw the revival of Lobato "as an instrument of political satire and liberation from the formal and thematic conventions of the previous decades."

Lima and Pereira also link influxes of incoming translations to expansions in Brazil's school system. They zoom in on the latest expansion, during the 1980s, which saw the Brazilian state become the main client of that country's publishers of books for children. They analyze the catalogue of Brazil's massive national school library program, which buys more than nineteen million books per year and serves twenty-two million primary and secondary school students. They found that the share of translations among the books purchased by the state for nurseries and kindergartens ranged between 18 and 35 percent of total books for the period 2008–2014, a sign that translations continue to play an important role in the ongoing development of Brazilian children's literature.

In "*Said, spoke, spluttered, spouted*: The role of text editors in stylistic shifts in translated children's literature," **Marija Zlatnar Moe** and **Tanja Žigon** turn their focus to the context of the editing process by examining the collaborative workflow between translator, text editor and book editor in the production of translated picture books. Drawing on original survey data from 235 Slovene translators, ninety-one text editors and twenty-six book editors, and a textual analysis of drafts, edited versions and published versions of a sample of Norwegian picture books in Slovene translation, they explore interpersonal power dynamics based on two indicators: (1) the relative ability of translators, text editors and book editors to make changes to the text after an initial translation has been drafted; and (2) the perceptions people in each of these roles have of their counterparts' authority to do so. Moe and Žigon show that, while the end result is always a compromise between all involved, in most cases the translator was seen by his/her collaborators as the 'author' of the target text and as such had significant power to influence the final version. Interestingly, translators tended to see themselves as overlooked agents in the translation process, despite others' perceptions of their authorial power. Moe and Žigon also found that text editors intervened more often in texts for children than in texts for adults. Text editors' changes neutralized non-standard orthographic, syntactic, grammatical and stylistic features in the draft translation, a (sometimes problematic) function of not speaking the source language of the translated text they were revising. These changes were often reversed in later editing stages, with book editors tending to defer to the opinion of the translator, particularly if that person was trusted, experienced and willing to take the time to explain his/her reasons for intervening.

Jan Van Coillie closes Part 1 with a wide-ranging reflection on the power of translated children's literature to bring children into contact with other cultures and perspectives. In "Diversity can change the world: Children's literature, translation and images of childhood," he approaches the 'foreign' in translated children's literature from four perspectives: selection, reduction, visualization and digitization. He strikes a critical tone, going so far as to ask whether translation itself, the mode by which many books for children circulate today, hinders or helps diversity. Underwriting the contributions by Lathey and O'Sullivan, he laments that the flood of translated children books from English, facilitated by Anglo-American processes of globalization and commercialization, has stifled diversity in many language areas. Anglophone dominance has been particularly strongly felt in smaller language markets in Europe and markets with emerging children's literatures in Southeast Asia, where anywhere between 60 and 80 percent of all translated children's books are from English. Even when non-Anglophone source texts *are* selected for translation, they are often stripped of their foreign elements, making it much more difficult for young readers to glean a sense of the source culture. These omissions and reductions of the foreign reveal target producers' commercial motivations as well as their own child images, which are often informed by the (for Van Coillie unfounded) belief that young readers are unable to understand and cope with foreign elements (strange sounding names, unfamiliar foods), let alone taboo subjects like sexuality, nudity, violence, and death. Van Coillie extends this to the visual medium in translated children's books, noting that it is not uncommon for illustrations to be adapted or replaced to suit the target culture. Many dominant source publishers circumvent this by instructing illustrators to "avoid culture-specific markers as well as references to sex, violence and anything else that could cause offence." Such practices limit diversity by filtering out visualizations of the foreign.

Van Coillie finishes his chapter with a discussion of digital books for children, where selection, reduction and visualization dynamics converge in potentially innovative ways. Digital children's books enrich the reading experience with in-story games, hotspots for interacting with items and characters in the story, reading comprehension exercises, and read-aloud functionality. Digital children's books also have the added advantage of being easily published in multilingual editions. This makes them not only a promising didactic tool for young readers and second-language learners but also an enriching potential site for encounters with the foreign. However, as with the print market, the market for digital children's books is currently dominated by English-only titles. Looking to the future, Van Coillie sees promise in digital children's books that combine multiple, high-quality translations/voice-over versions in many languages, each with localized supplemental content.

Many more examples of how a text's diversity is embraced or reduced upon entering a new context can be found in Part 2, "**Text » Context**." These contributions reflect a second, more well-established mode of studying translated children's literature oriented towards understanding the myriad ways individual translated texts or oeuvres are adapted to suit the context of a given target culture. Several contributions deal with retranslations, the study of which allows for a diachronic comparison of translation strategies across time and space. Retranslations invite investigations into the constraints imposed, explicitly or not, by (state) ideologies, pedagogic norms and dominant child images active in the target culture – all of which must be negotiated in one way or another by the translator. The translation strategies used and the various textual artefacts they render (shifts, omissions, subversions, changes in emphasis, reinterpretations) tell us something about the motivations of the translator and the cultural context in/for which s/he is translating.

In "The creative reinventions of nonsense and domesticating the implied child reader in Hungarian translations of *Alice's Adventures in Wonderland*," **Anna Kérchy** explores six different Hungarian translations of Lewis Carroll's Victorian classic produced over the last century and a half. She begins with a reflection on the (un)translatability of literary nonsense, a genre unique for its dual address and crossover appeal: literary nonsense offers "a retreat from structures of authority" for children and a "return to a child-like state" for grown-ups. Kérchy then comments on the six translations, using Venuti's terminology to identify a progression in the Hungarian translation history of Alice from "domesticating translations bordering on creative adaptations [to] foreignizing translations intent on respecting criteria of fidelity to the source-text." Some domesticating choices had major ramifications for the story. For example, in the third Hungarian Alice (1935), which Kérchy calls "the most exciting take on Carroll's classic to date," the decision to use Hungarian playing cards instead of French ones necessitated replacing the Red Queen with "a schizoid king figure" since Hungarian decks do not contain a queen card.

Kérchy argues that dominant images of the child and childhood prevailing in the target culture at the time a translation is produced are likely to influence the translation strategies used by the translator. This explains why most of the Hungarian translations transform Alice from an active, empowered co-creator of the narrative in Carroll's original to a passive, vulnerable listener in all but one (the latest, 2013) translation: until very recently, the dominant child image in Hungary infantilized the child reader.

Michał Borodo looks at another case of domesticating translation but suggests that, paradoxically, domestication can sometimes achieve a foreignizing effect. In "'Better watch it, mate' and 'Listen 'ere, lads': The cultural specificity of the English translation of Janusz Korczak's classic *Król Maciuś Pierwszy* [King Matt the First]," Borodo compares three English translations (two North American, one British) of this widely translated Polish classic for children. He pays special attention to the translation for British readers, created by Adam Czasak and published in London in 1990 with the title *Little King Matty*. In addition to the more obvious domesticating choices (adapting child protagonists' names and culture-specific items), the translator introduced an array of lexical items – 'lads,' 'mates,' 'mingy,' 'barmy,' 'to nick,' 'to take the mickey,' 'righto,' 'blimey' and 'flippin' 'eck' – associated with the British working class. This decision contrasts with the other two English translations, which use standard 'literary' English. Borodo concludes that Czasak's use of a marginal, non-standard discourse actually achieves the effect of a foreignizing translation in Venuti's terms, making for a more complex source–target dynamic. He credits Czasak with "breathing new life" into the Polish classic for children by giving it a "colloquial and distinctively British character."

Complementing the contribution by Lima and Pereira in Part 1, **Anna Olga Prudente de Oliveira** shows in "Brazilian rewritings of Perrault's short stories: Nineteenth- and twentieth-century versus twenty-first-century retellings and consequences for the moral message" how rewritings of Charles Perrault's *Tales of Mother Goose* contributed to the emergence of a Brazilian children's literature. She retraces three centuries of Perrault's tales in Brazil to show that whereas early rewritings challenged conventions in their time, newer rewritings tended to adhere to dominant ideological and aesthetic currents. The latter dictated that retranslations of canonical works should adhere closely to the original. Oliveira holds up the early omission and eventual reappearance of Perrault's morals (the witty codas in verse that followed each of Perrault's prose tales) to illustrate this progression. Informed by Descriptive Translation Studies and Lefevere's notions of rewriting and patronage, she shows how rewritings exerted a central role in establishing and maintaining Perrault's tales in the Brazilian children's literature canon. Monteiro Lobato reappears here as a central intermediary figure: his translations of eight tales from *Mother Goose* (he excluded the morals), published in 1934, cemented a place for Perrault in the Brazilian literary system.

Two contributions explore the complex relationship between text and image in translated picture books. In "Translating crossover picture books: The Italian translations of *Bear Hunt* by Anthony Browne," **Annalisa Sezzi** considers the translation problems that arise from having to handle two semiotic systems (the verbal and the visual), two addressees (child and adult) and difficult, taboo themes (in this case, war). Her investigation focuses on the Italian translation (1990) and retranslation (1999) of *Bear Hunt* (1979), a story revolving around a little white bear being chased by hunters who draws himself out of problematic situations with a magic pencil. The case study shows how the two Italian translators adopted different solutions when tackling the relationship between visual and verbal, the read-aloud situation posed by the adult reading aloud, and the various layers of meaning in Browne's picture book. Sezzi finds inspiration in O'Sullivan's (2003) scheme on narrative communication for translation, using it to compare the implied child reader and the implied adult reading aloud in the source and target texts. She finds that both the Italian translation and the retranslation make light of the picture book's disquieting yet central theme of war, suggesting that the child image *and* the adult image informing both translators' strategies question both audiences' ability to cope.

Sara Van Meerbergen and **Charlotte Lindgren** focus on the depiction of movement in images and words in two spreads from a popular series of Swedish picture books, showing how globally disseminated images receive local meanings when translated. Their chapter, "Pettson and Findus go glocal: Recontextualization of images and multimodal analysis of simultaneous action in Dutch and French translations," combines insights from social semiotics and Descriptive Translation Studies to "see translation and the act of translating as motivated by and within its specific social and situational context, depending on the signs that are culturally available within this context." On this basis, they discuss the Dutch and French translations of a Pettson and Findus picture book, describing the conditions of each translation's coming into being (the production context) and analyzing their multimodal features (the text-internal context containing the visual and verbal depiction of characters and their actions). They focus specifically on simultaneous action, where a character is depicted multiple times on one spread in a succession of different actions. (In their examples, Grandpa Pettson is going about various chores in his garden.) They find that the Dutch translation tends to neutralize and reduce ongoing simultaneous actions, reformulating them into sequential actions performed one after another, which requires less complex verb structures. In contrast, the French translation tends to use complex stylistic verb structures to depict simultaneous and ongoing action. Van Meerbergen and Lindgren relate these differing strategies to different translation norms in each production context. They also note the wider tendency in translations for children to avoid repetition and simplify difficult syntax. They conclude that the picture books about Pettson and Findus can be described as "'glocal' artifacts, where globally spread images receive different meanings due to local choices made in the translations."

Two final contributions examine the translation of violence in children's literature. **Marija Todorova** looks at the English translation (2011) and musical stage adaptation (2012) of Branko Ćopić's *Ježeva kućica* [Hedgehog's Home] (1949), one of the most enduring books for children from the former Yugoslavia. She opens her chapter, "Translating violence in children's picture books: A view from the former Yugoslavia," with a reflection on violence itself, parsing its various forms. She then goes on to explore how the violence foregrounded in the original book – direct violence caused by fighting in the Western Balkans during World War II – was recast in a different context to illustrate another form of violence: ecological violence to the natural environment. The musical stage adaptation, set in 1920s England, makes a similar move, combining references to ecological violence with references to class violence: whereas the Hedgehog is dressed to represent a British peasant, the bad animals of the forest are costumed as the upper class (with the Fox dressed in traditional foxhunting attire). Like Sezzi and Van Coillie, Todorova finds that direct mentions of war and death in the source text were either removed or rendered indirectly in the translation and stage adaptation "so that the dark forest is not so dark anymore." However, despite the fact that both target texts radically decontextualize the story from its geographical and historical context and fractalize its notion of violence, the story's recontextualization in a new time and place "arguably offers target readers a more complex and nuanced understanding of the issue of violence and its psychological and structural manifestations."

Valérie Alfvén examines another form of violence in the volume's final contribution: "Defying norms through unprovoked violence: The translation and reception of two Swedish young adult novels in France." She reconstructs the French careers of two Swedish young adult novels – *Spelar död* [Play Dead] (1999, translated into French in 2004) and *När tågen går förbi* [When the Trains Pass By] (2005, translated into French in 2007). Both books broach the sensitive topic of unprovoked violence perpetrated by young people on their peers. The translations sparked a 'moral panic' among French book producers that compelled the books' French editor, Thierry Manier, to explain his editorial choices in the media. He and others defended the books on the grounds that young readers were intelligent enough to read "literary works (...) [and were] capable of knowing the difference between being a voyeur (...) and being a reader" (Alfvén quoting *Le Monde des livres* 2007). Others disagreed, admitting that there were "taboo topics" and that "not everything is publishable" even if its literary merits are uncontested (*ibid.*). Using Toury's notions of adequate and acceptable translation, Alfvén gives a textual analysis of the translators' strategies for rendering violence. Given a French context of "strong pedagogical norms and reticence about dark and difficult topics, the risk that the Swedish texts would undergo restrictions in the translation was high." To her surprise, Alfvén finds that the French translators chose to translate in an adequate manner, that is, close to Swedish norms. (This is not the case for the English translation of *När tågen går förbi*, which she also briefly examines.) She then looks at the social conditions of the books' entry into the French system, concluding that they owe their existence to the clout of the well-established translators and editors attached to each title. Alfvén argues that the books are innovative in Even-Zohar's sense of the term: they arrived in France "at a historical moment where old models and norms were no longer tenable, as illustrated by the moral panic that ensued." By offering a new model, the works "filled a vacuum in the French system and injected it with a new dynamic." Since the publication of these books, some French authors for children and adolescents have dared to write about unprovoked violence themselves, an early indication that the Swedish model has found a foothold in France and another example – among the many compiled in this volume – of how translations can unsettle and innovate.

Bibliography

Alvstad, Cecilia. 2010. "Children's Literature and Translation." In *Handbook of Translation Studies Volume 1*, edited by Yves Gambier and Luc Van Doorslaer, 22–27. Amsterdam/Philadelphia: John Benjamins.

Baker, Mona. 2006. "Contextualization in Translator- and Interpreter-mediated Events." *Journal of Pragmatics* 38, no. 3: 321–337.

Bamberger, Richard. 1963. *Übersetzung von Jugendbüchers*. Vienna: International Board on Books for Young People [Schriftenreihe des Buchklubs der Jugend], 17.

Bamberger, Richard. 1978. "Influence of Translation on Children's Literature." In *Children's Books in Translation: The Situation and the Problems*, edited by Göte Klingberg, Mary Ørvig and Stuart Amor, 19–27. Stockholm: Almqvist & Wiksell International.

Bassnett, Susan and André Lefevere, eds. 1990. *Translation, History and Culture*. London/New York: Pinter.

Brownlie, Siobhan. 2006. "Narrative Theory and Retranslation Theory." *Across Languages and Cultures* 7, no. 2: 145–170.

Cronin, Michael. 2003. *Translation and Globalization*. London/New York: Routledge.

De La Rochère, Martine Hennard Dutheuil, Gillian Lathey and Monika Wozniak, eds. 2016. *Cinderella across Cultures: New Directions and Interdisciplinary Perspectives*. Detroit: Wayne State University Press.

Desmidt, Isabelle. 2006. "A Prototypical Approach within Descriptive Translation Studies? Colliding Norms in Translated Children's Literature." In *Children's Literature in Translation: Challenges and Strategies*, edited by Jan Van Coillie and Walter Verschueren, 123–139. Manchester: St. Jerome.

Dimitriu, Rodica. 2005. "The Many Contexts of Translation." *Linguaculture* 1: 5–23.

Dollerup, Cay. 1999. *Tales and Translation: The Grimm Tales from Pan-Germanic Narratives to Shared International Fairytales*. Amsterdam/Philadelphia: John Benjamins.

Douglas, Virginie and Florence Cabaret, eds. 2014. *La Retraduction en littérature de jeunesse / Retranslating Children's Literature*. Brussels: Peter Lang.

Du Nour, Miryam. 1995. "Retranslation of Children's Books as Evidence of Changes in Norms." *Target* 7, no. 2: 327–346.

Even-Zohar, Itamar. 1979. "Polysystem Theory." *Poetics Today* 1–2: 287–310.

Fischer, Beatrice and Matilde Nisbeth Jensen, eds. 2012. *Translation and the Reconfiguration of Power Relations: Revisiting Role and Context of Translation and Interpreting*. Graz: LIT Verlag.

Geerts, Sylvie and Sara Van den Bossche. 2014. *Never-ending Stories: Adaptation, Canonisation and Ideology in Children's Literature*. Ghent: Academia Press.

Ghesquiere, Rita. 2006. "Why Does Children's Literature Need Translations?" In *Children's Literature in Translation: Challenges and Strategies*, edited by Jan Van Coillie and Walter Verschueren, 19–33. Manchester: St. Jerome.

Hazard, Paul and Marguerite M. K. Mitchell. 1944. *Books, Children & Men*. Boston: The Horn Book.

Heilbron, Johan. 1999. "Towards a Sociology of Translation: Book Translations as a Cultural World-system." *European Journal of Social Theory* 2, no. 4: 429–444.

Hermans, Theo. 1999. *Translation in Systems*. Manchester: St. Jerome.

House, Juliane. 2006. "Text and Context in Translating." *Journal of Pragmatics* 38: 338–358.

Kaniklidou, Themis and Juliane House. 2017. "Discourse and Ideology in Translated Children's Literature: A Comparative Study." *Perspectives* 26, no. 2: 232–245.

Katan, David. 2004. *Translating Cultures: An Introduction for Translators, Interpreters and Mediators*. 2nd edition. Manchester: St. Jerome.

Kruger, Haidee. 2011a. "Exploring a New Narratological Paradigm for the Analysis of Narrative Communication in Translated Children's Literature." *Meta* 56, no. 4: 812–832.

Kruger, Haidee. 2011b. "Postcolonial Polysystems: Perceptions of Norms in the Translation of Children's Literature in South Africa." *The Translator* 17, no. 1: 105–136.

Lathey, Gillian. 2006. *The Translation of Children's Literature: A Reader*. Clevedon: Multilingual Matters.

Lathey, Gillian. 2010. *The Role of the Translator in Children's Literature*. London: Routledge.

Lathey, Gillian. 2015. *Translating Children's Literature*. New York/London: Routledge.

Lefevere, André. 1998. "Translation Practice(s) and the Circulation of Cultural Capital. Some Aeneids in English." In *Constructing Cultures*, edited by Susan Bassnett and André Lefevere, 25–40. Clevedon: Multilingual Matters.

Munday, Jeremy. 2001. *Introducing Translation Studies: Theories and Applications*. London/New York: Routledge.

Nida, Eugene A. 1964. *Toward a Science of Translating*. Leiden: E. J. Brill.

Nida, Eugene A. 2001. *Contexts in Translating*. Amsterdam/Philadelphia: John Benjamins.

Nord, Christiane. 1995. "Text-functions in Translation: Titles and Headings as a Case in Point." *Target* 7, no. 2: 261–284.

Nord, Christiane. 2003. "Proper Names in Translations for Children: *Alice in Wonderland* as a Case in Point." *Meta* 48, no. 1–2: 182–196.

Nord, Christiane. 1991. *Text Analysis in Translation*. Amsterdam/Atlanta: Rodopi.

Nord, Christiane. 1997. *Translating as a Purposeful Activity*. Manchester: St. Jerome.

O'Driscoll, Kieran. 2011. *Retranslation through the Centuries: Jules Verne in English*. Oxford/Bern: Peter Lang.

Oittinen, Riitta. 2000. *Translating for Children*. New York/London: Garland.

O'Sullivan, Emer. 2000. *Kinderliterarische Komparistik*. Heidelberg: C. Winter.

O'Sullivan, Emer. 2003. "Narratology Meets Translation Studies, or, the Voice of the Translator in Children's Literature." *Meta* 48, no. 1–2: 197–207.

O'Sullivan, Emer. 2005. *Comparative Children's Literature*. London: Routledge.

Persson, Lisa-Christina, ed. 1962. *Translations of Children's Books*. Lund: Bibliotekstjänst.

Reiss, Katharina. 1982. "Zur Übersetzung von Kinder- und Jugendbüchern: Theorie und Praxis." *Lebendige Sprachen* 17: 7–13.

Reiss, Katharina and Hans J. Vermeer. 1984. *Grundlegung einer allgemeinen Translationstheorie*. Tübingen: Niemeier.

Sapiro, Gisèle. 2010. "Globalization and Cultural Diversity in the Book Market: The Case of Literary Translations in the US and in France." *Poetics* 38: 419–439.

Seago, Karen. 2006. "Nursery Politics: *Sleeping Beauty* or the Acculturation of a Tale." In *The Translation of Children's Literature: A Reader*, edited by Gillian Lathey, 175–189. Clevedon: Multilingual Matters.

Shavit, Zohar. 1986. "Translation of Children's Literature." In *Poetics of Children's Literature*, 111–129, Athens/London: University of Georgia Press.

Shavit, Zohar. 1994. "Beyond the Restrictive Frameworks of the Past: Semiotics of Children's Literature – A New Perspective for the Study of the Field." In *Kinderliteratur im interkulturelle Prozess: Studien zur allgemeinen und vergleichenden Literaturwissenshaft*, edited by Hans-Heino Ewers, Gertrud Lehnert and Emer O'Sullivan, 4–15. Stuttgart/Weimar: J. B. Metzler.

Stephens, John and David McCallum. 1998. *Retelling Stories, Framing Culture: Traditional Story and Metanarratives in Children's Literature*. New York/London: Garland.

Tabbert, Reinbert. 2002. "Approaches to the Translation of Children's Literature: A Review of Critical Studies Since 1960." *Target* 14, no. 2: 303–351.

Toury, Gideon. 1995. *Descriptive Translation Studies – and Beyond*. Amsterdam/Philadelphia: John Benjamins.

Toury, Gideon. 1999. "A Handful of Paragraphs on 'Translation' and 'Norms'." In *Translation and Norms*, edited by Christina Schäffner, 10–32. Clevedon: Multilingual Matters.

Venuti, Lawrence, 1995. *The Translor's Invisibility: A History of Translation*. London/New York: Routledge.

Venuti, Lawrence, ed. 2012. *The Translation Studies Reader*. 3rd edition. London/New York: Routledge.

Wolf, Michaela. 2010. "Sociology of Translation." In *Handbook of Translation Studies Volume 1*, edited by Yves Gambier and Luc van Doorslaer, 337–343. Amsterdam/Philadelphia: John Benjamins.

Xu, Xu. 2013. "Translation, Hybridization, and Modernization: John Dewey and Children's Literature in Early Twentieth Century China." *Children's Literature in Education* 44, 222–237.

Part 1

Context » Text

"Only English books"

The mediation of translated children's literature in a resistant economy[1]

Gillian Lathey

Abstract

In 1802 Mrs. Sarah Trimmer, author of an influential monthly publication of reviews, articles and correspondence on children's books called *The Guardian of Education* (1802–1806), warned her readers against the corrupting influence of French literature. She argued that "only English books" (1802, 407) could guarantee a Christian basis for moral education. A resistance to translated children's literature – albeit with different causes – has continued in the UK since Mrs. Trimmer's day, resulting in a striking imbalance between the numbers of children's books translated into English (currently around 2 percent of publications for children per year) and from English into other languages. How, then, do publishers, editors, translators, critics and educators mediate those rare children's books that are translated into English? What effect does children's limited experience of reading translations have on translation strategies? What kinds of local and national initiatives exist in the UK to encourage the translation of children's books in the future? And what are the broader implications of this special British situation for the promotion and reception of translations for children?

Introduction

In 1803 the doughty Mrs. Sarah Trimmer published a dire warning to parents in *The Guardian of Education*, the monthly journal on children's books of which she was editor-in-chief. The teaching of French to English children, she argued, had become "the occasion of incalculable mischief, by opening a passage for

---

[1] A section of this chapter was previously published as Gillian Lathey. 2018. "Serendipity, Independent Publishing and Translation Flow: Recent Translations for Children in the UK." In *The Edinburgh Companion to Children's Literature*, edited by Clémentine Beauvais and Maria Nikolajeva, 232–244. Edinburgh: Edinburgh University Press.

that torrent of infidelity and immorality which has been poured upon the nation from the continent through the channel of French books" (Trimmer 1803, 406). Mrs. Trimmer's conclusion in the face of this intimidating deluge was that *"only English books"* could guarantee a Christian basis for a moral education (*ibid.*). A resistance to fiction for children originating outside the UK – albeit with entirely different causes – continues to this day to hamper its publication, resulting in a striking imbalance between the numbers of children's books translated from English into other languages and those translated into English. Indeed, on a list entitled "What Are the Best Books to Help Children Feel Connected to Europe" in the national newspaper *The Guardian* on Monday, June 6, 2016 – and in view of its publication just seventeen days before the Brexit vote one might well argue 'too little, too late' – *all* of the books reviewed were written by English-speaking authors with, as an afterthought, a link to a list of translations chosen by *Guardian* readers.[2]

This lasting and deep-seated wariness of the entity formerly known in the UK as 'the Continent' (pace Mrs. Trimmer) has resulted in erratic fluctuations in the publication of translated children's books. There have been some highpoints; it is ironic that Mrs. Trimmer's remarks, although indicative of a strand of contemporary anti-French sentiment, relate to an era when there was in fact a remarkably lively exchange of ideas and literature between France and the UK. In addition to translations, books in French, including Mme de Beaumont's *Magasin des Enfants* with the story of Beauty and the Beast (1756), were published in London. A further instance of increased translation activity occurred in the mid-twentieth century, between the 1950s and the 1970s, when British publishers introduced children to a variety of Nordic literature, including the work of Astrid Lindgren and Tove Jansson (Lathey 2010).

It is not my intention to attempt an exhaustive discussion of the disputed causes of this resistance to translated children's books but, rather, to highlight the steps being taken to overcome it. Nevertheless, a few basic preliminary and explanatory points should be noted. Firstly, research into global translation traffic indicates that there is a significant imbalance between translations into and from the English language. Recent sociological interpretations of international exchange include those of Johan Heilbron (2010) who posits a hierarchical system that governs world translation flows, with English currently in a central position as the source language for the world's published translations; or Pascale Casanova's (2007) political view of inequality and power struggle that identifies dominating and dominated languages, with

---

2   Thanks are due to Clémentine Beauvais for alerting me to this list.

English in the dominating category. Sources of data for the analysis of translation patterns are, as researchers admit, inevitably patchy and limited to statistics produced by individual countries or the incomplete UNESCO *Index Translationum*. It is nonetheless possible to echo Lawrence Venuti's conclusion that "English has become the most translated language worldwide, but despite the considerable size, technological sufficiency, and financial stability of the British and American publishing industries, it is one of the least translated into" (Venuti 1998, 160). Indeed, Venuti goes so far as to call this state of "unequal cultural exchange" "embarrassing" for the US and the UK, since it indicates cultural hegemony and the world dominance of English (*ibid.*, 159). Specific data on translations into English support Venuti's conclusion: a statistical report on all translated literature in the UK and Ireland compiled by Jasmine Donahaye of Swansea University in 2012 suggests that just 3 percent of all publications is the likely figure for the proportion of translated books in the sample years of 2000, 2005 and 2008 (Donahaye 2012).

In relation to material for young readers, the strong tradition of English-language children's literature since the mid-nineteenth century and its dominance on the international stage leads both to the saturation of the British market with very little space for imports, and to a high volume of translation from, rather than into, English. This disparity has only increased with the advent of globalization, with the *Harry Potter* series and associated franchises as a notable example of the ascendancy of the English language in relation to the intercultural transfer of children's fiction. Moreover, the position of English as a lingua franca leads to problems with a lack of confidence in young people in Britain as regards learning new languages (although many are, of course, bilingual), which in turn contributes to a reduced interest on the part of young British readers in European literature. Finally, from the all-important publishers' point of view, interviews, articles and research suggest that British publishers of children's books attribute their caution regarding translations to the high cost of production, the difficulty in identifying appropriate translators, the low level of sales, or – given a limited in-house knowledge of other languages – the uncomfortable process of having to trust a translator's report rather than their own gut instincts (see Flugge 1994; Lathey 2010, 159; Owen 2004).

The UK, a world leader in the global export of children's literature is, then, at a disadvantage in developing economic and cultural structures for the public reception of translations for children. In countries such as Finland, where translations account for up to 80 percent of children's books published in any one year, it is indigenous children's writers who require support in the face of an overwhelming tide of translations. Young readers in the UK, on the other hand, have limited access to the cultural, linguistic and aesthetic impetus that books originating in other countries provide. So how do publishers, editors, translators, critics and educators mediate those rare children's books that are translated into English? What effect does an awareness of children's limited experience of reading translations have on translators' attitudes to specific translation strategies? What motivates the publishers who do dare to publish translations in an unreceptive market, and what kinds of local and national initiatives exist in the UK to encourage the translation of children's books in the future? An exploration of these questions will address, in turn, the mediation of translated texts by publishers and translators, the pioneering work of a number of independent publishers determined to redress the balance in British children's publishing, and local and national initiatives to encourage publishers and to promote children's interest in the translation process. Each of these approaches and policies raises universal questions concerning the transfer of children's literature within the global economy.

Mediation

Across the history of translation of children's literature into English there exists evidence of multiple forms of mediation by publishers or translators designed to ease the passage of a 'foreign' work into the British market, and into the hearts and minds of young readers. A handful of historical and contemporary examples will indicate the tactics of diverse mediators seeking to align texts with British children's – or their parents' – expectations. In the mid-nineteenth century, children's poet Mary Howitt attached to her translation from the German of the fables of Wilhelm Hey a fey little verse that artfully diminishes the threat of the culturally alien:

> To English Children
> This little book comes from the hand,
> Dear Children, of a friend –
> Throughout the kindred German land,
> Tis loved from end to end. (Howitt 1844, 1)

Howitt addresses children almost as a benign, intermediary aunt would, introducing a "little" book that will not overwhelm them, and emphasizing kinship and friendship with Germany. In addition to such peritextual material by translators, publishers also adopt mediating strategies. One example is the tried and tested marketing ploy of adding the seal of approval of a well-known British children's writer to a translation. *Winnie-the-Pooh* author A. A. Milne's introduction to the first British edition of *The Story of Babar* in 1934, for example, closes with the words "I salute M. de Brunhoff. I am at his feet" (de Brunhoff 1934, 2). Children's poet Walter de la Mare, on the other hand, gently reassures young readers in his 1931 preface to Margaret Goldsmith's translation of Erich Kästner's *Emil and the Detectives* that "there is nothing in this German story that *might* not happen (in pretty much the same way as it does happen in the book) in London or Manchester or Glasgow to-morrow afternoon" (Kästner 1931, 13). There is therefore no need, de la Mare insists, for children to be alarmed by Emil's name and the Berlin setting of his adventures.

In the twenty-first century a number of publishers and editors have renewed efforts to render translators visible by introducing information in a child-friendly manner in blurbs, prefaces, profiles and postscripts, thus drawing the attention of young readers to the very fact that they are reading a translation. Guy Puzey, translator of Maria Parr's *Waffle Hearts* from Norwegian, is presented in a postscript to the book as a good choice because of his location: "Puzey grew up in the Highlands of Scotland, just a short swim from Norway" (Parr 2005, 240). In one original venture, it is the voice of the narrative's young protagonist that announces the name of the translator in the English versions of Johanne Mercier's French-Canadian books, a strategy that maintains the tenor and tune of the reading experience the child has just enjoyed. In a postscript to *Arthur and the Mystery of the Egg*, Arthur addresses young readers directly:

> Daniel Hahn translated the stories. He took my French words, and wrote them in English. He said it was quite a difficult job, but Cousin Eugene said he could have done it much better, only he was busy that day. So we got Daniel to do it, as he's translated loads and loads of books before. (Mercier 2013, 41)

Thus translators become real-life figures to children who might otherwise take linguistic transition for granted.

Such acts of mediation raise the question as to how British children's limited reading of translations might affect translation techniques. Discussion has to be largely speculative for want of a large-scale international and comparative study of strategies adopted in the translation of children's literature. However, taking Lawrence Venuti's (2008) delineation of 'foreignization' and 'domestication' strategies as a pertinent starting point, it is possible to offer some insights into translators' practices. Venuti's thesis that domestication amounts to cultural appropriation and that foreignization maintains the reader's awareness that s/he is reading the product of a different culture is, as translator and critic Riitta Oittinen asserts, a "delicate" one in relation to children's literature. Oittinen claims that whereas many adult readers "might not find foreignized texts offputting, the child reader may very well be unwilling to read the translated text, finding it too strange" (Oittinen 2006, 43). This argument carries some weight in the British context. Although it is essential to encourage children's natural eagerness to encounter difference, pragmatic compromises are sometimes necessary.

British translators express a variety of views on this issue. Patricia Crampton, translator of children's fiction across the second half of the twentieth century, conceded that "there is a need to counteract the reader's unfamiliarity with customs and cultural markers" (quoted in Lathey 2010, 190). Similarly, prize-winning translator Anthea Bell echoed Oittinen when she commented that "an adult may say: this is alien to us but foreign and interesting. A child may just lose interest" (Bell 1979, 50). On the other hand, Sarah Ardizzone, translator of children's books from French, aims to achieve a *décalage* or disjuncture at a linguistic level that is a reminder of the source language. She uses phrases such as "jet-lag," "being out of kilter" and "slippage" to convey the sense of a "healthy clash and jostle" as two languages meet (quoted in Lathey 2010, 190), thus highlighting the critically neglected significance of the "in-betweenness of languages and cultures" to which Clémentine Beauvais (2018, 10) has recently drawn attention. Even Ardizzone, however, has domesticated place names in her translations for the young, although she has acknowledged regret at altering 'Nice' and 'Paris' to the more neutral 'town' and 'city' in her translation of Daniel Pennac's *Dog* (quoted in Lathey 2010, 190). Anthea Bell's statement that the "atmosphere" of a narrative should not be reduced to an "inoffensive blandness," but rather that "[w]ith each individual book, you must gauge the precise degree of foreignness, and how far it is acceptable and can be preserved" (Bell 1985, 7), is a necessary cautionary note in a situation that calls for subtle linguistic and cultural negotiation to ensure that translations are read at all.

Independent publishers

It is common to hear the complaint from British children's publishers that translations do not sell well. As a result, mainstream publishing conglomerates issue single translations only sporadically. Of these larger publishing companies, Egmont created at the turn of the millennium a short-lived 'World Mammoth' series with the strapline "The finest literature from around the world," and Walker Books has published a number of translations in recent years, including Helen Wang's translation from Chinese of *Bronze and Sunflower* by Cao Wenxuan (2015), which won the 2017 Marsh Award for Children's Literature in Translation. It is, however, smaller companies that lead the way in publishing translations. Editors of the 2015 follow-up report to the Swansea University statistical analysis of translated literature in the UK and Ireland indicate that "translations are brought out mostly by smaller and medium-sized independent houses" (Büchler and Trentacosti 2015, 21). Companies of this kind make an invaluable contribution to the pool of translations available to children in the UK. On the logistical front it may well be the case that the small-scale publisher is able to expedite translations with a speed, efficiency and degree of personal contact that larger companies, with their hierarchies and complex marketing and approval systems, cannot match. Publishing a translation entails not only the possibility of limited editorial access to the language of the source text, but also a commitment to the time necessary for the translation process and, ideally, to close collaboration between editor and translator – all of which is easier to manage when only a limited number of employees are involved.

Comments taken from a series of telephone and email interviews with three independent publishers plying their trade at the precarious perimeter of the children's publishing scene in the UK in 2016 illustrates a phenomenon specific to the British situation, namely the impetus of a personal crusade by directors to address the lack of translations available to their own children.

Cheryl Robson's small company Aurora Metro extended its list to include books for young people after her daughter attended an interview at a prestigious school at the age of eleven and was the only girl to name a book other than *Harry Potter* as her favorite. (She chose *The Diary of Anne Frank*.) Robson decided to counteract the explosion of fantasy at the time by publishing "books about serious issues" (personal correspondence, April 16, 2016), and looked beyond the UK to find novels that met her requirements. Eight of the twelve titles on the Aurora Metro Young Adult list of 2017 were translations, with titles ranging from Jean Molla's *Sobibor* (2005) on the generational impact of the Holocaust, translated from French by Polly McLean, to a novel recounting the dangers faced by Cubans fleeing by sea to the US (*Letters from Alain* by Enrique Pérez Díaz, translated from Spanish by Simon Breden, 2008). Sadly, Robson is disappointed that despite her efforts the books have not been reviewed in the press, and that both the book trade and librarians have been reluctant to order them.

A second company, Tiny Owl Publishing, founded in 2014 by husband and wife team Karim Arghandehpour and Delaram Ghanimifard, owes its foundation to a concern similar to Robson's, although its remit is entirely different. Delaram Ghanimifard explains the decision she and her husband took to publish picture books from Iran as follows: "Tiny Owl is the result of my family's confrontation with immigration and facing the lack of translated books, diverse books, and children's books that reflected our cultural background for my son" (personal correspondence, May 19, 2016). A twofold purpose, firstly to enable her son to encounter his own culture in English, from the insights of thirteenth-century Persian mystic and poet Rumi to "contemporary authors such as Behrangi,"[3] and, secondly, to create the opportunity to learn about literature from other parts of the world "so that he could better understand his classmates" developed into a quest to broaden the perspectives of young British readers: "Many English books are translated in Iran every year and children read them and like them. Shouldn't this be a two-way road, allowing English children to learn about other cultures as well?" (personal correspondence, May 19, 2016). Currently there are fourteen titles on the Tiny Owl list. In an interview with Clive Barnes for the British section of the International Board on Books for Young People website, Ghanimifard insists that Iranian picture books are just the beginning of the venture, and has plans to match "the best authors that we know with the best illustrators and form a kind of a cultural dialogue" (Barnes 2016).

A third example is the rather larger independent Pushkin Press, founded in 1997 with a focus on literary quality and European fiction and essays for adults. Adam Freudenheim, one of the two managing directors, also refers to his own offspring and the "extreme lack of translations for children" (interview, June 29, 2016) when recounting the background to Pushkin's decision in 2013 to begin a children's list. Thanks to the successful adult list, Pushkin already had in place in-house speakers of German, French, Italian and Russian – all of which Freudenheim regards as 'gateway languages' providing access to books from a number of countries. Freudenheim and his team select books that have been successful in the source language, or have already sold well as translations in languages other than English. The Pushkin children's catalogue for 2017 lists seventy-nine children's titles. Over sixty of these are translations, including the first English editions of modern classics such as Tonke Dragt's *The Letter for the King* (2013, translated by Laura Watkinson) or Tomiko Inui's *The Secret of the Blue Glass* (2015, translated by Ginny Tapley Takemori), first published in the Netherlands in 1962 and Japan in 1959 respectively. Pushkin's publication of *The Adventures of Shola*

---

3   Samed Behrangi. 2015. *The Little Black Fish*. Translated by Azita Rassi. Illustrated by Farshid Mesghali. London: Tiny Owl Publishing.

by Bernardo Atxaga, translated from Spanish by Margaret Jull Costa, also won the Marsh Award for 2015.

Such a high volume of translations for children from one publisher is unprecedented, and has certainly enriched, shaken and stirred the translated children's book market in the UK in the last four years. Pushkin's success may well be attributable in part to an established following of literary-minded adult readers who have welcomed the feast of new and remembered children's classics, but a careful balance between new titles (for example Anne Plichota and Cendrine Wolf's French gothic fantasy series translated by Sue Rose) and beautifully presented classics likely to be bought as gifts has reduced the economic risk associated with translations for children. The commitment of Pushkin, Aurora Metro Books, Tiny Owl and other small-scale publishers to translations for the young represents a positive and much-needed contribution to the diversity of reading matter available to children in the UK.

Initiatives to promote translation and engage child readers

Neither the commitment of independent publishers nor the mediating strategies of translators and marketing departments alone can shift public opinion towards the reading of translations. The UK's resistance to foreign literature has led to much head-scratching and institutional debate, with national initiatives on translated children's literature funded by government arts and education departments, and the input of overseas cultural institutes promoting children's authors, particularly in London. The UK government's Arts Council has funded the touring Children's Bookshow, with its emphasis in recent years on translation, and also currently supports the Book Trust project "In Other Words," which annually showcases sample translations from 'outstanding' books originally written in a range of languages to British publishers at the Bologna Children's Book Fair. In 2006, in response to advice in the National Curriculum that children should read literature from a variety of cultures, a set of teaching materials entitled *Reading Differences: Introducing Children to World Literature* (QCA 2006) included translations. Moreover, since 1996 the biennial Marsh Award for Children's Literature in Translation sponsored by the Marsh Christian Trust – awarded biennially because there are quite simply insufficient translated books for an annual award – has drawn attention to translators and authors and illustrators from beyond the English-speaking world.

A new and promising development centering on translators and capitalizing on the existing linguistic knowledge and expertise of children aims to raise awareness both of the translation process and the qualities of literature written in other languages by encouraging children to translate. Prize-winning translator of children's books Sarah Ardizzone was, with teacher Sam Holmes, the first curator of the Translation Nation project, administered by charitable trusts and partly funded by Arts Council England. The project, intended for schoolchildren aged seven to eleven, ran from 2011 to 2014 and began both in London, where the first cohort of languages included Amharic, Gujarati, Italian, Polish, Portuguese, Somali, Spanish, Telugu (a Dravidian language spoken in south-eastern India) and Urdu, and on the Kent coast in schools with a large percentage of children from Poland, the Czech Republic and Slovakia. A series of three-day creative workshops run by literary translators and volunteer assistants enabled these children to work on the translation of a favorite story from their heritage language into English, with the aim of taking part in a competitive performance. The winning stories appeared on the Translation Nation website. One of the major aims of the initiative was to encourage the next generation of literary translators, and to enthuse monolingual English-speaking children by involving them in the editing and polishing of English versions of stories told or written by their classmates. As Ardizzone comments: "this is a project where we have to tear up the usual job description of what it means to be a literary translator – an energizing if challenging step for everyone's continuing professional development" (Ardizzone 2011, 7).

Such was the success of this first phase that the project has now developed into a "Translators in Schools" program, whereby trainee or professional translators spend three days on lesson planning, classroom management, visits to schools and on work with a mentor. Those taking part appreciate the opportunity to engage with a potential audience for their work, to develop children's writing skills in English and their understanding of differences between languages. For all children in the UK, whether mono-, bi- or multilingual, an understanding of translation and the aesthetic and linguistic processes involved is likely to enhance literary and general intellectual development and can only benefit the language-based aspect of diversity in British children's publishing in the long term. "Translators in Schools" is at present a small-scale project that deserves broader recognition and more substantial funding.

Valiant efforts by independent publishers, translators, government organizations, schools and charities are, therefore, working to make multiple facets of translation a part of children's lives in the UK. One brief, final point concerning the British context, however, indicates that the profile of translation still requires attention. In the UK of the 1980s and 1990s, there was a substantially funded impetus in larger cities to ensure the representation of children from a range of ethnic backgrounds in picture books and reading material in schools. Advocacy of diversity and plurality continues in organizations such as BAME in Publishing (Black Asian and Minority Ethnic) and Megaphone, an Arts Council and Publishers' Association-funded mentoring scheme for BAME writers wishing to publish a first book for children. Rarely, however, do such initiatives include any reference to the process of translation, which seems to be regarded as an entirely separate issue. A telling example of this disregard for translation is the list of the fifty best culturally diverse children's books published on October 13, 2014 in *The Guardian*, where only one title could be classed as a direct translation, namely Marjane Satrapi's account of her childhood in Tehran, *Persepolis I and II* (2003, 2004), translated from French by Mattias Ripa. Such a sidelining of the role of language in cultural diversity testifies once again to the centrality of the English language and the resulting invisibility of translation. Surely a united front to encourage publishers to embrace the linguistic, alongside the ethnic, variety of modern Britain, including the heritage languages of many children from across Europe currently residing in the UK, would more accurately reflect the country's multicultural population.

Conclusions

What kinds of general questions are posed for research into the economic and political contexts of translation for children by the present fragile situation in the UK? Firstly, with regard to mediation, there is a need for a more precise and broadly based account of relative degrees of peritextual mediation in blurbs, prefaces or child-friendly translator biographies within different countries. Comparative studies on the use of domestication strategies in translations published in children's literatures saturated with translations as opposed to those, like the UK, that are far less receptive to translations are also essential to an understanding of the impact of translation flows in the field of children's literature. Sample analysis of translations between selected languages in specific eras or genres might indicate whether translation strategies in a less penetrable economy differ from those in cultures where translations form a much larger percentage of children's reading material.

Furthermore, a theoretical advocacy of foreignization as a means of introducing children to difference has to be re-examined in relation to the context into which translations are received. The glocalization of globally distributed texts such as the *Harry Potter* series to meet local needs is now a recognized phenomenon; Michał Borodo's recently published *Translation,*

Globalization and Younger Audiences: The Situation in Poland (2017) is an informative and relevant case study. In the UK, such a study would have to take into account the specifics of a situation where the number of translations is limited. And there is still a need for further empirical research in order to establish children's responses to, say, two different translations with differing degrees of domestication; Haidee Kruger's (2012) investigation into the reception of translated children's literature in South Africa offers one model for this kind of inquiry. Are young British readers, for example, able to tolerate alien names and foodstuffs despite their lack of experience in reading translations? The answer might well be that they are, but whatever the result, such research would have wider international implications for translation practices in impenetrable markets.

In the meantime, both conglomerates and independent publishers require encouragement from government and charitable organizations to introduce British children to books from other languages. Again, comparative international insights into the role of national and local initiatives to support children's literature, and whether that support is channeled towards indigenous authors or translations, would be welcome. Research into the public role of translators as ambassadors and evidence of children as translators in classrooms or online, too, would benefit from a sharing of experience across a range of countries.

It is, then, possible to illustrate positive developments in the UK, including an increase in the number of translations for children from non-European languages, notably the books published by Tiny Owl from Iran and the winning title of the most recent Marsh Award from China. As for Europe and the cross-channel traffic so abhorred by Mrs. Trimmer, it is ironic that the second spike in the range and volume of translations for children published in the UK cited at the beginning of this chapter occurred in the mid-twentieth century, *before* Britain joined the EU. Who knows, perhaps Brexit will herald a new golden age of translations for children in the UK, as publishers and translators seek to maintain links with Europe and to overcome the echoing clarion call for "only English books."

Bibliography

Ardizzone, Sarah. 2011. "Translation Nation." *In Other Words: The Journal for Literary Translators*, no. 38: 6–11.

Barnes, Clive. 2016. "Tiny Owl Publishing." Accessed June 4, 2020. https://www.ibby.org.uk/tinyowlpublishing/.

Beauvais, Clémentine. 2018. "Translated into British: European Children's Literature, (In)difference and Écart in the Age of Brexit." *Bookbird: A Journal of International Children's Literature* 56, no. 1: 10–18.

Bell, Anthea. 1979. "Children's Books in Translation." *Signal*, no. 28: 47–53.

Bell, Anthea. 1985. "Translator's Notebook: The Naming of Names." *Signal*, no. 46: 3–11.

Borodo, Michał. 2017. *Translation, Globalization and Younger Audiences: The Situation in Poland.* Oxford: Peter Lang.

Brunhoff, Jean de. 1934. *The Story of Babar the Little Elephant.* Translated by Olive Jones. London: Methuen.

Büchler, Alexandra and Giulia Trentacosti. 2015. *Publishing Translated Literature in the United Kingdom and Ireland 1990–2012: Statistical Report.* Aberystwyth: Mercator Institute for Media, Languages and Culture, Aberystwyth University, Wales.

Casanova, Pascale. 2007. *The World Republic of Letters.* Translated by Malcolm de Bevoise. Cambridge, MA: Harvard University Press.

Donahaye, Jasmine. 2012. *Three Percent? Publishing Data and Statistics on Translated Literature in the United Kingdom and Ireland: Literature across Frontiers.* Aberystwyth: Mercator Institute for Media, Languages and Culture, Aberystwyth University, Wales.

Eccleshare, Julie. 2016. "What Are the Best Books to Help Children Feel Connected to Europe?" *The Guardian*, June 16, 2016. https://www.theguardian.com/childrens-books-site/2016/jun/06/best-childrens-books-on-europe-katherine-rundell-ludwig-belman.

Flugge, Klaus. 1994. "Crossing the Divide." *The Bookseller*, April 8, 1994: 18–20.

Heilbron, Johan. 2010. "Towards a Sociology of Translation: Book Translations as a Cultural World System." In *Critical Readings in Translation Studies*, edited by Mona Baker, 304–317. London: Routledge.

Howitt, Mary. 1844. *The Child's Picture and Verse Book: Commonly Called Otto Speckter's Fable Book with the Original German and with French Translated into English by Mary Howitt.* London: Longman, Brown, Green and Longmans.

Kästner, Erich. 1931. *Emil and the Detectives.* Preface by Walter de la Mare. Translated by Margaret Goldsmith. Illustrated by Walter Trier. London: Jonathan Cape.

Kruger, Haidee. 2012. *Postcolonial Polysystems: The Production and Reception of Translated Children's Literature in South Africa*. Amsterdam: John Benjamins.

Lathey, Gillian. 2010. *The Role of Translators in Children's Literature: Invisible Storytellers*. London/New York: Routledge.

Mercier, Johanne. 2013. *Arthur and the Mystery of the Egg*. Translated by Daniel Hahn. London: Phoenix Yard Books.

Oittinen, Riitta. 2006. "No Innocent Act: On the Ethics of Translating for Children." In *Children's Literature in Translation: Challenges and Strategies*, edited by Jan Van Coillie and Walter P. Verschueren, 35–45. Manchester: St. Jerome.

Owen, Joanne. 2005. "Lost in Translation." *The Children's Bookseller*, March 19, 2004: 20–23.

Parr, Maria. 2005. *Waffle Hearts*. Translated by Guy Puzey. London: Walker Books.

QCA. 2006. *Reading Differences: Introducing Children to World Literature*. Qualifications and Curriculum Authority and the Centre for Literacy in Primary Education.

Trimmer, Sarah, Mrs. 1803. *The Guardian of Education, Vol. 2*. London: J. Hatchard.

Venuti, Lawrence. 1998. *The Scandals of Translation*. New York/London: Routledge.

Venuti, Lawrence. 2008. *The Translator's Invisibility: A History of Translation*. 2nd edition. New York/London: Routledge.

Two languages, two children's literatures

Translation in Ireland today

Emer O'Sullivan

Abstract

The Anglosphere has a reputation for being unreceptive to fiction in translation, and this also applies to Ireland. Some of the reasons for the relative paucity of translations in Irish children's literature in English are indeed the same as for other Anglophone countries, but the situation and development of children's literature in Ireland differ so significantly from theirs that it calls for a more differentiated look. Ireland is not just an Anglophone country; the first official language of the state is Irish, a Gaelic language, spoken daily today by only a small percentage of the population. It is therefore a case of one country with two languages and two children's literatures, each with their own tradition, into which books are (or are not) translated under different conditions. While Irish-language publications (including translations) have been heavily state subsidized since Irish independence in 1922, those in English have to survive in economic competition with the huge publishing conglomerates on the neighboring island. This chapter discusses the conditions under which both traditions have developed and examines contemporary Irish publishers who issue translations into English and Irish.

Introduction

"The Anglophone world is notoriously unreceptive to fiction in translation" (Parkinson 2013, 151). This statement also applies to Ireland, the most western Anglophone country in Europe, but it does not tell the whole story.[1] Some

---

1   Although Ireland was included with Britain in the "Literature across Frontiers" study which discovered that the proportion of translations of literature between 1990 and 2012 was somewhere around the 4 percent mark (Büchler and Trentacosti 2015), this general finding cannot be taken to apply specifically to Ireland, where the figure is significantly lower. The only publishers regularly issuing translations into English are the Dedalus Press, which specializes in contemporary poetry, and the international publisher Dalkey Archive Press, which has links to Ireland. Little Island is

of the reasons for the relative paucity of translations into English in Irish children's literature are indeed the same as in other Anglophone ones, and these are well documented (by Gillian Lathey in the previous chapter, for instance). But the situation and development of children's literature in Ireland differ so significantly from theirs that it calls for a more differentiated look.

For a start, Ireland is not just an Anglophone country. The first official language of the state is Irish, a Gaelic language, spoken daily by only a small percentage of the population. So it is a case of one country, two languages, and two children's literatures, each with their own tradition, into which books are (or are not) translated under different conditions. While Irish-language publications (including translations) are heavily state subsidized, ones in English have to survive in economic competition with the huge publishing conglomerates on the neighboring island. In order to illuminate the place of translation in each of these coexisting children's literatures today, this chapter will sketch the conditions under which they have developed since Ireland became independent in 1922. It will start by looking at publishing for children in Irish, which was fostered from those early days on, and will give an account of important contemporary developments as well as issues relating to translation into that language.

Almost sixty years were to pass before an indigenous publishing industry of any size existed for its Anglophone counterpart, and the reasons for this, as well as a brief account of Irish publishing for children in English from 1980 onwards, will follow. While translations were vital for the project of revitalizing the Irish language, this was not, of course, the case for English, and hardly any books for children were published in English translation before 2010, when a small independent press, Little Island, was set up with the express intention of publishing emerging Irish writers and children's books in translation. This courageous enterprise is the focus of the final section of this chapter, which will offer insights into the difficult conditions pertaining to children's literature in English translation in Ireland.[2]

---

the major publisher of children's books in English translation in Ireland and, apart from theirs, hardly any others are issued.

2   I am very grateful to publishers Siobhán Parkinson of Little Island and Tadhg Mac Dhonnagáin of Futa Fata, and to Walker Books' agent in Ireland, Conor Hackett, for generously giving of their time and answering my questions on translating in Ireland in personal, telephone and email interviews.

Irish children's literature in Irish

The sole language of the majority of Irish people through most of the country's history was Irish. It came under severe pressure after the English conquest in the seventeenth century and, by the late eighteenth century, large numbers of the Irish population – and virtually all the urban population – had adopted English. The more remote and underdeveloped regions of the west and south of the island remained Irish-speaking. These were the areas most affected during the Great Famine of 1848–1849, when the starvation and emigration of millions further hastened the demise of the language. During the rise of political and cultural nationalism in the late nineteenth and early twentieth century, there was a revival of interest in the Irish language, and the translation of its literary legacy into English became "an agent of aesthetic and political renewal" (Cronin 2011, 54). After independence, Irish became the official national and first language of the country but was never again to become the language of the majority, despite various official measures such as making Irish compulsory in schools. In the 2016 census, 1.7 million of the 4.7 million inhabitants of the Republic of Ireland answered 'yes' to being able to speak Irish, but just 73,803, or 1.7 percent of the population, said they spoke it daily outside the education system (Central Statistics Office 2019). There are no monoglot speakers of Irish today.

The majority attitude to the language is ambivalent. Most pay lip service to it as an important part of their cultural heritage but are not inclined to invest any significant effort into using it; some regard it as a relic from the past, to be spoken by a turf fireplace in a remote cottage. However, a recent urban revival movement, encouraged by changes in legislation in 2011 with regard to patronage of new schools, has seen a dramatic rise in the number of *Gaelscoileanna*, Irish-medium schools. A survey in 2018 revealed that 23 percent of parents would choose a local *Gaelscoil* for their children if it was available. And while it is unlikely that Irish will ever again be spoken by a majority on a daily basis, this increased demand for Irish-medium education reflects an interest in the language indicating that the downward trend might, at the very least, have been arrested. "Irish is a lot cooler than it used to be," says publisher Tadhg Mac Dhonnagáin (interview with Tadhg Mac Dhonnagáin), citing as an example new work by the Belfast hip hop duo Kneecap.

As with other languages in need of revitalization and dissemination, such as modern Hebrew, literature in translation played and plays an important role in reviving and fostering the Irish language. In 1926, the publishing house An Gúm [The Scheme] was established under the aegis of the Department of Education with the task of publishing literature in Irish, especially educational textbooks. While only six Irish-language books were in print in 1893 (Kiberd 2018, 44), An Gúm produced 1,465 publications in that language between 1926 and 1964 (Kennedy 1990, 14),[3] aided by "an ambitious policy of translation" (An Gúm n.d.). Translations of over 250 classical and popular titles by British, American and European writers were published during the 1930s alone, and many of their translators went on to become creative writers themselves, making the need for translations gradually less acute.

A situation in which a single state-funded publishing house operates under no commercial pressure and with little competition is, however, not conducive to ensuring high production values, and many children's books issued in Irish towards the end of the twentieth and the beginning of the twenty-first centuries were unattractive by comparison with books in English. The recent rise in the number of *Gaelscoileanna* also meant a rise in the number of readers of Irish and an increased demand for reading material for them, as well as for the children of native speakers in the *Gaeltacht*, the primarily Irish-speaking regions.[4] The feeling in general among parents, teachers, publishers and translators was that there was a need for contemporary Irish-language children's books that were as attractive and exciting as their English-language counterparts. Walker Books agent Conor Hackett, for instance, named the unappealing material in Irish on offer to his primary school children at the beginning of the decade as one of the elements that motivated him to seek to issue Irish translations of Walker picture books (interview with Conor Hackett). These factors combined to herald an exciting new wave of Irish-language publishing for children in the first decade of the twentieth century. A number of small, new, innovative, independent Irish-language presses were established – Futa Fata (2005), An tSnáthaid Mhór (2005), Páistí Press (2011) and others – which mainly targeted the 12–15 percent of children who are either native speakers or attend *Gaelscoileanna*. Translations issued by some of these presses, as well as by individual British publishing houses, helped significantly to raise the profile and production quality of children's books in Irish.

The source language(s) from which works are translated has been a hotly debated issue. As translator Maire Nic Mhaolain remarked in 2019 (Irish Translators'), in the past "translation from English to Irish [was considered]

---

3   This included 1,108 general literary works, 230 pieces of music and 127 textbooks. A selection of covers of the translations and other publications by An Gúm can be seen in the "Free State Art: Judging Ireland by its Book Covers" virtual exhibition of the Burns Library.

4   The translator Máirín Ní Ghadhra (2016) wrote: "Children who take to reading in the middle classes of national school can read up to a book a day, and the challenge for those of us rearing native speakers in the Gaeltacht in [sic] to ensure a regular supply for them."

almost a betrayal of our native writers," although today "the old attitude is going, if not gone." When An Gúm began to publish translated picture books, they were mainly bought in from the USSR and former Eastern Bloc countries "partly because they were comparatively inexpensive, but also for ideological reasons: they were not original English-language publications" (Coghlan 2013, n.p.). There was a long-standing policy that state support for translation into Irish only funded translations from languages other than English, the reasoning being that, as most readers of Irish, being bilingual, already had access to books in English, funding translation from other languages added to the diversity of material available. The economies of scale of the Irish-language book market are such that publishers depend on this state funding in order to survive (selling 8,000 copies of a book in Irish would, according to Conor Hackett, be exceptional (interview with Conor Hackett)), and all translation into Irish is supported by grants.[5] A refusal to support translation of English source texts meant that they were unlikely to be translated.

In the wake of the Good Friday Agreement, a new body, Foras Na Gaeilge [Irish Institute], was set up in December 1999. It was responsible for the promotion of the Irish language throughout the whole island of Ireland, with the activities of earlier state organizations – including An Gúm – being transferred to the new organization. After much debate they decided to revise the English language ruling, which resulted in a substantial amount of material being translated from English, some even issued by British publishers. The first popular title was *Harry Potter agus an Órchloch,* translated by Maire Nic Mhaolain and issued by Bloomsbury UK in 2004.[6] An Irish translation of Eoin Colfer's *Artemis Fowl*, also by Nic Mhaolain, was the next popular title to follow, published in the Penguin Ireland imprint in 2006. In 2012, Conor Hackett headed a project to issue translations into Irish of Walker's most popular picture books by Irish authors or illustrators, and ten books in total by Martin Waddell, Sam McBratney, Chris Haughton, Niamh Sharkey

---

5   In the case of non-Irish publishing houses, only the translation costs are covered; indigenous publishers receive more substantial support. Foras na Gaeilge is the main funder of publishing in Irish today. The Arts Council also funds individual projects and An Chomhairle um Oideachas Gaeltachta agus Gaelscolaíochta (COGG), an organization that supports Irish-medium education, also assists publishers financially (interview with Mac Dhonnagáin).

6   Bloomsbury commissioned translations of *Harry Potter and the Philosopher's Stone* into Welsh, Latin, Ancient Greek, and Irish, obviously with the educational market in view. They may not have been as commercially successful as hoped, as the only language into which the second volume of *Harry Potter* was translated is Welsh. The Irish bookseller Des Kenny said that *Harry Potter* had to be "the fastest children's classic to find itself in the Irish language," and that the initial print run of 25,000 was not only remarkable but also a vote of confidence in Irish by an English publisher (Siggins 2004).

and others were published under Walker's Éireann imprint. The fact that the books were already recognizable and successful gave them a commercial edge when sold in an Irish-language version, and this, according to Hackett, even led to some bookshops committing to maintaining a permanent children's Irish-language section. He expressed the hope that the strength of these books would "also direct attention of the market to the wealth of Irish language publishing from indigenous publishing houses" (quoted in O'Loughlin 2012), mentioning especially the quality picture books by the publishing house Futa Fata, which was already making its mark on the Irish-language market around that time.

Two important effects of translating popular British children's books into Irish is that they motivate young readers to read in Irish and raise the perceived status of the language. Since 2010, Cló Iar-Chonnacht, one of the largest private Irish-language firms, has issued several of the *Horrid Henry* [*Dónall Dána*] series by Francesca Simon and Tony Ross as well as eight Blyton *Famous Five* [*An Cuigear Croga*] volumes in translation. Máirín Ní Ghadhra, the translator, remarked:

> You are trying to ensure that children who are learning Irish as a second language in the education system will be able to read the book and – more importantly – enjoy it. (…) The perception of Gaeilge [Irish] as old-fashioned (…) can now be put to bed. (…) It is about providing more books to children who read Gaeilge, books that their peers read in English. And it is about persuading the children that their language is equally as cool as the one spoken by readers of Enid Blyton's *Famous Five*, *Horrid Henry*, *Dork Diaries* and Roald Dahl. It is also about demonstrating to those who have a mortal dread of our native tongue that Gaeilge is accessible, fun and trendy. (Ní Ghadhra 2016)

And booksellers were keen to stock known books by Blyton, David Walliams or Jeff Kinney in Irish translation, as "brand awareness is very high" amongst booksellers whose proficiency in Irish is not great (interview with Mac Dhonnagáin).[7]

However, the vast number of books translated from English after Foras changed their policy led to the Irish-language writers' organization, Aontas na Scríbhneoirí Gaeilge, lobbying to have the volume restricted, as they felt these translations undermined the development of original work in Irish.

---

7   Tadhg Mac Dhonnagáin believes that probably less than 2 percent of Irish booksellers speak or read Irish with confidence (interview with Mac Dhonnagáin).

The rules were once more revised, and today established publishers can apply for support for up to a maximum of 20 percent of their output to be translated – from any language, including English.

The innovative Futa Fata is an interesting case study for these contemporary developments. When it began publishing in 2005, it translated a number of picture books from French, originated by Belgian publisher Mijade, and also a few from German. Since 2016, it has published an Irish version of *Diary of a Wimpy Kid* by Jeff Kinney and books by David Walliams, all of which have succeeded commercially. Tadhg Mac Dhonnagáin explains: "We print in the 2,500–3,000 range and we reprint regularly. For a language with a base population of around 75,000 daily speakers, that's pretty good going. The commercial success of the books has helped our company to get on a more secure financial footing" (interview with Mac Dhonnagáin). But the concern of Irish-language writers prompted Futa Fata "to take a change of direction in our approach to translation" (*ibid.*). Its emphasis is now on replacing translations with original work, and it has done well in selling its quality picture books on the international market, which is highly unusual for an Irish-language publisher. The only picture books it has translated recently are by Julia Donaldson and Axel Scheffler, as they sell very well in Irish. The striking and original picture books issued by Belfast publishing house An tSnáthaid Mhór have also enjoyed international success.

There are a few anomalies peculiar to translating into Irish. Unusually for a literature in a first national language, a difficulty in producing attractive reading material for older children and young adults in Irish is connected to the fact that the vast majority learn it as a foreign language, so their level of linguistic competence is not apace with their intellectual and emotional development (Uí Mhaicín 1996, 132). A recent innovative move by publisher Tadhg Mac Dhonnagáin to address this anomaly involved having translations done of a series of short novels for children aged eight to twelve, originally commissioned from recognized UK writers and illustrators such as Malorie Blackman, Frank Cottrell Boyce, Cathy Brett and others by Barrington Stoke, a dyslexia-friendly, reluctant-reader publisher. These 5,000–7,000-word-long stories, where the content is appropriate for eight- to twelve-year-olds but the reading age is lower, have proved so popular in schools that Futa Fata is now planning to publish a similar original series of short novels in Irish. This further step by Futa Fata to replace translations with original work is also a good example of translation having had a sustainably positive influence on the target literature and directly influencing indigenous production.

An anomaly of a different kind can be found in the translation of certain kinds of historical children's novels. English is the source language of Marita

Conlon McKenna's much-lauded *Under the Hawthorn Tree* (1990), set during the Great Famine in the mid-nineteenth century and one of the few contemporary Irish novels to be translated into Irish. But the target language, Irish, is the one that would actually have been spoken by the fictional children in the setting of the novel. Alan Titley thus found the translation into Irish, *Faoin Sceach Gheal* by Maire Nic Mhaolain (2000), superior to the original. Conlon McKenna's book, he writes, "is superbly interesting in itself, but the Irish translation succeeds in drawing us back into the maw of time and recreating the conditions of talk and conversation and atmosphere which existed during the famine in a way that the English version simply cannot do" (Titley 2000, 104). The paradox of this situation can be summed up by asking which of the two translation strategies – in Lawrence Venuti's terminology 'domestication' or 'foreignization'– have been applied here. On the one hand it could be declared a domesticating one, because it apparently brings the text closer to the culture of the target language. However, it does so not by virtue of cultural adaptation but by rendering an already Irish story in one Irish source language into, according to Titley, a 'more Irish' story in the other Irish target language.

From the early Irish translations in the 1920s onward, a trend favoring cultural adaptation – domestication in the more traditional sense – has prevailed. Caoimhe Nic Lochlainn identifies a clear domestication policy in translations into Irish starting with *Eibhlís I dTír na nIongantas,* the first Irish version of *Alice in Wonderland* by Pádraig Ó Cadhla in 1922, which relocated the text to Ireland, changed the name of the protagonist to the Irish Eibhlís, and inserted (non-parodied) traditional Irish myths and poems in place of Carroll's parodies.[8] And she sees it continuing up to the 1994 translation of Blyton's *The Secret Mountain* as *Eachtra San Afraic* [An Adventure in Africa] by Tomás Mac Aodha Bhuí, which renders it as a "self-consciously anticolonial and often overtly didactic text" (Nic Lochlainn 2013, 85). Nic Lochlainn concludes: "While manifestations of domestication are not always as evident as in these texts, this methodology has clearly found a foothold in Irish translations for children, without any properly articulated justification" (*ibid.,* 86). In the most recent Blyton translations issued by Cló Iar-Chonnacht, the names of the characters of the Famous Five were not translated or domesticated.

---

[8] Nic Lochlainn translates a 1923 review written in Irish, which writes appraisingly: "Padraig O Cadhla takes this little girl and, with the magic wand of the Irish language, makes her so Irish that you would swear that she had always been living in the Ring Gaeltacht" (Nic Lochlainn 2013, 75). The retranslation of *Alice in Wonderland* by Nicholas J. A. Williams in 2003 is also domesticated; see Titley (2015, 309).

However, as translator Máirín Ní Ghadhra (2016) remarks, "efforts were made to make the script as relevant to Irish children as possible."

These forms of domestication can be especially problematic in translations from English to Irish, where all potential readers are bilingual, and could theoretically be familiar with the 'foreign' elements changed or eliminated in translation, especially if the text is a classic or popular one (Nic Lochlainn 2013, 86). Nonetheless, there would seem to be one area where this does not hold true: picture books. While Julia Donaldson and Axel Scheffler are very well known in Ireland, Tadhg Mac Dhonnagáin finds that Irish-speaking children are not necessarily familiar with the original books. He thinks this is because in Irish-speaking homes, people tend to read in Irish to young children, as parents "want the child's experience of Irish in the early years to be as full and as fun-filled as possible" (interview with Mac Dhonnagáin). This they can achieve reading Mac Dhonnagáin's own translations of Donaldson (apart from being a publisher, Mac Dhonnagáin is also a songwriter) or the poet Gabriel Rosenstock's rhythmic, often alliterative translations of the Walker picture books. Mac Dhonnagáin believes that these rhyming books therefore have the potential to be perceived and remembered by many children as original Irish works.

He also points out a further, significant aspect which underscores how the translations of these kinds of picture books can dovetail with older forms of oral Irish culture:

> Rhyming stories also integrate beautifully with our 'agallamh beirte' [dialogue for two] tradition, the (...) dialogue dramas very popular in Gaeltacht communities. Irish is basically an oral culture with an enormous heritage. Certain elements of the tradition are thriving – our thing is to connect that oral, performative energy with the world of books. (*ibid.*)

Irish children's literature in English

Until the 1980s, almost all English-language books for children in Ireland – including those by Irish writers – were imported from the UK. The last two decades of the century saw an astounding proliferation of domestic publishing activity encouraged by Arts Council subsidies introduced in 1980, by the school curriculum putting greater emphasis on reading and, later in the decade, by the increasing affluence which would lead to the phenomenon known as the 'Celtic Tiger.' The growth peaked in the mid-1990s, when seven Irish publishers were regularly issuing books in English for young readers. The declared intention of many of these publishers was to produce Irish books for Irish children. At a time when traditional notions of Irishness were being challenged in a rapidly altering society, home-produced children's literature was a vital forum in which Irish identity could be examined (see O'Sullivan 2011). This spectacular growth was followed by a gradual decline. Of the seven (English-language) publishers for children active in the Irish market in the 1990s, only two were still in regular operation in 2007. The main reason lay in "the economics of publishers surviving in a small market" (Coghlan 2004, 1099). Paradoxically, as Valerie Coghlan points out, the very strength of the Irish market in the 1990s and the availability of Irish authors led to UK publishing conglomerates such as Penguin Random House setting up publishing divisions in Ireland (*ibid*.). This, in turn, further hastened the decline of local publishing. A vital problem for Irish publishers was that, although they had linguistic access to a larger market, they made "virtually no impression on bookshops in Britain" (Webb 2003, 10). Claire Reniero made a revealing comparison between the sales of two books by Irish authors in 2002, one published by an Irish publisher, the other by a British publisher. *The Love Bean* by Siobhán Parkinson was the most promoted book by The O'Brien Press, the largest children's publisher in Ireland, and was the best-selling book for young adults that year, but Eoin Colfer's *Artemis Fowl*, published by Penguin in Britain, sold over ten times more copies (Reniero 2005, 106). This says a lot about the comparative scales and possibilities of the Irish and British markets and explains why most Irish authors publish, when they can, in Britain, where they have access to the world market (see Keenan 2007; O'Sullivan 2011). Since 2005, Siobhán Parkinson's English novels have been published in Britain, mainly with Puffin and Hodder.

There is some sign today of the Irish market picking up, and new or rebranded publishers, such as Gill, are now publishing in English for children. Speaking at Publishing Ireland's annual trade day in November 2018, Oliver Beldham of the metadata service provider Nielsen Book Research said sales of Irish-published Anglophone books were rising with "the Children's market (…) now larger than Fiction and at its highest point in ten years!" (Publishing Ireland 2018). However, as Tadhg Mac Dhonnagáin claimed, "[t]here are now more books for children published in Irish than English in this country. (…) [B]ecause we are working in Irish, we're more immune to the very challenging competition that Irish publishers working in English face" (quoted in Gleeson 2011).

It is nonetheless difficult for Irish publishers in English to compete with the large British market. From the perspective of the publisher she has now become, Siobhán Parkinson writes:

> Children's publishing is fun, it is important (...) but it is not remotely lucrative, at least not for a small publishing house on the edge of Europe, working in the shadow of a world centre of children's publishing. Our proximity to London, with its enormous publishing conglomerates and its output of several thousand children's titles a year, is of course problematic. London sets the tone, London sets the prices, London dominates the market – and London is not particularly interested in what is happening in a tiny market like ours. And that makes it very difficult for small publishers to make any inroads into the British bookshops. (Parkinson 2015)

During the publishing boom from 1980 to 2005, almost no translations into English from other languages were issued. Poolbeg Press brought out an English version of a Christine Nöstlinger novel in 1992, and Wolfhound Press issued translations of three novels by Belgian author Ron Langenus. Apart from an English version of the Irish classic *Jimeen*, The O'Brien Press published two titles from French. However, it did not consider this excursion into foreign waters as an importer rather than an exporter of books a success, and "no longer has an active interest in sourcing children's books for translation" (Parkinson 2013, 153). The reason, apparently, has to do with the difficulty in finding satisfactory translators.

Little Island Books

In 2010, in the aftermath of the collapse or withdrawal from children's publishing of almost every English-language Irish publisher but The O'Brien Press, a new independent player arrived on the scene: Little Island. It was set up to publish both emerging Irish authors and – something totally new for this branch in Ireland – books in translation. Several Little Island books have since won or been nominated for awards, and the press itself won the Reading Association of Ireland Award in 2011. The publisher, commissioning editor and translator Siobhán Parkinson is well known as an award-winning and much-translated writer for children and teenagers in English and Irish. She was Ireland's first *Laureate na nÓg* [Children's Laureate] from 2010 to 2012 and has edited Irish and international journals on children's literature.

Little Island publishes eight to ten books a year for children and young adults – two of which are, on average, translations. The commitment to publishing books in translation began with Parkinson's own interest in translating, and she believes "passionately in the importance of making books available to children that bring them the message that not everyone interacts with the world through the medium of English" (Parkinson 2015). Connected to this cultural aim is Little Island's translation policy:

> We do not set out to localize the books we translate, or to erase the markers of the originating culture. On the contrary, we encourage translators to leave personal and place names in the original language, for example, so that readers are aware that they are reading a book that was written out of a different language and culture.[9] (Parkinson 2013, 156)

In stark contrast to the domestication strategy at work in the Irish translations discussed above, this policy clearly favors a foreignizing strategy. The only exception concerns the titles, because, as Parkinson comments, they are "an important marketing tool, and a title that is faithful to the original but is unlikely to appeal to our market is self-defeating" (ibid., 157).

Parkinson challenges the reasons put forward to explain the notorious unreceptiveness to fiction in translation in English-speaking countries. She agrees that there is some truth in the claim that the general public is intimidated by authors with foreign names that are difficult to pronounce, but points out that "English-speaking football fans are quite comfortable with foreign players' and managers' names" (ibid., 152). Publishers often complain about the difficulty in sourcing and assessing suitable titles and in identifying appropriate translators (see Lathey 2017, 233). Parkinson, who gives a detailed insight into how she goes about this herself, believes that "it is not difficult to build up a network of international children's books contacts, for instance by attending the Bologna book fair, by joining the International Board on Books for Young People (IBBY) and keeping in touch with organisations like the International Youth Library (IYL)" (Parkinson 2013, 154), whose annual *White Ravens* catalogue recommends a selection of 200 children's books in all languages for translation. Finding titles to publish is, in her opinion, "a mixture of adventure, luck and skill" (Parkinson 2016),

---

9   Parkinson elaborates on this for young readers in a chatty mode on the Little Island website: "Reading a book that comes from a different country is a bit like travel – it broadens the mind. And we at Little Island are all in favour of nice broad minds – they are so much more interesting than minds that never read a book originally written in French or German." See http://littleisland.ie/.

and she advises publishers: "The secret is not to feel that you have to find *THE* German or French or Swahili book – that way madness lies; the secret is to find *A* German or French or Swahili book that you love enough to want to publish it for Irish and other Anglophone children" (*ibid.*).

A relevant factor in Parkinson's own selection of titles is the fact that she speaks German, which not only gives her access to literature in that language but also "serves as a useful gateway language" (Parkinson 2013, 154) to, for example, Swedish, Danish and Dutch. Since 2010 Little Island has published fifteen translations: nine from German, translated by Parkinson herself, and one each from Swedish, Finnish, Brazilian Portuguese, Irish,[10] French and Latvian, the latter, like Irish, one of the least translated European languages (Büchler and Trentacosti 2015, 16–17). The books in translation get financial support, to varying degrees, from the countries of origin, as it would not be possible for a small publishing house to translate a novel from another language at a cost of thousands of euros without significant subsidy. Little Island has therefore naturally tended to look towards countries that do subsidize translation. Germany is reasonably generous, according to Parkinson, but the Scandinavian countries are even more so. However, as the list of languages/countries of origin of the translations shows, it is not the amount of subsidy alone that dictates her selection. Little Island has, for practical reasons, published far more German than Scandinavian titles (interview with Siobhán Parkinson).

Just as the range of languages has expanded over time, so too has the range of genres. The first two translations were German novels by Renate Ahrens and Burkhard Spinnen, translated by Parkinson, and they, and those that followed, were predominantly fiction for children aged nine and up. But the generic and formal scope has now expanded to include picture books for younger readers, poetry and non-fiction. The eclecticism of the list reflects the serendipity involved in finding suitable books, but also the publisher's experience gathered in terms of how successful they are. The consequence of this is that Little Island is currently giving fiction a rest to focus on other forms. Examples of two recent books which are a new departure are *All Better*, a collection of entertaining poems on the topic of being sick or injured written by one of Latvia's foremost poets, Inese Zandere and illustrated by Reinis Pētersons. It was translated literally and then retold by the award-winning Irish poet Catherine Ann Cullen. And the funny, illustrated non-fiction picture book *Declaration of the Rights of Boys and Girls* (2017) by Élisabeth

---

10   To protect Irish-language publications and give them a head start before making them available in English, an embargo of two years is imposed before a translation may be published.

Brami and Estelle Billon-Spagnol, originally published in French, which in the Little Island translated version is issued not as two separate books, as in the original publication, but innovatively as a flipbook to be read from either end. In the case of the recent picture books, Parkinson has said that Little Island neither expected nor sought any subsidies for the translation due to the very small amount of text (interview with Siobhán Parkinson).

With a wide range of source languages, genres and age groups addressed, it would be foolish to try to find a common denominator, other than the fact that all these Little Island books are translations. However, it is striking that there is hardly a title among them which does not display some degree of humor or wit, a feature dominant in Parkinson's own work as a writer. And in that, they perhaps reflect the publisher's own enjoyment in her work, about which she says: "It is tremendous fun and hugely worthwhile" (Parkinson 2016).

Conclusion

Two languages, two literatures. While children's literature in Irish has traditionally had to struggle with factors which limit its potential reception, such as the sometimes backward image of the language and the fact that most Irish people learn it as a second language in school, it would seem to have been experiencing a very dynamic phase over the past decade. This is thanks in part to translations, towards which it has always been open. Irish children's literature could not survive without generous state subsidies, which reduce the commercial risk for publishers issuing translations. Anglophone children's literature published in Ireland, on the other hand, has always had to compete under difficult commercial conditions with the mighty neighboring British publishers. Publishing translations into English in Ireland is a brave venture indeed, but one which the independent publisher of Little Island, Siobhán Parkinson, feels passionate about. In this, she echoes some of the enthusiasm of recent new independent publishing initiatives in Britain documented by Gillian Lathey (2017).

During the boom of Irish children's literature in English, there was huge European and worldwide interest, with ensuing translations, aided by Ireland being showcased as the Guest of Honour at the Frankfurt Book Fair in 1996. Irish publishing in English has not been correspondingly welcoming to voices from abroad, but at least a step is being taken in this direction today by a single, courageous and creative independent publisher – an important symbolic step, even if only on a relatively small scale.

Bibliography

An Gúm / Foras na Gaeilge. n.d. "About Foras na Gaeilge." Accessed April 14, 2020. https://www.forasnagaeilge.ie/about/about-foras-na-gaeilge/?lang=en.

Büchler, Alexandra and Giulia Trentacosti. 2015. *Publishing Translated Literature in the United Kingdom and Ireland 1990–2012: Statistical Report*. Aberystwyth: Mercator Institute for Media, Languages and Culture, Aberystwyth University, Wales.

Burns Library. 2004. "Free State Art: Judging Ireland by its Book Covers: Virtual Exhibit Summer 2004." Accessed April 14, 2020. https://www.bc.edu/libraries/about/exhibits/burnsvirtual/bkcovers.html.

Central Statistics Office. 2019. "Census of Population 2016 – Profile 10 Education, Skills and the Irish Language." Accessed April 14, 2020. https://www.cso.ie/en/releasesandpublications/ep/p-cp10esil/p10esil/.

Coghlan, Valerie. 2004. "Ireland." In *International Companion Encyclopedia of Children's Literature*, edited by Peter Hunt, 1099–1103. 2nd edition, 2 volumes. London: Routledge.

Coghlan, Valerie. 2013. "The Bold Beast, Irish Children's Book Illustration." In *Pictúir: Contemporary Book Illustrators from Ireland / Maisitheoirí Comhaimseartha Leabhar Páisti as Éirinn*. Edited by Children's Books Ireland, n.p. Dublin: Children's Books Ireland.

Cronin, Michael. 2011. "Ireland in Translation." *English Today: The International Review of the English Language* 27, no. 2 [106]: 53–57.

Gleeson, Sinead. 2011. "A Christmas Tale That Puts Language in the Picture." *The Irish Times*, December 21, 2011. https://www.irishtimes.com/culture/books/a-christmas-tale-that-puts-language-in-the-picture-1.14095.

Hackett, Conor. 2019. Telephone interview by Emer O'Sullivan. April 18, 2019.

Irish Translators' and Interpreters' Association. 2019. "Interview with ITIA member Maire Nic Mhaolain." Accessed April 26, 2019. https://www.translatorsassociation.ie/maire-nic-mhaolain/.

Keenan, Celia. 2007. "Divisions in the World of Irish Publishing for Children: Recolonization or Globalization?" In *Divided Worlds: Studies in Children's Literature*, edited by Mary S. Thompson and Valerie Coghlan, 196–208. Dublin: Four Courts Press.

Kennedy, Brian P. 1990. *Dreams and Responsibilities: The State and the Arts in Independent Ireland*. Dublin: Arts Council/An Chomhairle Ealaíon.

Kiberd, Declan. 2018. *After Ireland: Writing the Nation from Beckett to the Present*. 1st Harvard University Press edition. Cambridge, MA: Harvard University Press.

Lathey, Gillian. 2017. "Serendipity, Independent Publishing and Translation Flow: Recent Translations for Children in the UK." In *The Edinburgh Companion to*

Children's Literature, edited by Clémentine Beauvais and Maria Nikolajeva, 232–244. Edinburgh: Edinburgh University Press.

Mac Dhonnagáin, Tadhg. 2019. Email interview by Emer O'Sullivan. April 14, 2019.

Maguire, Nora and Beth Rodgers, eds. 2013. *Children's Literature on the Move: Nations, Translations, Migrations*. Dublin: Four Courts Press.

Ní Ghadhra, Máirín. 2016. "Meet Dónall Dána – Translating Kids' Classics into Irish." Updated November 11, 2016. Accessed February 11, 2019. https://www.rte.ie/culture/2016/1116/832188-meet-donall-dana-translating-kids-classics/.

Nic Lochlainn, Caoimhe. 2013. "Tarts and Treacle, Roast Potatoes and Buttermilk: Domestication in Irish-language Translations of Children's Literature." In *Children's Literature on the Move: Nations, Translations, Migrations*, edited by Nora Maguire and Beth Rodgers, 73–86. Dublin: Four Courts Press.

O'Loughlin, Vanessa. 2012. "Walker Eireann." *Writing.ie: The Complete Online Writing Magazine*, September 2012. https://www.writing.ie/readers/walker-eireann/.

O'Sullivan, Emer. 2011. "Insularity and Internationalism: Between Local Production and the Global Marketplace." In *Irish Children's Literature and Culture: New Perspectives on Contemporary Writing*, edited by Valerie Coghlan and Keith O'Sullivan, 183–196. New York: Routledge.

Parkinson, Siobhán. 2013. "English That for Me! Publishing Children's Books in Translation." In *Children's Literature on the Move: Nations, Translations, Migrations*, edited by Nora Maguire and Beth Rodgers, 151–160. Dublin: Four Courts Press.

Parkinson, Siobhán. 2015. "Happy 5th Birthday, Little Island: Siobhán Parkinson Traces the History, Successes, Challenges and Ambitions of the Children's Publisher She Helped Found in 2010 as It Launches Its 50th Book." *The Irish Times*, May 13, 2015. https://www.irishtimes.com/culture/books/happy-5th-birthday-little-island-1.2211315.

Parkinson, Siobhán. 2016. "Watch out for the Umlauts! Children's Books in Translation from Little Island." *Writing.ie: The Complete Online Writing Magazine*, April 28, 2016. https://www.writing.ie/interviews/children-young-adult/watch-out-for-the-umlauts-childrens-books-in-translation-from-little-island-by-siobhan-parkinson/.

Parkinson, Siobhán. 2019. Interview by Emer O'Sullivan. February 14, 2019, Dublin.

Publishing Ireland. 2018. "The Business of Books 2018 Roundup." Accessed February 6, 2019. https://www.publishingireland.com/trade-day-2016-interview-series/

Reniero, Claire. 2005. "Panorama historique de l'édition de jeunesse en Irlande / A Historical Survey of Children's Book Publishing in Ireland." *Revue LISA/LISA e-journal* 3, no. 1: 99–109.

Siggins, Lorna. 2004. "It's All Greek to Harry Potter as Philosopher's Stone Turns into Orcloch." *The Irish Times*, October 11, 2004. Accessed April 26, 2019. https://

www.irishtimes.com/news/it-s-all-greek-to-harry-potter-as-philosopher-s-stone-turns-into-orcloch-1.1161323.

Titley, Alan. 2000. "Children's Books in Irish." In *The Big Guide 2: Irish Children's Books*, edited by Valerie Coghlan and Celia Keenan, 103–110. Dublin: CBI.

Titley, Alan. 2015. "On Eilís in the Irish Language: 'To Gaelicise the References to English Culture'." In *Alice in a World of Wonderlands: The Translations of Lewis Carroll's Masterpiece*, edited by Jon A. Lindseth and Alan Tannenbaum, 307–310. 3 volumes. New Castle, Del.: Oak Knoll Press.

Uí Mhaicín, Máire. 1996. "Irish Books." In *The Big Guide to Irish Children's Books*, edited by Valerie Coghlan and Celia Keenan, 131–147. Dublin: Irish Children's Book Trust.

Webb, Sarah. 2003. "What's Happening to Irish Children's Publishing?" *Inis*, no. 5: 10–13.

Cultural translation and the recruitment of translated texts to induce social change

The case of the *Haskalah*[1]

Zohar Shavit

Abstract

This chapter challenges the common usage of the notion of cultural translation. It argues that since every translation is the result of an ongoing dialogue between at least two cultural systems and of continuous tensions between the demands of the source and target systems, every translation is 'cultural,' making the general concept of cultural translation superfluous. The chapter proposes a narrower definition which reserves the term for cases where translations play an active role in the dynamics of a given society, for instance when translations function as agents of social change and serve as a vehicle for presenting and exhibiting a desired social change. As a test case, the chapter analyzes how translations functioned as agents of social change in Central European Jewish society at the turn of the nineteenth century. Members of the *Haskalah* – the Jewish Enlightenment movement – aspired to induce social change in Jewish society pertaining not only to the Jewish *Weltanschauung* but also, and perhaps more significantly, to Jewish daily practices. This involved the intentional use of translated texts for disseminating the modern *Maskilic* habitus and the values of *Bürgerlichkeit*, presenting these ideals as everyday practices and social models.

Introduction

This chapter discusses the function of translations in mobilizing sociocultural change. As a test case, it examines the emergence of a new system of books

---

1   This contribution is dedicated to Jan Van Coillie. The research reported here was conducted in the framework of the DFG-funded research project "Innovation durch Tradition? Jüdische Bildungsmedien als Zugang zum Wandel kultureller Ordnungen während der 'Sattelzeit'" (with Prof. Dr. Simone Lässig, German Historical Institute, Washington).

that was one of the most significant endeavors of the *Haskalah* movement (the Jewish Enlightenment movement) (Feiner 2004). This new system, which developed towards the end of the eighteenth century in German-speaking Jewish communities in Europe, attempted to offer an alternative repertoire of books, most of them translations, that would differ drastically from those on the traditional rabbinical bookshelf. It voiced an unprecedented, revolutionary process of modernization in European Jewish society (see Katz 1973; Lässig 2004; Lowenstein 1993; Schochat 1956, 1960; Toury 1972). These books not only effected a radical transformation in the corpus of Jewish literature, but also performed a key role in the transition of Central European Jewry from its pre-modern, traditional stage to the modernity of the *Haskalah*.

As part of the attempt to challenge the monopoly of the Ashkenazi religious elite over culture, a new sub-system of books emerged as well – books that were written specifically for Jewish children. This was part of the efforts of the *Maskilim*, a group of young Jewish intellectuals belonging to the *Haskalah* movement, to reshape Jewish society by propelling it into a civilizing process. One of the central objectives of the *Haskalah* movement was the reformation of the Jewish educational system. To this end, the *Maskilim* established a network of schools (Eliav 1960) based on Philanthropinist ideas of education. The Philanthropinist movement (in German, *Philanthropinismus*) blossomed in the 1770s in northern Germany. It sought to implement educational reforms based on Enlightenment values and to correct the flaws of traditional education (Schmitt 2007). The Jewish *Maskilim* saw Philanthropinism as a source of inspiration for the revolutionary change they desired to bring to Jewish education. In its early stages, their connection to Philanthropinism stemmed from Moses Mendelssohn's personal relationships with central members of that movement, primarily with Joachim Heinrich Campe and Johann Bernhard Basedow, who founded the *Philanthropinum* school in Dessau.

These schools, in turn, created an urgent need for books for children and young adults that would articulate the change that the *Haskalah* movement endeavored to engender in Jewish society. A major *Maskilic* project thus emerged toward the end of the eighteenth century to publish books for Jewish children and young adults that would serve the *Maskilic* agenda.

Most of the books, if not all, were translations. Translations were chosen to serve as a platform for inducing social change in Jewish society because it was the easiest way to supply the needs of the new, emerging cultural field. Translations were also part of the desire to import 'goods' from the German culture. German culture, which was regarded as an ideal model to borrow from, served as a source system for most of the translations – direct or mediated.

The notion of cultural translation

Before turning to the case study, I would like to examine briefly the notion of 'cultural translation' and suggest a different understanding of it. As is commonly known, the act of translation involves a process by which the textual and cultural models of a source system – not just texts – are transferred to a target system, whether in the same macro-system or not. This transfer, as Gideon Toury (1984, 1995) and Itamar Even-Zohar (1990a, 1990b, 1990c, 1997; see also Weissbrod 2004) have argued, often involves an adaptation and adjustment of the source system's texts and models to the texts and models of the target system, while subordinating them to the systemic constraints of the latter in response to its needs and requirements.

In light of understanding the act of translation as such, we may well ask whether there is a translation that is not cultural. In fact, every translation *is* cultural in the sense that it is always the result of an ongoing dialogue between at least two cultural systems and of continuous tensions between the demands of the source and the target systems. As such, I contend, the concept of cultural translation becomes rather superfluous. This is why I propose to adopt a narrow definition of 'cultural translation' in which this notion will be reserved for cases where translations play an active role in the dynamics of a certain society; in my case study, they played a role as agents of social change in Jewish society during the *Haskalah* period.

In many cases of cultural translation, the source text is often regarded as no more than a starting point for the introduction of cultural and social models into the target system and is thus used as raw material, subject to considerable changes directed to meet the needs and demands of the target system. In passing, I would like to remark that the translators' treatment of source texts as no more than raw material to be molded for the translators' purposes often makes it difficult or even impossible to identify the source texts themselves.

The Maskilic adoption of the Philanthropinist educational program and their translational project

According to Akiva Simon (1953) and Tsemach Tsamriyon (1988), prominent scholars of the *Haskalah* and the history of education, the *Maskilim* adopted the Philanthropinist educational program and implemented it in the network of schools they established. In addition to adopting the pedagogical practices of Philanthropinism in schools, the movement's ideas were also incorporated into the Jewish education system through a massive translation project that provided a huge influx of translated texts into the emerging body of *Haskalah* literature. In fact, there are scholars, like Gideon Toury (1998, 112), who maintain that every text produced by the *Maskilim* should be treated as a translation unless proven otherwise.

The new habitus

I contend that these translations functioned as agents of social change because they were the vehicle for presenting and exhibiting a desired social change. The social change that the *Maskilim* aspired to induce in Jewish society implied not only changing the Jewish *Weltanschauung* but also, and perhaps more significantly, Jewish daily practices.

Simple matters – such as what one should do after waking in the morning; whether one should bathe, and, if so, when; how one should behave at the table; and how one should dress, employ one's leisure time, or interact with other people, including non-Jews – were among the aspects of daily practice addressed by the translated *Maskilic* texts. It must be emphasized that, trifling as they may seem, practices such as these that organize a person's life are not spontaneous actions; rather, they are derived from social norms and cultural codes that comprise the habitus of individuals.

There is no need to delve in detail into the concept of habitus as developed by Pierre Bourdieu (1977, 1984), building on the work of Norbert Elias.[2] In brief, habitus refers to pre-existing dispositions that provide guidelines for the daily practices that organize a person's life, such as how one behaves, what one wears or eats or reads, which pre-existing formulas one uses in everyday and professional interactions, and what one's personal space looks like. This set of implicit behavioral codes, which determines individual conduct within a certain group, also plays a role in distinguishing a given individual or a given social group from other individuals and groups.

The members of the *Haskalah* movement realized that in order to make their project of modernizing Jewish society viable, they must change the models of the Jewish habitus. As written texts were the main media of the *Haskalah* movement and the new educational system was one of their main organs, they recruited translated texts to help them present new forms of habitus to the Jewish public. Moreover, translations were used to introduce the values of *Bürgertum* and *Bildung* underlying the new social models.

---

2   On Elias' influence on Bourdieu, see Sela-Sheffy (1997) and Algazi (2002).

What makes the *Maskilim*'s efforts to construct a new Jewish habitus so interesting is how explicit their guidelines were. Normally, the set of behavioral codes that determines a given habitus is a doxa – in other words, it is taken for granted and hence needs not explicitly be formulated. The case of the *Haskalah* is of particular interest because it involves the introduction of explicit instructions.

In order to understand how substantial the social change the *Maskilim* aspired to enact in Jewish society was, one need only compare typical depictions of Jewish peddlers or Jewish villagers (taking into account, of course, their stereotypical representations) (see for instance Rowlandson 1954) with portraits of members of the *Haskalah* movement and of the Jewish economic elite. When one looks at these portraits, it is impossible not to notice how the *Maskilim* posed for the artist in a manner expressing self-confidence and self-esteem. Several wear eighteenth-century wigs, and their dress and hairstyle are similar to that of the German bourgeoisie. Consider, for example, the portrait of Isaac Daniel Itzig,[3] a wealthy Jewish entrepreneur. Nothing in his appearance discloses his ethnic identity as a Jew. We see that he has adopted practices common to the eighteenth-century German high bourgeoisie: his face is clean-shaven, and he sports a short wig with an arrangement of 'side curls,' fashionable among the German bourgeoisie of the time. His clothing, too – a blue velvet jacket – is the dress of the German upper middle class. His overall appearance reveals his wealth and his attachment to the higher bourgeoisie. This is also true of the portraits of several other *Maskilim*, such as Dr. Elieser Marcus Bloch[4] and Dr. Marcus Herz, who each wear a plaited wig and a fashionable jacket over a shirt with ruffles, or of Hartwig Wessely[5] [Naphtali Herz Weisel].

In 1833, a German writer, Michael Benedict Lessing (of whom we know little), published a description of (likely urban) Jewish society in the German-speaking sphere. In particular, he noted the "tremendous change" he observed:[6]

> Let us take a hard look at some of these individuals; let us consider the tremendous change that has taken place in the language, dress, way of life, needs and leisure activities, customs and habits of the Jews! (…) Their appearance – how much it has changed. Who would not have noticed Jews immediately by their cumbersome Eastern dress, their large, dark caftan,

---

3   Joseph Friedrich August Darbes, *Portrait of Daniel Itzig*, https://www.preussenchronik.de/person_jsp/key=person_daniel_itzig.html.
4   Unknown artist, *Portrait of Marcus Elieser Bloch*, https://en.wikipedia.org/wiki/Marcus_Elieser_Bloch#/media/File:Marcus_Elieser_Bloch.jpg.
5   Unknown artist, *Protrait of Hartwig Wessely*, https://de.wikipedia.org/wiki/Hartwig_Wessely#/media/File:Naphtali_Herz_Wessely.JPG.
6   Unless otherwise noted, translations of quotations of Hebrew and German citations are mine.

their fur hat weighing down the forehead, their slippers and their beard disfiguring the face? Who would not immediately have noticed a Jewish matron by her silver-embroidered cap, her stern-looking face, lacking any ornament? And how many Jews still look like that today, except for those remnants of the past or those coming from Poland? How carefully they once adhered to the pettiest customs, and who would have ventured even thirty years ago to open his shop on a Saturday, or engage in business, or write, or travel? (…) Would one have seen them thirty years ago in inns and restaurants sitting next to Christian guests, chatting with them freely, eating the same food, drinking the same drinks? (…) When comparing the records of Christian schools from the last thirty years of the previous century and the first third of ours, one cannot fail to notice that back then a Jewish boy among Christian students was as rare as a white raven, whereas nowadays Christian schools in every city accept almost all the children of the Jewish inhabitants, especially in the higher grades. (…) Only in a few households is the Jewish dialect still used, and only by the elderly, whereas children, above all children in the great cities, speak at home and outside their home the same language as their fellow Christian citizens (…) Hundreds of thousands of people can still testify to the once absolute absence of Jews from concerts, parties, balls, public festivities, (…) in coffee shops and in the offices of the exchange market; they can testify as to whether they ever used to show any interest in daily newspapers (…); whether they had ever then met Jews equal to their Christian peers in manners and knowledge, met a Jew in the theatre, music hall, or art exhibitions, (…) whether they had ever encountered Jews in scientific and other educated circles, or whether Christian scholars and statesmen would frequent the salons of a Jewish lady? (Lessing 1833, 129–132; cited partially in Hebrew translation by Toury 1972, 81)

The presentation of the new habitus in translated children's literature

Lessing's description points to the very aspects of daily life where a transformation began to take place in Jewish daily practices, such as personal hygiene, dress, language, leisure time, and interactions with one's surroundings (Lowenstein 2005). Notably, they were typical of the guidelines included in the *Maskilic* translated texts.[7]

---

7   'Translated' in the broad sense, where any kind of a linkage exists between two texts that are defined as a source and a translated text.

CULTURAL TRANSLATION AND SOCIAL CHANGE   79

Remarkably, such guidelines could be found not only in a variety of books addressed to Jewish children, but also in one of the most important books of the *Haskalah* movement – the manifesto *Divrei Shalom ve-Emet* [Words of Peace and Truth] written by Naphtali Herz Weisel, a Jewish Hebraist and educator. In this manifesto, Weisel presented the universal nature of the Enlightenment and the place of the 'Torah of the Jew' within it. At the same time, he did not refrain from addressing more mundane matters, such as daily practices, and noted that his manifesto was aimed, inter alia, at teaching his readers proper table manners and dress and how to interact with other people, in both private and public spheres:

> These lessons teach a person how to behave in the company of his friends, when he enters and when he leaves: He should speak calmly and not raise his voice, nor whisper. [They also teach him] table manners, comportment, and dress, how he should behave with his household, how he should negotiate, so that other people will enjoy his company and his business and will wish to do business with him, and so on. (Weisel 1886 [1782], 237)

Otherwise, the guidelines are to be found in passages of the most significant books officially addressed to children and young adults. These books were reissued time and again in many editions and continued to be published in Eastern Europe, some even until the end of the nineteenth century: *Avtalion*, by Aaron Wolfsohn-Halle (1790); *Mesilat ha-Limud*, the first part of *Bet ha-Sefer*, by Judah Leib Ben-Ze'ev (1836 [1802]); **Sefer Toldot Israel**, by Peter Beer (1796); and *Moda le-Yaldei Bnei Israel*, by Moses Hirsch Bock (1811). One could further add the epistolary *Igrot Meshulam ben Uriya ha-Eshtemoi* by Isaac Abraham Euchel (1789–1790), whose instructions were less explicit.

The texts mentioned above were based on a translation of passages from several popular books from that period. Among these popular works, Basedow's *Elementarwerk*, published in 1774 (Basedow 1972 [1774]), and the German translation of Rousseau's *Émile*, translated into German immediately after its publication in 1762, stand out.[8] I will briefly discuss these two works in order to illustrate my case.

---

8   On Rousseau's place in the Jewish *Haskalah* see Kuperty-Tzur (1999).

Basedow's Elementarwerk

The encyclopedic and voluminous *Elementarwerk* by Johann Bernhard Basedow, one of the founding fathers of the Philantropinism school, served as the source text for the translation of several passages that were included in the above-mentioned *Maskilic* books for children and young adults. The choice of Basedow's *Elementarwerk* was rooted in the close relationship between the Jewish and the Philantropin movements (Simon 1953, 175; see also Tsamriyon 1988, 181–182) and requires a separate and thorough examination.[9]

Here I will briefly discuss how the translation of passages from Basedow's *Elementarwerk* helped present Jewish children and young adults with guidelines for daily practices that, as already mentioned, were intended to lead eventually to the construction of a new habitus. In passing, it is interesting to note that the German title of one of the most popular *Maskilic* books for children even reads *Israelitische Kinderfreund. Ein Elementarwerk* (Bock 1811).

The various translations of passages of the *Elementarwerk* did not adopt all the topics discussed by Basedow; they borrowed only those that best suited the *Maskilic* agenda – topics such as personal hygiene and cleanliness of clothing, table manners, social integration, leisure culture, and interactions with others.

Let us look at one citation from the *Elementarwerk* and then examine several translated passages.[10]

> Kinder, die schon etwas älter sind, und die man nicht mehr an dem ganzen Leibe waschen kann, müssen täglich und zwar so oft, als sie sich besudelt haben, an Händen, Gesicht und Füßen gewaschen werden, im Gesicht und an den Händen aber insbesondere vor und nach jeder Mahlzeit. Hierzu ist bei dem Gesicht und Händen das reine und kalte Wasser das beste. Weil solches aber die Fettigkeiten nicht zulänglich wegnimmt, so kann man allemal, wenn es nötig ist, etwas Seife zur Hilfe nehmen. Bei dem Waschen des Gesichts müssen jedesmal die Augen, vorzüglich das, was sich in dem inneren Augenwinkel festzusetzen pflegt, ausgewaschen und die Ohren

---

9   Johann Bernhard Basedow and Moses Mendelssohn corresponded on philosophical issues (see Altmann 1973, 323); however, the relationship between them went beyond intellectual exchange. Basedow asked Mendelssohn to help him obtain financial support for his Philantropin Institute in Dessau, and indeed the Jews of Berlin donated 518 talers to the school (Simon 1953, 159). In his *Elementarwerk*, Basedow devoted an entire table [*Tafel*] (number 80) to Jewish matters, including Mendelssohn's profile.

10 As already mentioned in note 7, 'translated' is meant here in the broad sense, where any kind of a linkage exists between two texts that are defined as a source and a translated text.

sowohl inwendig als hinter denselben gereinigt werden. Die Füße müssen besonders bei Kindern, die schon angefangen viel herumzulaufen, alle Abende mit lauwarmen Wasser, wozu das Flußwasser mit etwas Kleie vermischt am besten ist, abgewaschen werden. (Basedow 1972 [1774], 189)

[The hands, face, and feet of children who are older and whose entire body cannot be washed [by an adult] must be washed daily once they have dirtied themselves, but especially before and after meals. To this end, the best means is clean and cold water. However, in case of a need to get rid of greasiness, one can use soap as well. In the washing of the face, the eyes must be washed each time, especially the inner corner of the eye, and the ears must be cleaned both internally and behind. The feet must be washed daily in the evenings with lukewarm water, for which the best is water mixed with a little bit of bran, especially by children who have started to walk around a lot.]

The text continues, in the same manner, to discuss other daily practices, including appropriate clothing, table manners, and interactions with others.

In order to briefly illustrate my case, the following discussion of several translated passages will focus on guidelines that deal with one dominant subject: personal hygiene.

In his reader *Mesilat ha-Limud*, one of the *Haskalah's* bestsellers, Judah Leib Ben-Ze'ev, a grammarian and lexicographer, meticulously prescribed the rules of personal hygiene, with specific instructions for rising from bed, washing, and maintaining the cleanliness of one's clothes:

You shall wake up and wash your face and hands, and brush and rinse your mouth with water and clean it and purify it of mucus and filth; and you should put on clean and splendid clothes and go over your hair with a comb so that you will not be called by shameful names. (Ben Ze'ev [1802] 1836, 114)

The need to keep one's clothing clean is mentioned repeatedly in almost all the guidelines. For example, Ben-Ze'ev states: "Your clothes should always be white and your dress clean of filth and spots, because a man is respected for the splendor of his clothing" (*ibid.*). Similarly, in *Moda le-Yaldei Bnei Israel*, Moses Hirsch Bock (a pedagogue and writer) offered general instructions on the use of soap: "Remove all filth from your body, wash it and clean it with soap, because cleanliness is very conducive to bodily health" (Bock, 1811, 189).

In his popular book *Sefer Toldot Israel*, Peter (Peretz) Beer, a radical *maskil* (an educationalist and writer) gives his readers concrete instructions concerning personal hygiene. Beer emphasizes time and again the need to keep one's body clean:

> Wash your hands and your face and also your neck with water / Do not forget to rinse [your] mouth and teeth, and keep your nails short / And [keep] your head combed every day and your hair in order. (Beer 1796, 285)

> My child! Before you lie down in your bed, / Go and kiss your father's hands and do not forget to rinse your mouth and teeth / before you lie down to sleep, in clean water. So that in the morning your mouth will not smell bad, / and you will not disgust and repulse all who encounter you. (*ibid.*, 294)

> When you eat and your hands become grubby and soiled, / wash them afterwards so that you do not dirty your clothes. (*ibid.*, 290)

These representative examples dealing with personal hygiene suffice, I believe, to illustrate my argument about the use of translated texts as agents of social change. Imparting these daily practices was part of the *Maskilic* attempt to advocate the notion of *Bildung*, whose adoption was a prerequisite for making Jews part of bourgeois civil society (Hettling 2015). In the view of the *Maskilim*, it was the only way to assure Jews' integration into non-Jewish bourgeois society.

I would like to stress that such detailed guidelines appeared in *Maskilic* books for children not only with respect to hygiene but also to the other daily practices I mentioned above, such as dress, language, leisure, and interaction with one's surroundings. Furthermore, one must remember that although the *Maskilic* books officially addressed children and young adults, they were often read by adults as well, especially by those who were looking for a path towards Enlightenment, and thus they actually reached a much larger audience.

Rousseau's Émile

Another source for guidelines was Rousseau's *Émile*. Elsewhere (Shavit 2014) I have extensively discussed the strategies employed by translators to introduce, in disguise, Rousseau's *Émile* into the Jewish cultural and educational system. Here I will refer briefly to one example, a translation of a passage in *Émile* that gives a detailed account of how and why children should be bathed in cold water:

Lavez souvent les enfants; leur malpropreté en montre le besoin. Quand on ne fait que les essuyer, on les déchire; mais, à mesure qu'ils se renforcent, diminuez par degré la tiédeur de l'eau, jusqu'à ce qu'enfin vous les laviez été et hiver à l'eau froide et même glacée. Comme, pour ne pas les exposer, il importe que cette diminution soit lente, successive et insensible, on peut se servir du thermomètre pour la mesurer exactement.

Cet usage du bain une fois établi ne doit plus être interrompu, et il importe de le garder toute sa vie. Je le considère non seulement du côté de la propreté et de la santé actuelle, mais aussi comme une précaution salutaire pour rendre plus flexible la texture des fibres, et les faire céder sans effort et sans risque aux divers degrés de chaleur et de froid. Pour cela je voudrais qu'en grandissant on s'accoutumât peu à peu à se baigner quelquefois dans des eaux chaudes à tous les degrés supportables, et souvent dans des eaux froides à tous les degrés possibles. Ainsi, après s'être habitué à supporter les diverses températures de l'eau, qui, étant un fluide plus dense, nous touche par plus de points et nous affecte davantage, on deviendrait presque insensible à celles de l'air. (Rousseau 1762, 50)

[Wash the children often; their dirtiness proves the need for it; when one only wipes them, one lacerates them. But to the extent that they regain strength, diminish by degrees the warmth of the water, until at the end you wash them summer and winter in cold and even chilly water. Since in order not to expose them it is important that this diminution be slow, successive, and imperceptible, a thermometer can be used to measure it exactly.

This practice of bathing, once established, ought never again be interrupted, and it is important to keep to it for the whole of life. I am considering it not only from the point of view of cleanliness and present health; but I also see it as a salutary precaution for making the texture of the fibers more flexible and able to adapt to various degrees of heat and cold without effort and without risk. For that purpose I would want him in growing up to become accustomed little by little to bathing sometimes in hot water at all bearable degrees and often in cold water at all possible degrees. Thus, after being habituated to bear the various temperatures of water which, being a denser fluid, touches us at more points and affects us more, one would become almost insensitive to the various temperatures of the air.] (Rousseau 1979, 59–60, trans. Bloom)

A concise translation of this passage was published posthumously in Hebrew in 1787[11] by *Ha-Me'asef*, the most important journal of the *Haskalah*:

> They [parents and caregivers] will also make a habit of bathing children / at least twice a week in cold water / so they will be strong and healthy / because apart from this being in keeping with cleanliness and ritual purity / it is also good and conducive to bodily health. (Baraz 1787, 37)

The translator, Shimon Baraz, was a virtually anonymous writer who belonged to *Maskilic* circles in Königsberg. He was probably motivated by *Émile*'s enormous success in Germany.[12] After *Émile* had been translated into German in 1762, it was then retranslated multiple times and became a frequently cited text. Shimon Baraz adapted into Hebrew several paragraphs of Rousseau's *Émile* and published them in an article titled "The Education of Boys: On the Necessity of Educating Boys Properly" [Chinukh Ne'arim: Al Devar Chinukh ha-Banim ka-Ra'uyi] (Baraz 1787, 33–43). We may assume that he had not read *Émile* in French but rather had read one of the many German translations. Furthermore, we may even assume that Baraz did not necessarily have access to the complete German translation, but only to one or more of the numerous summaries, reviews, and articles written by various intermediaries who introduced the ideas of *Émile* into the German cultural system.

Baraz himself does not mention Rousseau as his source but refers to the work of the "Sages," which a detailed comparison suggests was Rousseau. Baraz translated and adapted several paragraphs of *Émile* that deal with concrete issues of child-raising and provide detailed guidelines on different phases of everyday life: how to dress, bathe, and feed children, and even teach them how to swim. While not referring directly to Rousseau, the translator mentions Maimonides as his source and selects from *Émile* those passages that corresponded best with Maimonides' view of the need to maintain bodily health as a prerequisite for mental health. In so doing, Baraz tried to connect Rousseau's discussion of the body with Maimonides' ideas (Maimonides, n.d.). He also strove to associate his adaptation of Rousseau with rabbinical writings. For instance, to Rousseau's recommendation to teach a child how to swim, Baraz added a quotation from the tractate *Kiddushin*, which is the most significant source in rabbinical literature on the education of children. Baraz followed Rousseau faithfully even at the

---

11 Shimon Baraz died on October 4, 1787.
12 On Rousseau's place in the German Enlightenment, see Mounier (1979, 1980).

expense of contradicting Maimonides – for instance, advising that children be bathed in cold water, which contradicts Maimonides' instruction to keep the body warm.

Baraz's presentation of passages taken from *Émile* masquerading as those of Maimonides was part of the strategies employed by the *Maskilim* to minimize opposition and hostility to the translation of 'foreign' texts. Among the principal strategies of disguise was the method of composing a text based on ready-made phrases taken from canonical Jewish literature. This method was commonly used in traditional Jewish literature, in which the authors constructed the text as a puzzle whose phrases consist of, or allude to, various canonical Jewish texts. Baraz embedded ready-made phrases of the Hebrew Bible, rabbinical writings, and Maimonides (Shavit 2014) into the paragraphs taken from Rousseau, interweaving them to create a coherent puzzle. In this way, he made the translation seem familiar to his Jewish readers, making it appear as part of the Jewish tradition.

Staging bourgeois society

In addition to the presentation of new daily practices, translated texts were also used by the *Maskilim* to introduce the new social model they aspired to implement in Jewish society. This model was based on the values of the German bourgeoisie, particularly in terms of familial relations, *Bildung*, vocational training, and relations with non-Jews. The translation of Campe's *Robinson der Jüngere* [The Young Robinson] by David Samostz (1824) was part of these *Maskilic* efforts to promote and disseminate *Bildung* values with the aim of becoming part of bourgeois civil society.[13] This, in the spirit of Christian Wilhelm von Dohm's (1972 [1781]) recommendation that Jews be granted equal civil rights, provided that they adopt the *Bildung* values and the behavioral codes of the civil society's bourgeoisie. The *Maskilim* enthusiastically supported the adoption of such values, which could open new horizons for Jews' integration into non-Jewish bourgeois society, where one was judged by one's ability to achieve independent status through the acquisition of a profession, broad education, and financial and cultural capital.

---

13 Campe's decision to adapt Defoe's *Robinson Crusoe* for children was part of the new 'Robinsonade' genre that inundated Europe, especially Germany. Nevertheless, only Campe's adaptation enjoyed such remarkable success, becoming one of the most-translated books of his day; it was translated into French, English, Italian, Latin, Greek, Croatian, Czech, Serbian, Romanian, Spanish, Danish, Swedish, Finnish, Dutch, Yiddish, and Lithuanian, among others.

David Samostz's translation was designed to provide teachers and parents (primarily fathers) with a text that could be used to impart this new set of values to children.

A detailed analysis of Samostz's translation is beyond the scope of this chapter. Nonetheless, I would like to present here the conclusions that derive from this analysis.[14]

Following Joachim Heinrich Campe, Samostz presented in Hebrew a model of bourgeois life and 'staged' or dramatized various principles of Philantropinic pedagogy, such as a constant dialogue between parents and children and between teachers and children. Staging scenes of family life and intrafamilial dialogues furthermore provided a way to illustrate the ideal model of interaction between fathers and children and between teacher and students. As is well known, Campe's *Robinson der Jüngere* evolves as a dialogue between a father and his children (Ewers 1996, 162–163), thus enabling the dramatization of various scenarios in a 'typical' bourgeois family and providing an almost visual illustration of the ideal model of bourgeois life in which children are educated according to the principles of Philanthropinism. Campe received acclaim for his extensive use of dialogue and conversations (*Gesprächform*), primarily between an adult and children. Through his constant use of dialogues, Campe presented – in a concrete, rather than abstract, way – the normative rules for dialogue between adults and children, and the differences between such dialogue and conversation among children themselves (ibid., 174).

The visualization of Philanthropinist principles, as well as the story of Robinson Crusoe, were perfectly in line with the *Maskilim*'s aspiration to broaden Jews' horizons beyond their narrow and provincial world. In his translation of *Robinson der Jüngere*, Samostz depicts a society open to the world and characterized by social mobility, rationality, and a universalist outlook – a society of people who attained a profession, were knowledgeable about the world, and lived off their own hard work. In place of the isolated Jew remaining in the confines of his home, Samostz sought to portray a Jew who lives in an open, inclusive society enjoying fruitful relations with his surroundings. The 'new Jew' in this society adopts the daily practices of non-Jews, speaks the language of the society in which he lives, and is familiar with its culture. He makes his living in various professions and enriches his spiritual world not only through religious but also through secular studies.

Digressing slightly, I believe it is important to note the difficulties translators faced due to the need to translate the dialogues into Hebrew. Hebrew at

---

[14] For a comprehensive analysis, see Shavit (in press).

the time was not yet a spoken, colloquial language; Samostz thus had to devise *ad hoc* solutions for translating the dialogues and had to invent patterns for conversations taking place in the family, in a language that did not yet offer a reserve of ready-made and formulaic exchanges for everyday situations.[15] In this way, translations of texts for children played a role in the renaissance of the Hebrew language – especially in the depiction of spoken language in written texts – and offered models for dialogue and conversation, just as the letter-writing manuals that were common at the time provided templates for written correspondence (Kogman 2016).

The effectiveness of the translated texts

Can we maintain that the Jewish public indeed adopted a new habitus? And if so, can we point to a link between the new habitus and the educational projects of the *Haskalah* movement at the turn of the eighteenth century and the beginning of the nineteenth century? In other words, can we point to the extent to which the guidelines were effective?

Based on the small number of pupils in *Maskilic* schools and on their socioeconomic profile, it is difficult to imagine that the dramatic change described by Michael Lessing could have resulted exclusively from such *Maskilic* projects. We do not have at our disposal much evidence concerning the extent to which these guidelines were indeed followed. Nevertheless, we can point to the gradual growing awareness of those daily practices, especially in Jewish schools. Thus, for instance, the Wilhelm School in Breslau received an order from the authorities concerning personal hygiene "[to] pay more attention to cleanliness of the body, clothing, and books, which is generally neglected in education in Jewish homes" (quoted in Eliav 1960, 86). Furthermore, awareness of modern hygiene changed as indicated in the memoir of Shmuel Meyer Ehrenberg, where he writes about the time he spent as a student at the Samson School in Wolfenbüttel stating, "[at first] there was no bathtub, and toothbrushes were introduced only three years later" (*ibid.*, 103, note 5).

We know that several of the graduates of the *Maskilic* schools became leading figures in Jewish communities and helped disseminate *Maskilic* values and ways of life. Thus, for instance, graduates of the Dessau school became teachers in large and small Jewish communities (*ibid.*, 91). Five of the pupils at Chinukh Ne'arim in Berlin went on to study at the prestigious

---

15 On the development of dialogue in literary texts, see Shavit (2012).

Joachimsthalsches Gymnasium, "some to study medicine [*chochmat ha-refu'a*] and others to study religion," (Anonymous 1862 [1783]). Other pupils in the *Maskilic* schools later became teachers at those schools. Several would become prominent figures of the *Wissenschaft des Judentums* [*Chochmat Israel*] movement.

Of course, graduates of these schools were not the only agents to disseminate the *Maskilic* agenda. However, those graduates were more likely to serve as role models because of their status and position. In addition, one must remember that, as already mentioned, though the texts themselves officially addressed young readers, they were nevertheless read by adults as well, and, at times, primarily so.

Thus, the efforts to reform Jewish society involved the intentional use of translated texts as agents to disseminate the modern *Maskilic* habitus and the values of *Bürgertum*. These translated texts were written both as propaganda and for practical purposes. In fact, they laid bare the ideals of the *Haskalah* movement since they were not simply 'translated texts,' but rather they translated, so to speak, these ideals into everyday practices and social models. It appears, then, that in addition to the personal example set by the *Maskilim* themselves, it was the translated texts that presented the new habitus and social models and values to the Jewish public in German-speaking areas – even those who did not read the books directly or attend the *Haskalah* movement's schools. These *Maskilic* projects played a major role in the efforts to generate social and cultural reform in Jewish society, a change that gradually characterized growing circles of Jews in the German-speaking sphere, and a change that in many ways opened the door to the creation of a modern Jewish society whose source of authority would be based less and less on religious values and that would maintain a continuous cultural dialogue with the non-Jewish world.

Bibliography

Algazi, Gadi. 2002. "The Shaping of the Concept of Habitus in Bourdieu's Work." *Israeli Sociology* 4, no. 2: 401–410. [Hebrew]

Altmann, Alexander. 1973. *Moses Mendelssohn: A Biographical Study*. London: Routledge & Kegan Paul.

Anonymous. "Toldot ha-Zeman. Igeret Ne'etak mi-Sefer Chacham Nozri al Devar Chinukh Ne'arim be-Berlin." *Ha-me'asef* (Tevet 5544 [1862] [1783]): 61. [Hebrew]

Baraz, Shimon. "Chinukh Ne'arim: Al Devar Chinukh ha-Banim ka-Ra'uyi." *Ha-Me'asef* (Tishrei 5548 [1787]): 37. [Hebrew]

Basedow, Johann Bernhard. 1972 [1774]. *Elementarwerk*. Hildesheim: Georg Olms.
Beer, Peretz. 1796. *Sefer Toldot Israel*. Prague: n.p. [Hebrew]
Ben-Ze'ev, J. Lev. 1835 [1802]. *Mesilat ha-Limud*. Vienna: Anton Edlen von Scmid. [Hebrew]
Bock, Moses Hirsch. 1811. *Moda le-Yaldei Bnei Israel*. Berlin: Chevrat chinukh ne'arim. [Hebrew]
Bourdieu, Pierre. 1977. *Outline of a Theory of Practice*. Cambridge: Cambridge University Press.
Bourdieu, Pierre. 1984. "The Habitus and the Space of Life-styles." In *Distinction: A Social Critique of the Judgement of Taste*, 171–175. Translated by Richard Nice. Cambridge, MA: Harvard University Press.
Campe, Joachim Heinrich. 1824. *Robinson der Jingeree, Ein Lesebuch für Kinder*. Translated by David Samostz. Breslau: Sulzbach.
Dohm, Christian Wilhelm von. 1973 [1781]. *Über die bürgerliche Verbesserung der Juden*. Hildesheim/New York: Georg Olms.
Elias, Norbert. 2000. *The Civilizing Process: Sociogenetic and Psychogenetic Investigations*. Translated by Edmund Jephcott. Oxford: Blackwell.
Eliav, Mordechai. 1960. *Jewish Education in Germany in the Period of Enlightenment and Emancipation*. Tel Aviv: The Jewish Agency for Israel Publishing House. [Hebrew]
Euchel, Isaac. "Igrot Meshulam ben Uriah ha-Eshtemoi." *Ha-Me'asef*, Part 1 (Cheshvan 5550): 38–50, Part 2 (Kislev 5550): 80–85, Part 3 (Adar 5550): 171–176, Part 4 (Iyar 5550): 245–249. [Hebrew]
Even-Zohar, Itamar. 1990a. "Translation and Transfer." *Polysystem Studies*, a special issue of *Poetics Today* 11, no. 1: 73–78.
Even-Zohar, Itamar. 1990b. "Polysystem Theory." *Polysystem Studies*, a special issue of *Poetics Today* 11, no. 1: 9–26.
Even-Zohar, Itamar. 1990c. "Laws of Literary Interference." *Polysystem Studies*, a special issue of *Poetics Today* 11, no. 1: 53–72.
Even-Zohar, Itamar. 1997. "The Making of Culture Repertoire and the Role of Transfer." *Target* 9, no. 2: 373–381.
Ewers, Hans-Heino. 1996. "Joachim Heinrich Campe als Kinderliterat und als Jugendschriftsteller." In *Visionäre Lebensklugheit, Joachim Heinrich Campe in seiner Zeit (1746–1818)*, edited by Hanno Schmitt and Peter Albrecht. Wiesbaden: Harrasowitz: 159–178.
Feiner, Shmuel. 2004. *The Jewish Enlightenment*. Philadelphia: University of Pennsylvania Press.
Hettling, Manfred. 2015. "Bürger, Bürgertum, Bürgerlichkeit." Accessed April 28, 2020. http://docupedia.de/zg/hettling_buerger_v1_2015.
Katz, Jacob. 1973. *Out of the Ghetto: The Social Background of Jewish Emancipation, 1880–1870*. Cambridge, MA: Harvard University Press.

Kogman, Tal. 2016. "'Do Not Turn a Deaf Ear or a Blind Eye on Me, as I Am Your Son': New Conceptions of Childhood and Parenthood in 18th- and 19th-Century Jewish Letter-Writing Manuals." *Journal of Jewish Education* 82, no. 1: 4–27.

Kuperty-Tzur, Nadine. "Afterword." In *The Confessions*, Jean-Jacques Rousseau, 567–579. Translated by Irit Akrabi. Jerusalem: Carmel. [Hebrew]

Lässig, Simone. 2004. *Jüdische Wege ins Bürgertum*. Göttingen: Vandenhoeck & Ruprecht.

Lessing, Michael Benedikt. 1833. *Die Juden und die öffentliche Meinung im preussischen Staate*. Altona: J. F. Hammerich.

Lowenstein, Steven M. 1993. "The Lifestyle of Modernizing Berlin Jews." In *The Berlin Jewish Community*, 43–54. New York/Oxford: Oxford University Press.

Lowenstein, Steven M. 2005. "The Beginning of Integration, 1780–1870," in *Jewish Daily Life in Germany, 1618–1945*, edited by Marion A. Kaplan, 93–171. Oxford: Oxford University Press.

Maimonides. n.d. *The Guide for the Perplexed*. Translated [to the Hebrew] by David Kapah. Part 3, Chapter 27. Accessed April 28, 2020. http://www.daat.ac.il/daat/mahshevt/more/c9-2.htm#2.

Mounier, Jacques. 1979. *La fortune des écrits de Jean-Jacques Rousseau dans les pays de langue allemande de 1782 à 1813*. Doctoral diss., La nouvelle Sorbonne [Sorbonne 3].

Mounier, Jacques. 1980. *La fortune des écrits de Jean-Jacques Rousseau dans les pays de langue allemande de 1782 à 1813*. Paris: Presses universitaires de France.

Rousseau, Jean-Jacques. 1762. *Émile, ou De l'éducation*. Accessed April 28, 2020. https://fr.wikisource.org/wiki/Émile,_ou_De_l'éducation/Édition_1782/Livre_I.

Rousseau, Jean-Jacques. 1979. *Emile or On Education*. Translated by Allan Bloom. New York: Basic Books.

Rowlandson, Thomas. 1954. "Jewish Peddler." in *A Jewish Iconography*, edited by Alfred Rubens. London: The Jewish Museum.

Schmitt, Hanno. 2007. *Vernunft und Menschlichkeit: Studien zur Philanthropischen Erziehungsbewegung*. Bad Heilbrunn: Julius Klinkhardt.

Schochat, Azriel. 1956. "The German Jews' Integration within Their Non-Jewish Environment in the First Half of the Eighteenth Century." *Zion* 21, no. 3: 207–235. [Hebrew with English summary]

Schochat, Azriel. 1960. *Beginnings of the Haskalah among German Jewry*. Jerusalem: Bialik Institute. [Hebrew]

Sela-Sheffy, Rakefet. 1997. "Models and Habituses: Problems in the Idea of Cultural Repertoires." *Canadian Review of Comparative Literature* 24, no. 1: 35–47.

Shavit, Zohar. 2012. "From Time to Time: Fictional Dialogue in Hebrew Texts for Children." In *Translating Fictional Dialogue for Children and Young People*, edited by Martin B. Fischer and Mari Wirf Naro, 17–42. Berlin: Frank & Timme Verlag.

Shavit, Zohar. 2014. "Rousseau under Maimonides' Cloak: The Strategy of Introducing Enlightenment Literature into the New Jewish Library: The Case of Publication of Paragraphs of Jean-Jacques Rousseau's Émile in *Hame'asef*." *Zion* 79, no. 2: 135–174. [Hebrew, English summary: xiii–xiv].

Shavit, Zohar. In press. "*Robinson der Jüngere* in the Service of the Haskalah: Joachim Heinrich Campe, the Haskalah and the *Bildung* Project in Jewish Society." To be published in *Wie aus Kindern Juden oreig*, edited by Dorothea Salzer. Berlin: De Gruyter.

Simon, Ernst A. 1953. "Pedagogical Philanthropism and Jewish Education." In *Jubilee Book in Honor of Mordecai Menahem Kaplan*, edited by Moshe Davis, 149–187. New York: Jewish Theological Seminary. [Hebrew]

Toury, Gideon. 1984. "Transfer Operations and Translation." In *Semiotics Unfolding: Proceedings of the Second Congress of the International Association for Semiotic Studies, Vienna, July 1979*, edited by Tasso Borbé, 1041–1048. Berlin/New York/Amsterdam: Mouton.

Toury, Gideon. 1995. *Descriptive Translation Studies – and Beyond*. Amsterdam/Philadelphia: John Benjamins.

Toury, Gideon. 1998. "The Beginnings of Modern Translation into Hebrew: Yet another Look." *Dappim: Research in Literature* 2: 112. [Hebrew]

Toury, Jacob. 1972. *Prolegomena to the Entrance of Jews into German Citizenry*. Tel Aviv: The Diaspora Research Center. [Hebrew]

Tsamriyon, Tsemach. 1988. *Ha-Me'assef, The First Modern Periodical in Hebrew*. Tel Aviv: University Publishing Projects. [Hebrew]

Weisel, Naftali Herz. 1886 [1782]. "Fourth Letter." In *Sefer Divrei Shalom ve-Emet*, 237. Warsaw: Y. Kh. Zabelinski Bookshop. [Hebrew]

Weissbrod, Rachel. 2004. "From Translation to Transfer." *Across Languages and Cultures* 5, no. 1: 23–41.

Wolfsohn-Halle, Aaron. 1790. *Avtalion*. Berlin: Chevrat chinukh ne'arim. [Hebrew]

Associative practices and translations in children's book publishing

Co-editions in France and Spain

Delia Guijarro Arribas

Abstract

This chapter analyzes the associative practices developed by French and Spanish children's book publishers to export their books beyond their national boundaries. It examines the case of co-editions in particular, differentiating them from co-productions and co-prints. Comparing the French and Spanish subfields for children's literature, it identifies and analyzes the logics and mechanisms attached to co-editions in the French and Spanish national subfields, and in the global translation market. The comparison reveals how dominant publishers use co-editions as a tool of economic and/or cultural conquest of foreign markets. It also provides a measure of the symbolic capital of nations and languages and how this can be leveraged in cross-border literary exchange.

The sociology of translation allows us to reveal the mechanisms and logic at the heart of the global book market. This market has been studied since the 1990s by sociologists of culture, and more specifically within the framework of a research program piloted by Pierre Bourdieu, which focuses on the social conditions of the international circulation of cultural goods (see Heilbron and Sapiro 2002a, 2002b). These works connect Bourdieu's field-theoretical framework with the center-periphery model proposed by Abram de Swaan in order to analyze power dynamics within and between languages (see Bourdieu 1984, 1999, 2002; de Swaan 1993, 2001). In the introduction to her book *Translatio* (2008), Gisèle Sapiro lays out a research structure with which to analyze the global market for book translations. She focuses on two main issues: the distribution of books in their original language, which leads to the creation of transnational publishing fields corresponding to linguistic areas; and translation flows between these linguistic areas as an essential vector for measuring the economic and cultural conquest of foreign markets, and, consequently, the symbolic capital accumulated by nations and languages. In the same way, the global translation market has come to be structured according to professional rules and specific logics imposed by the specialization of its agents in the exportation and importation of (translated) books, and by the establishment of international institutions with legitimacy-conferring power such as book fairs.

Drawing on this theoretical and methodological framework, this chapter aims to reflect upon the various associative practices children's book publishers undertake around issues related to translation: namely, the co-production, co-edition and co-printing of children's books. A comparison of two national subfields of children's book publishing, in France and in Spain, allows us to detect the different meanings attached to these practices in the functioning of each national context.

International co-editions: The French strategy

Since the 1950s, technological advances in printing (the 'offset' method, in particular) enabled the widespread use of illustrations in fiction and non-fiction picture books for children. These processes implied an increase in editing and production costs. However, the construction and expansion of a common European market facilitated international cooperation between European publishers. Indeed, publishers sought to collaborate more and more through co-productions, co-editions, and co-printing practices in order to increase print runs and reduce the costs of production (Piquard 2005). This dual process constituted a new stage in the internationalization and renewal of children's book publishing in Europe.

Collaborations between publishers were not unique to children's books. Initially, such collaboration was focused around the publication of encyclopedias. However, as the share of children's literature in the book market grew over the course of the second half of the twentieth century, the sector became a privileged space for such associative practices. While co-productions have been quite common since the 1950s, French publishers have shown an increasing preference for co-editions, particularly as the subfield of children's book publishing autonomized throughout the 1970s. Philippe Schuwer, an editor at Hachette and later Nathan, set out to define and distinguish between the often-confused terms 'co-edition' and 'co-production' in his *Traité de coédition et de coproduction internationales* (1981).[1] Co-production

---

1 Schuwer's work builds on his master's thesis completed at the EHESS (School for Advanced Studies in the Social Sciences) in 1975, entitled *Coproduction et coéditions dans l'édition d'albums pour la jeunesse*.

allows for the realization of particularly ambitious and costly projects. Pierre Marchand used it within the first years of Gallimard Jeunesse for the creation of collections such as *Kinkajou* (1974), a series of books designed to guide children in different kinds of play. The books were richly illustrated and rather long (96 pages) and would not have been viable without partners. Nonetheless, co-production entails several constraints. Pierre Marchand explains the difficulties involved:

> *Kinkajou* was a success: 135,000 copies across forty titles. We had up to twelve co-publishers. But our discussions went on and on and the traveling was ceaseless. It was exhausting. These grand alliances can never last for too long, not least because of these kinds of arbitrations.[2] (Livres Hebdo 1985, 70)

Indeed, co-production necessitates a strong and sustained collaboration between publishers because they must conceive, finance, and print the works together, as well as share publishing rights.

It is precisely the matter of rights that constitutes one of the principal differences between co-productions and co-editions. In the case of co-editions, the originating publisher seeks out rights buyers abroad, generally prior to the publication of a given work. This practice ensures certain benefits for the originating publisher, who maintains control over the editorial design and publishing rights, which can then be exploited through the sale of foreign rights to publishers in other languages or territories. For their part, the co-publishers benefit because the burdens of production are taken on by the originating publisher. Co-editions thus make it possible for co-publishers to gain access to skills and techniques that they may not have in-house.

Most of the time, co-edition schemes include a co-printing strategy as well, which enables larger print runs because all co-edition partners pool their orders, which reduces per-book printing costs. In other cases, when printing is carried out remotely (in the country of the co-publishers), the originating publisher delivers the printing plates of the finished book to its

---

2   Unless otherwise indicated, all translations are by the author. In the French original: "Kinkajou a été une belle réussite, 135.000 exemplaires pour une quarantaine de titres. Nous avons eu jusqu'à douze coéditeurs. Mais les discussions devenaient interminables. Les voyages n'en finissaient pas. C'était épuisant. Ces grandes alliances ne peuvent jamais durer très longtemps, ne serait-ce qu'à cause des arbitrages."

partners, who then print locally. Writing in 1971, Catherine Deloraine, an editor at Flammarion, explained this practice in the following terms:

> For co-editions, either we buy the French rights to a foreign work and the French version is entirely produced abroad, or we receive the plates and produce the French version ourselves. In other cases, we may act as the originating publisher and either we fabricate the foreign versions [for our partners] (for example, the English and German versions of *Roi Brioche Ier*) or we send the plates.[3] (Livres Hebdo 1971, 34)

Such co-edition agreements between publishing houses in different countries are facilitated by low-cost printers in countries like China. They also benefit from the rise of international book fairs, which serve as hubs for negotiating co-edition deals. For children's book publishers, the Bologna Children's Book Fair is an ideal moment to present new projects and search for potential partners. Since the 1980s, French children's book publishers have cultivated an international reputation for 'know-how' around co-editions, which has given them a competitive boost in the face of stiff international competition. This can be seen alongside the broader trend toward a French specialization in the production of picture books (fiction and non-fiction). Both trends reinforced the autonomization of the French subfield of children's book publishing and the international recognition of French picture books. Indeed, co-editions carry certain undeniable benefits: greater distribution and promotion levels, and better chances of gaining recognition from international institutions of literary consecration. Co-editions can thus be a means of consecration for a given work, but also for its authors, its originating publisher and, to a lesser degree, its co-publishers.

Throughout the 1970s and 1980s, Pierre Marchand invoked the international prestige of Gallimard to maximize the number of co-edition partners. The assured success of his projects reinforced co-publishers' trust and guaranteed their support for future projects. For the majority of its co-editions, Gallimard Jeunesse required co-publishers to work with Gallimard's own printers. It thus developed into a significant children's literature printing hub,

---

3   In French: "Pour les coéditions, ou bien nous achetons les droits français d'un ouvrage étranger, et alors tantôt la version française est entièrement réalisée à l'étranger, tantôt nous recevons le film des illustrations et fabriquons nous-mêmes l'édition française. Ou bien nous sommes l'éditeur original et, soit nous fabriquons les versions étrangères (par exemple anglaise et allemande du Roi Brioche Ier) ou bien nous envoyons les films des illustrations."

which gave it the capacity to print books in foreign languages to which it did not possess rights as a legal assignee (Livres Hebdo 1983, 76).

Other economic and political factors help explain the international success of French co-editions as well. In the 1980s, the franc was weaker than the dollar, the pound, the mark, or the yen, which allowed French editors to propose more competitive prices, while publishers in the two other dominant European national fields for children's literature, the UK and Italy, suffered significant regressions, in part due to cultural politics at the national level. In 1985, Philippe Schuwer provided an analysis of the situation at the time in the following terms:

> On a global level, the crisis has reached Great Britain and Italy. Across the Channel in particular, fewer books are being checked out at libraries and print runs have consequently dropped. For encyclopedias, we've dropped from 15,000 to 10,000, even to 5,000 copies. The prices secured for co-editions have thus risen, and sales have become more competitive. In Italy, it's another case. There, the development of media conglomerates has imposed such a great degree of competition on children's books that the market has significantly tightened. With print runs diminishing, the costs of creation and production have increased such that we've looked for [other] economic formulas.[4] (Livres Hebdo 1985, 68)

According to the figures of the French Publishers Association (Syndicat national de l'edition, hereafter SNE), more co-editions are struck in the children's book sector than anywhere else in the French book market. In 2017, the children's book sector accounted for 68 percent of the 1,791 co-editions concluded in France, good for 1,213 titles (SNE 2018, 3). Most countries do not distinguish book rights from co-editions in their statistics on book exports. The mere fact that the SNE chooses to specify the proportion of co-editions within the totality of rights sales attests to the economic and symbolic weight of these practices within French publishing, and particularly within French children's book publishing.

---

4   In French: "La crise a globalement atteint la Grande-Bretagne et l'Italie. Outre-Manche particulièrement, les crédits aux bibliothèques diminuant, les tirages ont baissé. On est passé, pour les encyclopédies, de 15.000 à 10.000, voire 5.000 exemplaires. Les prix de coéditions proposées ont donc monté et les achats sont devenus moins compétitifs. En Italie, c'est un autre cas de figure. Le développement des groupes de communication ont fait subir une telle concurrence au livre jeunesse que le marché s'est fortement réduit. Les tirages diminuants, les coûts de création et de fabrication ont atteint une telle proportion qu'on a recherché des formules économiques."

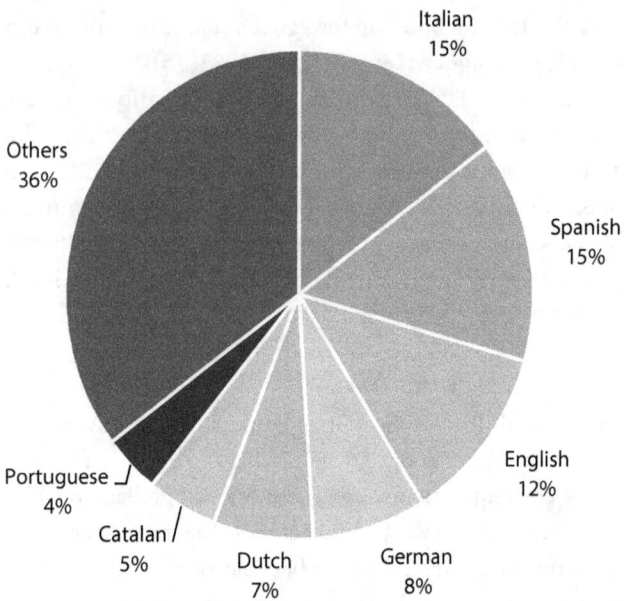

Figure 1. SNE's co-publication statistics according to language zones for the year 2017

Co-edition deals take place in an international context characterized by unequal power relations between nations and languages. Indeed, the originating publisher must generally occupy a dominant position in the global publishing market. In the words of the publisher Valérie Cussaguet, "one must be well positioned" (interview, October 25, 2018). Figure 1 shows SNE's co-edition statistics for 2017, organized by languages. It is evident that French publishers struck more co-edition agreements with Italian and Spanish publishers than with any others. These two semi-peripheral languages, which represent 15 percent of co-editions for the French children's publishing sector, is followed by English, a "hyper-central" language, and German, a central language (Heilbron 1999). It seems, thus, that co-editions are facilitated when the power relation between the participating languages is slightly asymmetric (Sapiro 2009).

The SNE also provides figures for co-editions by country, without distinguishing between market sectors (SNE 2017, 16). Even though these figures represent the entire French book market, they nonetheless reveal that co-editions occur primarily between the neighboring countries of Western Europe. Thus, co-edition projects with publishers working in Spanish are undertaken predominantly with editors from Spain rather than Latin America. The same is true for Portuguese. Only for English were co-editions equally distributed between the US and the UK. Nonetheless, discussions with French publishers suggest that co-publications with English-language publishers occur mostly with UK editors when it comes to children's books, and with US editors for all other publishing sectors.

Looking at the figures for Spanish and Catalan, we see that Spain is the first country in which French publishers find co-edition partners. The comparison of co-edition practices in France and Spain is complicated by the fact that the export statistics of the Spanish Association of Publishers Guilds (Federación de Gremios de Editores de España, FGEE) do not distinguish co-editions among book rights. It is thus impossible to know what proportion of outgoing rights agreements initiated by Spanish publishers are co-editions. However, interviews with Spanish publishers lead us to believe that, when they do enter into co-edition agreements, it tends to be as co-publishers and not as originating publishers.

Smaller children's book publishers in France, which do not generally possess the prestige necessary to easily attract co-edition partners in the way Gallimard Jeunesse does, have developed other strategies. These include specializing in pop-up books, as well as co-printing in later print runs after a first run in France. Pop-up books are illustrated books with (often quite sophisticated) interactive mechanisms. They are expensive to produce, but they can be quite profitable when done in the framework of an international co-edition. The publishing house Hélium, associated with the group Actes Sud Junior, has specialized in this type of book, mostly co-published with international partners. The small French publishing house L'Agrume, created in 2013, also publishes pop-up books. However, it lacks the symbolic capital required to attract foreign publishers for co-edition schemes. It therefore first publishes its books in France in small print runs (no more than 2,000 copies), and then works to find co-printers abroad. While its international clients tend to call themselves co-publishers, in practice the exchange is actually just a question of transferring rights to a foreign publisher, plus a co-printing clause. L'Agrume then manages the simultaneous co-printing processes, which can reach up to 20,000 or 25,000 copies. L'Agrume thus enjoys the option to reprint at a lower price for its own new print runs. While this strategy is much riskier from an economic perspective, it seems to be paying off. Indeed, only five years after its creation, the publishing house has already obtained awards at the Bologna Book Fair, including the prestigious Opera Prima award. L'Agrume's strategy nicely illustrates the principle of 'economic denial' that often characterizes actors within the market for symbolic goods, where, according to Pierre Bourdieu, "only those who know how to come to terms with the 'economic' constraints inherent in that hypocritical economy will prove able to fully reap the 'economic' profits of their symbolic capital" (Bourdieu 1997, 5).[5]

It is important to note that the majority of pop-up books are printed in China. To facilitate deals, many Chinese printing enterprises have opened offices in large European publishing centers such as Paris or Barcelona, where their commercial agents can more easily link up with European publishers. These agents have also developed expertise in the domain of paper engineering, skills that are necessary to ensure pop-up projects' success, but which are far too costly for smaller publishers to employ in-house. Guillaume Griffon, director of L'Agrume, explained this in an interview:

> We never have paper engineers because that is a supplementary post, so it's the author who constructs his models and it's the Chinese printer, instead of a paper engineer, who takes it from there and works out any kinks. We've had a number of problems with the book *Inventions*, which is very complicated. It was our Taiwanese sales representative based in France who presented us with a number of options – to such an extent that I even told her she should start pitching me new projects. She is actually the one who pitched the book *Une faim de Loup* to me, after which I hired an illustrator to do the illustrations. But the concept itself was hers.[6] (Interview with Guillaume Griffon, November 22, 2018)

We have just evoked the practices of international co-editions between publishers working in different languages. However, international co-editions also exist within linguistic areas, as Hélène Buzelin has shown in the case of adult literature co-editions between French and Quebecois publishers. These projects were predominantly initiated by Quebecois publishers as a means to penetrate the French market (Buzelin 2009). Turning to the children's book sector, we observe that co-editions between France and other Francophone countries are rare due to the domination exerted by the French

---

5   In French: "Seuls ceux d'entre eux qui savent composer avec les contraintes 'économiques' inscrites dans cette économie de la mauvaise foi pourront recueillir pleinement les profits 'économiques' de leur capital symbolique."
6   In French: "Nous n'avons jamais d'ingénieur papier, parce que c'est un poste supplémentaire, donc c'est l'auteur qui fait ses maquettes et après c'est l'imprimeur chinois qui fait un peu le relai et qui remplace l'ingénieur papier, et qui va donc trouver des solutions. Nous avons eu pleins de problèmes avec le livre Inventions, qui est très compliqué et c'est la commerciale taiwanaise qui habite en France qui nous a proposé pleins de choses, à tel point que je lui ai dit qu'elle devrait proposer des projets. Alors le livre Une faim de Loup, c'est elle, la commerciale de mon imprimeur chinois, qui me l'a proposé et je l'ai fait illustrer par un illustrateur, mais le concept est d'elle."

subfield within the Francophone linguistic area. Indeed, French editors do not need to use co-editions in order to access Francophone markets outside France. This observation holds even more true for the relationship between children's book publishers in Spain and other publishers within the Spanish-speaking area: co-editions between them are non-existent. To bypass the center, some periphery-based publishers have developed co-edition strategies amongst themselves, as Martin Dore demonstrates in the case of co-editions between Quebecois publishers and Francophone African publishers (Dore 2009). A similar strategy, albeit rather minor, was implemented by the ten Latin American children's book publishers that joined to form the *Coedición Latinoamericana* project.[7]

Plurilingual co-editions and co-printing at the national level: The Spanish strategy

Within Spain, a number of co-printing and co-edition projects exist between publishing houses in the various autonomous communities. These projects ensure that books can be simultaneously distributed in as many of the country's co-official languages as possible. To understand this strategy, it is necessary first to understand the singularity of the Spanish case with respect to plurilingualism and translation. The Spanish state defines itself as a monolingual state composed of officially monolingual territories on the one hand and officially bilingual territories on the other. Within these territories, "more or less marked regional identity clusters cohabitate" (Córdoba Serrano 2013, 9).[8] Although there are six co-official languages within the country (Spanish, Catalan, Galician, Basque, Valencian, and Aranese), bilingualism is only perceptible and encouraged within certain regions. The public education system in Spain does not allow pupils to learn other 'Spanish' languages that are not the official language(s) of the autonomous community where they attend school. A pupil from Andalusia cannot learn Basque at school, and a pupil from Catalonia will never have the possibility of taking courses in Galician. However, all pupils are required to study English from the age of

---

7 They include: Aique Grupo Editor in Argentina, Editora Melhoramentos in Brazil, Babel Libros in Columbia, LOM Ediciones in Chile, Editorial Piedra Santa in Guatemala, CIDCLI in Mexico, Anamá Ediciones in Niguaragua, Ediciones PEISA in Peru, Ediciones Huracán in Puerto Rico and Ediciones Taller in the Dominican Republic. This project benefited from financing from UNESCO via its regional center (CERLALC) headquartered in Bogota.
8 In French: "cohabitent différents noyaux identitaires régionaux plus ou moins marqués."

six. Depending on where they go to school, pupils are also required to study French, German or Italian.

After the Franco dictatorship (1939–1975), bilingualism was introduced in schools across certain autonomous communities. In the 1980s, in a context of regional identity creation (which sometimes took on a linguistic or nationalistic tenor), the governments of these autonomous communities financed translations into regional languages. This system promoted the development of large groups specialized in publishing for children (both schoolbooks and children's literature). Publishing houses such as Santillana, SM, Edebe, Edelvives and Anaya established more or less autonomous subsidiaries in each of these communities or bought up existing regional publishing houses. These subsidiaries would produce textbooks following the regional education programs and translate the national production of children's literature into regional languages. The subsidiaries were required to purchase translation rights from their parent publishing house, which handled the simultaneous co-printing of works into all pertinent languages. The same process is also widely used when buying rights for a book from outside Spain: the parent publishing house buys the translation rights to the work for the entire Spanish territory (and sometimes for the entire Spanish linguistic area, known as 'world Spanish rights'), and the subsidiaries, in turn, buy the rights for each regional language with all printing managed by the parent publishing house. In the same vein, the subsidiaries of Spanish children's book publishers in America are given priority when it comes to buying exploitation rights for the country in question.

In Spain, 98.9 percent of the population can speak Spanish. Spanish is a supercentral language within Spain according to the global linguistic system described by Abram de Swaan, who calculates the centrality of a language according to the number of plurilingual speakers (polyglots) who choose it as a mode of communication (de Swaan 2001, 4). Spanish is the mother tongue of the majority of people within all of Spain's autonomous communities except Galicia (see Table 1) (Instituto Nacional de Estadística 2016, 5). Whereas bilingualism is largely dominant in Catalonia, in the Balearic Islands and in Galicia, only a little over half of the population in the Basque Country and in the Community of Valencia are bilingual. Both regions are marked by very intense language-based territorial inequalities.

Regarding children's book publishing, the data from the Monitoring Center for Reading and Books (Observatorio del libro y de la lectura) show that, in 2014, Spanish is the only language with nationwide distribution and is the main publishing language for children's books. According to ISBN, 69.4 percent of children's book titles in Spain are published in Spanish

Table 1. Percentage of mother tongue speakers in the Autonomous Communities by co-language

Autonomous Communities	Spanish (%)	Co-official languages (%)	Both equally (%)	Other languages (%)
Catalonia	55.1	31	2.8	11.1
Valencian Community	60.8	28.8	9.5	0.9
Galicia	30.9	40.9	25.3	2.9
Basque Country	76.4	17.5	6	0.1
Balearic Islands	48.6	37.9	3.6	9.9

Table 2. Titles published in Spain by language and market sector in 2014 (children's book publishing versus the book market in Spain overall)

	Children's book publishing (%)	Overall publishing market (%)
Spanish	69.4	84.7
Catalan	18.5	10
Basque	3.9	1.9
Galician	3.5	1.7
Other languages	9.7	1.7

and 18.5 percent in Catalan. Far behind these languages, we find Basque (3.9 percent) and Galician (3.5 percent). Comparing these figures with figures for the entire Spanish publishing industry shows that the share of titles published in regional languages is higher within the children's publishing sector (see Table 2). This sector also seems to attract the greatest number of translations (almost 42 percent of all titles). As is the case globally, the major language from which books are translated remains English, which accounted for 46.3 percent of all translations in Spain. Nonetheless, the second most common source language of translated works in this sector is Spanish (20 percent), followed by Italian (11 percent), and French (7.6 percent) (Observatorio del libro y de la lectura 2016, 18). These proportions have remained constant since at least the middle of the 2000s, with some fluctuations for French and Italian.

The position of Spanish as the second most translated language in Spain's children's book publishing sector can be explained by the high number of translations into other co-official languages in Spain. This phenomenon, which is present throughout the Spanish publishing market, is all the more notable in the children's book sector. It is interesting to observe how the statistics concerning translations within the children's book sector are noticeably different from those relative to the general publishing market. For the year 2014, English represented 58 percent of translated books for the entire sector, compared with 46.3 percent for children's books. In the same year, Italian accounted for 3.7 percent of the entire sector (fifth, behind German) compared with 11 percent within the children's book sector (third). The lesser domination of English and the increased presence of Italian testify to the sector's relative autonomy and to the specific literary capital accumulated by the different languages present within this sector relative to others.[9]

Spain is not the only country where plurilingualism has had consequences for the structuration of literary and publishing fields. Unlike the Belgian case, however, where linguistic separation is heavily territorialized (Bourdieu 1985, 3–6), or even the Algerian case, where languages are socially hierarchical (Leperlier 2018), the Spanish publishing field is characterized by a high degree of interdependence and interpenetration between regional language markets and the dominant market (that is to say, the Spanish-language market). Spain's regional language markets are also quite interdependent, despite their geographical segmentation. Even though they are inscribed at the local or community level according to the Spanish model of decentralized public action, most of the subfield structures exist and are shared at the national level. Publishing houses in Spain publish works in different languages simultaneously, either directly or, as we have just explained, through subsidiaries. The same national literary criticism spheres take an interest in publications of all the state's co-official languages. The interpenetration of linguistic book markets concerns not only authors (a number of whom write in two languages and produce their own translations) but also the public, as all those who read in Catalan, Galician, Basque or Valencian also read in Spanish.

This interpenetration also structures translation practices in Spanish children's book publishing. The translation of a work from a foreign language or a regional language into Spanish implies that the original version will not then be translated into the country's other regional languages unless the translations into regional languages occur simultaneously with the Spanish translation. During an interview carried out in 2017, Isabelle Torrubia, who

---

9   Looking at adult literature translated in France, Gisèle Sapiro observes this phenomenon of symbolic capital accumulation for certain languages within certain genres, particularly for German in theatre works and for Spanish and Hebrew in poetry (see Sapiro 2008, 163).

directs a literary agency specialized in the sales of rights for French children's books in Barcelona, explains this phenomenon in the following terms:

> Catalans purchase translation rights for Spanish and Catalan simultaneously. The same goes for Galicians. The Basques only buy for Basque. If a book is published first in Catalan, it can then be published later in Spanish. If a book is published first in Spanish and not simultaneously in Catalan, I will never be able to sell it in Catalan because the Spanish version will devour the Catalonian market.[10] (Interview with Isabelle Torrubia, March 24, 2017)

Some children's book specialists that are well recognized in their respective autonomous communities describe the perverse effects of such a polysystem. Applying Itamar Even-Zohar's polysystem theory to Spain, Sierra Cordoba (2013, 26) states that "the Spanish system occupies a central place in the polysystem, the Galician and Basque systems inhabit the periphery, while the Catalan system is situated somewhere in between." The writer and Spanish-Galician literary translator of children's books Xosé Antonio Neira Cruz explains that one of the weak points of the Galician publishing sector is its lack of international literary classics, the vast majority of which have already been translated into Spanish: "The fact that we had to wait until 2004 to see the translation of a classic such as *The Diary of Anne Frank* is symptomatic of the sector's relative weakness" (Aguiar 2005, 65).[11] For her part, Teresa Maña, a specialist in Catalan children's books, questions the pertinence of translating such an abundance of children's books from Spanish into Catalan given the fact that all those who read Catalan also read Spanish.

> Publishing books in Catalan presents a number of coincidences with publishing in Spanish, given that the Catalan books are edited simultaneously, or shortly afterwards, in both languages. This practice, desirable when it's a question of translating [a foreign book] or a book originally written in Catalan, becomes a perversion when it becomes a question of a book initially written in Spanish that is then translated into Catalan. What's the

---

10   In French: "Les catalans achètent de manière simultanée les droits pour l'espagnol et le catalan. Ceux de Galice aussi, les basques n'achètent que pour le basque. Si un livre est d'abord publié uniquement en catalan il pourra être publié en espagnol. Si le livre est publié d'abord en espagnol et pas simultanément en catalan, je ne pourrais jamais le vendre en catalan, parce que l'espagnol va manger le marché en Catalan."

11   In Spanish: "Es sintomático de la debilidad de este sector el hecho de que tuviéramos que esperar a 2004 para ver traducido un clásico como *El diario de Ana Frank*."

use of readers knowing both languages if, either due to social dictates or ignorance, they will opt for the translation? (Aguiar 2005, 45).[12]

Studying translation flows in light of the power dynamics at work between languages, as Johan Heilbron and Gisèle Sapiro have done, allows us to understand why the majority of translations are undertaken from Spanish (a central language) into other regional languages (peripheral languages), irrespective of the number of speakers and their reading capacities (Heilbron and Sapiro 2008). Based on data collected between 2012 and 2014 for three peripheral languages in Spain (Basque, Galician, and Catalan, which includes figures for Valencian) these languages exhibited a higher proportion of translations (nearly 60 percent of titles published for children in these languages) than the same sector in Spanish. Spanish is the principal source language for translations into Galician (30 percent of all children's book translations) and into Basque (43 percent). For Catalan, the most common source language alternates between English and Spanish (each around 30 percent). The share of children's book translations in the opposite direction, from Spain's regional languages into Spanish, accounts for 3 percent of all children's books translated into Spanish (Ministerio de Cultura 2010). Despite the fact that translations between regional languages remain marginal – 8 percent of all translations, or 1.8 percent of total domestic production (Observatorio del libro y de la lectura 2015, 22) – there are number of co-edition arrangements between publishing houses based in different autonomous communities committed to publishing works simultaneously in each co-official language. The group Editores Asociados, which brings together La Galera (Catalonia), Galaxia (Galicia), Tàndem (Valencian Community), Elkar (Basque Country), Llibros del Pexe (Asturias), and Xordica (Aragon), is a case in point. The latter two publishing houses publish respectively in Bable (also called Asturian) and in Aragonese, two languages among a large number of languages and dialects spoken in Spain that are relegated to an ultra-minority status and are not recognized as co-official languages.

---

12 In Spanish: "La edición de libros en catalán presenta muchas coincidencias con la edición castellana puesto que los libros se editan simultáneamente, o al cabo de poco tiempo, en ambas lenguas. Esta práctica, deseable cuando se trata de un libro traducido o de un original catalán, resulta una perversión cuando se trata de un original castellano que se vierte al catalán. ¿De que les sirve a los lectores conocer dos lenguas si, ya sea por prescripción o por desconocimiento, lo leerán traducido?"

Conclusion

The development of international co-edition schemes has been favored by French children's book publishers as a means to export their production internationally, beyond the French linguistic area. By contrast, Spanish publishers undertake relatively few co-edition projects on an international scale, opting instead for a strategy of direct distribution within a powerful linguistic area. However, they use co-edition and co-printing partnerships widely to translate works into each co-official state language, thereby conquering Spain's plurilingual market. Although they operate at different levels, the French and Spanish co-edition strategies are subject to the symbolic capital possessed by each respective language, nation and publishing house involved in the exchange. These strategies both adapt to and reinforce specialization patterns in national production. The Spanish subfield of children's book publishing largely dominates the Spanish linguistic area but occupies a less central position within the world market, which makes it difficult for Spanish publishers to find co-publishers for co-edition projects. In contrast, French children's books enjoy widespread international circulation thanks to their immense international prestige, which itself can be attributed in part to the exportation of French publishers' editorial 'know-how' when it comes to co-editions.

Bibliography

Aguilar, Elsa. 2005. *Anuario sobre el libro infantil y juvenil*. Madrid: Ediciones SM.

Bourdieu, Pierre. 1977. "La production de la croyance [contribution à une économie des biens symboliques]." *Actes de la recherche en sciences sociales*, no. 13: 3–43.

Bourdieu, Pierre, ed. 1984. "Quelques propriétés des champs." In *Questions de sociologie*, 113–120. Paris: Minuit.

Bourdieu, Pierre. 1985. "Existe-t-il une littérature belge? Limites d'un champ et frontières politiques." *Études de lettres*, no. 3: 3–6.

Bourdieu, Pierre. 1998. *Les Règles de l'art: Genèse et structure du champ littéraire*. Paris: Le Seuil.

Bourdieu, Pierre. 2002. "Les conditions sociales de la circulation international des idées." *Actes de la recherche en sciences sociales*, no. 145: 3–8.

Buzelin, Hélène. 2009. "Les contradictions de la coédition international: des pratiques aux représentations." In *Les contradictions de la globalisation éditoriale*, edited by Gisèle Sapiro, 45–79. Paris: Nouveau Monde Éditions.

Córdoba Serrano, María Sierra. 2013. *Le Québec traduit en France: Analyse sociologique de l'exportation d'une culture périphérique*. Ottawa: Presse de l'Université d'Ottawa.

de Swaan, Abram. 1993. "The Emergent World Language System." *International Political Science Review* 14, no. 3: 219–226.

Dore, Martin. 2009. "Stratégies éditoriales et marche international: Le cas d'un éditeur canadien francophone, Hurtubise HMH." In *Les contradictions de la globalisation éditoriale*, edited by Gisèle Sapiro, 201–225. Paris: Nouveau Monde Éditions.

Ferrand, Christine. 1983. "Gallimard Jeunesse fête ses dix ans, les coulisses d'une réussite." *Livres Hebdo*, February 8, 1983.

Grangié, Marianne. 1985. "Les éditeurs de jeunesse français créent pour le monde entier." *Livres Hebdo*. March 11/11: 68.

Heilbron, Johan. 1999. "Towards a Sociology of Translation: Book Translations as Cultural World System." *European Journal of Social Theory* 2, no. 4: 429–444.

Heilbron, Johan and Gisèle Sapiro, eds. 2002a. "Traduction, les échanges littéraires internationaux." *Actes de la recherche en sciences sociales*, no. 144.

Heilbron, Johan and Gisèle Sapiro, eds. 2002b. "La circulation internationale des idées." *Actes de la recherche en sciences sociales*, no. 145.

Heilbron, Johan and Gisèle Sapiro. 2008. "La traduction comme vecteur des échanges culturels internationaux." In *Translatio: Le marché de la traduction en France à l'heure de la mondialisation*, edited by Gisèle Sapiro, 25–44. Paris: CNRS-Editions.

Instituto Nacional de Estadística. 2016. "Nota de Prensa de la Encuesta sobre la participación de la población adulta en las actividades de aprendizaje." Accessed April 14, 2020. https://www.ine.es/prensa/eada_2016.pdf.

Le Bulletin du Livre. 1971. "Les livres de jeunesse en France." March 186: 34.

Leperlier, Tristan. 2018. *Algérie, les écrivains de la décennie noir*. Paris: CNRS-Editions.

Ministerio de Cultura. 2010. "La Traducción Editorial en España Servicio de Estudios." Accessed April 28, 2020. https://repositorio.comillas.edu/jspui/retrieve/108170/libro_blanco_acett_2010.pdf.

Observatorio del libro y de la lectura. 2015. "El sector del libro en España 2013–2015." Accessed April 28, 2020. https://www.cegal.es/wp-content/uploads/2016/05/Sector-del-Libro-en-España-Enero-2016.pdf.

Observatorio del libro y de la lectura. 2016. "Los Libros infantiles y juveniles en España 2014–2015." Accessed April 28, 2020. https://www.observatoriodelainfancia.es/ficherosoia/documentos/5414_d_informelij-2017.pdf.

Piquard, Michèle. 2005. *L'édition pour la jeunesse en France de 1945 à 1980*. Lyon: Presses de l'Enssib.

Sapiro, Gisèle, ed. 2008. *Translatio: Le marché de la traduction en France à l'heure de la mondialisation*. Paris: CNRS-Editions.

Sapiro, Gisèle. 2009. "Mondialisation et diversité culturelle: Les enjeux de la circulation transnationale des livres." In *Les contradictions de la globalisation éditoriale*, edited by Gisèle Sapiro, 275–301. Paris: Nouveau Monde Éditions.

Schuwer, Philippe. 1981. *Traité de coédition et de coproduction internationales*. Paris: Promodis.

Syndicat national de l'édition. 2017. "Repères statistiques: France et international 2016–2017." Accessed April 16, 2020. https://www.sne.fr/document/synthese-des-reperes-statistiques-20162017/.

Syndicat national de l'édition. 2018. "Repères statistiques, l'édition jeunesse: France et international 2017–2018" Accessed April 16, 2020. https://fill-livrelecture.org/wp-content/uploads/2018/07/RS18_BatWEBSignet.pdf.

Swaan, Abram de. 2001. *Words of the World: The Global Language System*. Cambridge: Polity Press.

Translation and the formation of a Brazilian children's literature

Lia A. Miranda de Lima & Germana H. Pereira

Abstract

This chapter examines the historical role of translations in the constitution of Brazilian children's literature. Resting on a systemic view informed by Antonio Candido and Itamar Even-Zohar, it provides a historical panorama of the translation of children's literature in Brazil since the end of the nineteenth century to the present day. It also presents a brief analysis of the current state of translated literature for children in Brazil, looking particularly at books for small children. Translations are shown to be a fundamental aspect in the building of a literary tradition and in the emergence of a national canon of Brazilian works and authors.

Introduction

This chapter embraces a historical perspective in order to provide an overview of Brazilian children's literature (BCL). Using a theoretical framework informed by the studies of Itamar Even-Zohar and the Brazilian scholar and literary critic Antonio Candido, its aim is to emphasize the historical role of translations in the constitution of a local children's literary system and demonstrate the persistent importance of translations in the emergence and development of BCL. This historical perspective consists in examining the interrelations between literary works over time and connecting their internal, aesthetic components to the position these texts take up in a certain social context. This approach demands the integration of translated works into the reconstruction and analysis of the historical course of a national literature.[1]

This chapter is organized in four parts. First, we consider the notions of 'literary system' and 'formation' of a literature according to Candido, and of 'polysystem' according to Even-Zohar. Second, we present a historical

---

1 For a similar approach to the development of Hebrew children's literature, see Shavit (1995, 1996, 1997, 2002). See also Shavit's contribution in this volume.

overview of the first literary works for children in Brazil. Third, we focus on the period between 1930 and 1945, known as *Estado Novo* [New State], during which Brazil lived under the dictatorial regime of Getúlio Vargas. During these years, Brazil experienced significant economic and social changes that boosted the production of books for children. One particularly important change was the expansion of the educational system. Finally, adding to the already well-developed historiographical works on BCL (see Hallewell 1982; Arroyo 1990; Lajolo and Zilberman 2007; Coelho 2010), we situate foreign works in the contemporary Brazilian literary children's system, taking as examples the books distributed by the state to nurseries and kindergartens.[2] Our analysis points to the centrality of translation in the development of BLC.

The literary system

Translation, alongside criticism and anthologizing, is one of the main forms of rewriting literature. It impacts the circulation of literary works, their reception, the reputation of writers and the constitution of the canon (Lefevere 1992). We understand the canon as a group of works that are "accepted as legitimate by the dominant circles within a culture and whose conspicuous products are preserved by the community to become part of its historical heritage" (Even-Zohar 1990, 16). Translation is also an instrument for universalizing literature by introducing foreign works into the receiving literary system (Casanova 2007). Therefore, the study of translations becomes imperative to a more complete understanding of a literature's development. This point has been aptly made by scholars in the last two decades of the twentieth century, especially in the field of Descriptive Translation Studies.

Drawing on these contributions, we follow polysystem theory as formulated by Itamar Even-Zohar here. According to Even-Zohar, a literature is seldom a uni-system, but is rather a multiple system (polysystem) of activities considered by its members to be literary. In the polysystem, these members define their values in relation to one another. Such an approach allows for the examination of correlations between repertoire and system, production, products, and consumption. It rejects the idea of literature as a conglomerate of disconnected items. Translations constitute a system of their own, which connects to the polysystem via a net of cultural and verbal relations. According to Even-Zohar, translated works correlate in at least two ways: in the principles of source text selection by the target literature, and in the way translations

---

[2] In Brazil, children attend kindergarten from birth to five years of age.

use the literary repertoire, adopting norms, behaviors and specific policies (Even-Zohar 1990, 47). Even-Zohar considers translations not as a closed system within a literary polysystem but as an active system that can assume a central or a peripheral position within a literature (*ibid*). In the case of the Brazilian literary system for children's literature, translations occupied a central position at least until the 1960s and remain significant today.[3]

Another related theoretical perspective is that of Antonio Candido. Candido has devoted himself to the historical study of Brazilian literature, consistently in connection to literary criticism. In 1962, he published his most important work, *Formação da Literatura Brasileira* [Formation of Brazilian Literature]. In this book, Candido understands the *literary system* as the corollary of the historical shaping of a literature, which follows the phases of the first literary manifestations (single productions of little repercussion) and the early configuration of the system (the drafting of a literature as a shaped cultural fact). He calls *formation* the whole process of emergence and development of a literature until it becomes a system. Candido distinguishes between *literary manifestations* and *literature* as such, which constitutes a "system of works connected by common denominators, which allow recognizing the dominant tones of a phase" (Candido 2000, 23).[4] This system consists of producers of literature, readers, means of distribution and circulation, and elements of style. It acts as a symbolic whole that organically integrates civilization. The system presumes a literary continuity, aesthetically punctuated by phases of rupture, surpassing, and recovering, which originate a tradition. Candido's method consists in articulating each one of these stages, outlining a flow that allows us to picture literary phenomena in a complex way.

In his essay "The First Baudelarians" (1989), Antonio Candido uses several terms and expressions to refer to a foreign author's position in the receiving system (in this case, Baudelaire in Brazil), in each historical moment. Candido uses the term '*sistema receptor*' [receiving system] to refer to a literature that welcomes translations. (We have chosen to keep his expression instead of

---

3   In the 1940s, translations represented more than 70 percent of children's books in Brazil. Between 1975 and 1978, the share of translations dropped to around 50 percent according to Marisa Lajolo and Regina Zilberman (2007, 121). Currently, there are no statistics regarding translated children's literature in particular, but more general data can point to tendencies. The survey *Produção e Vendas no Setor Editorial Brasileiro* [Production and Sales in Brazilian Editorial Sector], carried out by the Câmara Brasileira do Livro (CBL), Sindicato Nacional dos Editores de Livros (SNEL) and Fundação Instituto de Pesquisas Econômicas (Fipe), indicated that in 2016 and 2017, 40 percent of new titles (across all genres) were translations.
4   In Portuguese: "sistema de obras ligadas por denominadores comuns, que permitem reconhecer as notas dominantes duma fase." All English translations are by Lia Miranda.

replacing it with the most current term in translation studies: 'target system'). The foreign author can be an influence, an inspiration, nourishment, a master, a model; s/he can be translated, adapted, paraphrased, imitated, assimilated, unfolded; s/he can be emulated by others in his/her themes, ways and typical images; or s/he can have "a normal presence in the writers' sensitivity" (*ibid.*).[5] According to Candido, Baudelaire's historical importance in Brazilian literature was a result of deformations and adjustments in his poetry in order to meet the needs of the society that received his work. This partial, altered, and modified vision of the foreign author, which highlights certain elements and attenuates others, is what allows the receiving system to evolve. Therefore, the theoretical framework that we embrace to observe translations is primarily descriptive, avoiding prescribing rules for the translation process. Otherwise, it would be impossible to situate translations in the receiving system and understand their role in the evolution of this system.

We regard translations as a fundamental aspect of literary continuity in BLC and in the constitution of its tradition, which has enabled the emergence of a national canon. In other words, following Even-Zohar, we postulate the feasibility and the relevance of integrating translated literature into the historical trajectory of children's literature.

Historical background

As seems to be the rule among young or small literary systems (Even-Zohar 1990, 49), the first stage of literary production for children in Brazil was the importation of foreign literary works. The first translations came from Portugal during the second half of the nineteenth century and were intended especially for schools. Among the translated authors were Marquise de Lambert, Madame de Beaumont, Fedro, Andersen, De Amicis, Verne, Giulio Cesare Croce, Emilio Salgari, and Christoph von Schmid. The first Brazilian translations, which were actually localized adaptations, emerged soon afterwards, motivated by protests of intellectuals against the European translations. The pioneers who undertook this task were educators who left us abridged versions of classics such as *Gulliver's Travels*, *Robinson Crusoe*, and *Don Quixote*, as well as fables and short stories by Perrault, Andersen, and the Brothers Grimm, between the 1880s and 1890s.

These first translations blended external references and local re-creation and constituted the germ of the autochthonous children's literature that flourished

---

5   In Portuguese: "presença normal na sensibilidade dos escritores."

during the following decades. With the abolition of slavery in 1888 and the Proclamation of the Republic in 1889, Brazil met the political, economic, social, and productive conditions to allow the emergence of a system of books for children. The young Republic promoted the industrialization and the urbanization of the country, which, combined with the emergence of a consumer market, made the regular circulation of children's books possible for the first time.

Antonio Candido argues that Brazilian literature, although modified by the conditions of the New World, is an organic part of Western literature (Candido 2000, 11). The same holds true for BCL. Its beginnings are distinguished by a project of stating a national identity in accordance with the ideals of Romanticism that spread in Brazil after its independence from Portugal in 1822. The wish of the new independent state to affirm its disconnection from the Portuguese colonizers (only to align itself with other influences) required that BCL embraced Brazilian themes and language.

Nonetheless, in the absence of a national children's repertoire that could serve as a reference, Brazilian authors sought out models for these first literary productions in European works. Maybe the most remarkable example is the Italian *Cuore* (1886), by Edmondo de Amicis and translated into Portuguese by João Ribeiro (1891), a book that circulated with great success in Brazil and which bequeathed patriotism to national production. Another emblematic case is *Le tour de la France par deux garçons* (1877), by G. Bruno, which inspired *Através do Brasil* (1910) by Olavo Bilac and Manuel Bonfim, a book that marked the childhood of several generations of Brazilians.

An increase in the production of children's books by Brazilian authors at the turn of the twentieth century, especially for school use, did not hinder translations. On the contrary: the increase in the means of production and circulation, and the school demand, boosted the publishing of translations and local works simultaneously. Moreover, several authors both wrote and translated children's literature. Prominent authors who also translated include the Parnassian poet Olavo Bilac, who translated *Max und Moritz* (1865) by Wilhelm Busch, Monteiro Lobato (active in the 1930s and 1940s), and other authors of Brazilian modernism, such as Henriqueta Lisboa.

It is only from the 1930s on, during the New State regime, that we may speak of regular literary activities for children in Brazil, with a set of authors, dissemination vehicles, and a dedicated audience. Monteiro Lobato (1882–1948) was a pioneer, not only due to the literary works he left to children but also for his editorial activities, which were innovative in the production and the circulation of books in the country at a time where there was not yet a strong national tradition that could serve as a model for new authors.

Monteiro Lobato: When inspiration becomes originality

In the late 1920s, Brazil experienced an economic crisis that was aggravated by the Great Depression. This situation displeased the industrial elites, the new politicians, and the army, who planned a coup d'état that led to the so-called Revolution of 1930. Getúlio Vargas was made president and Brazil's economic structures underwent significant transformations, including an accelerated process of industrialization and the expansion of the school system.

During the 1930s, modernist aesthetics already dominated Brazilian literature, and BCL started to show autonomous and original elements, overcoming the imitations of its first stages. Monteiro Lobato was the great figure in this transitional period and became an inspiration for authors that would emerge in the following decades. Lobato radically renovated the language in BCL and appropriated a European collection of works as well as Brazilian folklore in an innovative fashion, with an anthropophagic spirit consonant with modernist aesthetics.

Lobato is a remarkable example of the participation of foreign literature in the formation of Brazil's national literature. His children's books comprise a series of fantastic stories situated on a family farm called 'Sítio do Picapau Amarelo' [Yellow Woodpecker Farm]. In this series, he evokes the European tradition of fairy tales and retrieves characters from the European and North American cultural industries, such as Peter Pan and Felix the Cat, merging them with national folklore figures – *saci-pererê* and *cuca*, for instance. Furthermore, Lobato punctuated a change in influences in Brazilian literature: from French to British and North American literature. In 1908, he wrote:

> French is making me sick. How dull is that same old tale of a man that has taken someone else's woman – as if life were nothing, nothing but this! English literature is far more airy, varied, with more horizons, trees, and beasts. There are no tigers or elephants in French literature, while English literature is a whole Noah's Ark.[6] (Lobato 2010)

English literature had a significant influence on the Farm's exuberance, with its varied characters (children, old women, a talking cloth doll, a wise

---

6   In Portuguese: "O francês anda a me engulhar todas as tripas. Como cansa aquela eterna historinha dum homem que pegou a mulher do outro – como se a vida fosse só, só, só isso! A literatura inglesa é muito mais arejada, variada, mais cheia de horizontes, árvores e bichos. Não há tigres nem elefantes na literatura francesa, e a inglesa é toda uma arca de Noé."

corncob, a pig), its agile narrative, and the striking presence of fantasy, which was recovered in BCL in this modernist phase.

Besides his authorial activities, Monteiro Lobato devoted himself to the translation and adaptation of world literature classics such as *Robinson Crusoe* (1930), *Alice in Wonderland* (1931), *Pinocchio* (1933) and *Gulliver's Travels* (1937). His production was so abundant that the critics of his day came to doubt that all translations were his. Lobato's adapting procedures were conscious and intentional, as indicated in his correspondence with his friend and writer Godofredo Rangel: "I need a D. Quixote for children, more fluent and more in the local language than the editions by Garnier and the Portuguese" (Lobato 2010).[7]

Although theoretical approaches that value foreignizing translations are nowadays in vogue, Lobato's domesticating adaptations should not be condemned without considering their place in history. Lobato, as Brazil's first Baudelairian poets (Candido 1989, 26) had done before him, deformed foreign literature according to the expressive needs of BCL, selecting from the texts the aspects more suitable to the renewal that he intended to promote.

We argue that the well-worn discussions over fidelity and equivalence should be dealt with from a historical perspective, considering the role of translations in a certain stage of the development of a literary system. The deforming appropriation of foreign literature by Lobato enabled his dissent from the conservative aesthetics that dominated Brazil's incipient children's literature. One could say that, for the first time, the pleasure of reading overtook pedagogical goals in children's books, and Lobato searched in Anglophone literature for the ingredients to compose works that combined fantasy, adventure, humor, and irony.

The 1930s and 1940s can be considered decisive moments in the formation of BCL. The adaptation of universal forms to the local reality, which had been happening since the end of the nineteenth century, now questioned the universal project for the first time. Monteiro Lobato, alongside other authors such as Graciliano Ramos, one of the greatest Brazilian novelists who also wrote for children, took up a new, critical relationship with the Brazilian national project. They mistrusted the official propaganda of progress – at least the rural ideal – being spread in the young Republic and exposed its contradictions, as we may observe in *Geografia de D. Benta* (1935), by Lobato, and *Histórias de Alexandre* (1944), by Graciliano. In these books, the authors suggest to children that there is a difference between the official story that the dominant classes tell and the real story of the defeated. Monteiro

---

7 In Portuguese: "Estou precisando de um D. Quixote para crianças, mais correntio e mais em língua da terra que as edições do Garnier e dos portugueses."

Lobato, along with other less prolific yet representative authors such as the above-mentioned Graciliano Ramos and José Lins do Rego, were not yet fully inserted into an earlier tradition of Brazilian authors for children. They would form their own tradition for posterity. This process of accumulation had its upshot during the 1960s and 1970s, when, after a short democratic period (1945–1964), Brazil was again under a dictatorship. This regime was legitimated by discourses against the threat of communism and the social agenda of the legally constituted government of João Goulart.

A military coup took place in 1964. Only in 1979 did a progressive re-democratization process begin. During these years of political repression and censorship, original and politically engaged books for children emerged in a phenomenon that became known among scholars and educators as the BCL boom. At that moment, authors felt the need to refer to the national tradition, even if to question it, and external influences began to be offset (Lajolo and Zilberman 2007). The legacy of Monteiro Lobato was retrieved as an instrument of political satire and liberation from the formal and thematic conventions of the previous decades. Two authors who emerged in the 1960s and 1970s would go on to become Hans Christian Andersen Prize-winners: Lygia Bojunga (1982) and Ana Maria Machado (2000).

Although translations still dominated the Brazilian literary market for children in the 1970s, during that period the dynamics between national and translated children's literature did not curtail the aesthetic development of BCL, which found grounds for innovation departing from external references, just as Lobato had done.

Translations in Brazilian schools

The re-democratization process initiated in the late 1970s was characterized by contradictions that exist to the present day. On the one hand, freedom of the press and the end of censorship seemed to favor artistic creation. On the other hand, the political shift was followed by an economic and cultural liberalization that allowed cultural projects to be imported in large quantities. Books became consumer goods, and book producers and distributors turned more and more to pulpy, commercially motivated titles. At the same time, and in contrast, from the 1980s onward, specialists began to participate in the selection of books to be published (in publishing houses) and purchased (in governmental institutions). Opportunities increased for new writers and illustrators, and the printing quality of books improved. Bordini describes this dialectic as follows:

Alongside these tendencies of renewal or of productive and provoking continuity, the need to serve a market with consumption features and to professionalize the authors led children's literature of the 80s to other not always so well-recommended paths. Series and collections, often single-authored, multiplied. (...) The ravenous demand for novelties led to a thematic and stylistic pulverization where a lot is written, but always on the same subject.[8] (Bordini quoted in Serra 1998)

Contemporary BCL is a result of these contradictions. Many of the authors who emerged during the 1970s, such as Ana Maria Machado, are still working, while young authors have emerged during the last decades with more up-to-date offerings, especially in the field of illustration, such as Ângela-Lago and Roger Mello – the latter a 2014 Andersen Illustrator's Award-winner. However, books of dubious literary quality still have considerable room in the market, among which we find translations with no authorship, perpetuating the same old public domain narratives that barely differ from one another.

During the 1980s, the school system was expanded significantly, and the state, faced with stocking literature books for many new schools and libraries, became the main customer of the publishing industry. Two other relevant moments of expansion of the Brazilian school system came at the end of the nineteenth century, with the proclamation of the Republic, and in the 1930s, under Getúlio Vargas. Until 2014, the main channel of distribution of literature to state schools was the Programa Nacional Biblioteca da Escola (PNBE) [National School Library Program], of the Ministry of Education, created in 1997. To give an idea of the program's size, in 2014 more than nineteen million books were delivered to more than 253,520 schools all over the country serving more than twenty-two million students in basic and secondary education (FNDE 2016). Citing a lack of resources due to the economic crisis in the country, the program was discontinued in 2015. In 2017, following a project of dismantling the Brazilian social state, the Ministry of Education proposed alterations to the PNBE, integrating the purchase of literature books in the Programa Nacional do Livro Didático (PNLD) [National Didactic Books Program]. This measure put books directly in the hands of students rather than on school libraries' shelves.

---

8   In Portuguese: "A par dessas tendências de renovação ou de uma continuidade produtiva e instigante, as necessidades de atender a um mercado com características de consumo e de profissionalizar os autores conduziram a literatura infanto-juvenil dos anos 80 por outros caminhos às vezes nem tão recomendáveis. Multiplicaram-se as séries ou coleções, frequentemente de autoria única. (...) A demanda gulosa por novidades conduziu a uma pulverização temática e estilística em que muito se escreve, mas sempre sobre o mesmo."

Based on the collections delivered to nurseries and kindergartens in 2008, 2010, 2012 and 2014, we have compiled the following table:

Table 1. Distribution of translations in the PNBE collections (2008–2014)

Year	Number of translations	Number of titles (total)	% share of translations
2008	15	60	25
2010	18	100	18
2012	28	100	28
2014	35	100	35

We observe that non-translations prevail but that the share of translations trended upward from 2010 onward. One hypothesis is that publishing houses might be presenting more and more translations to the PNBE, offering the evaluators a wider range of foreign options in contrast to Brazilian ones.

In the past few years, the state has issued between twice and four times as many non-translated books to state nurseries and kindergartens than translated books. However, this does not necessarily mean that translations are not prevailing in the Brazilian book market. The PNBE's evaluating committee had the option to intervene to design the profile of the collections according to the guidelines of the Public Notice, and not according to the proportion of applications for selection. Parallel research (Lima and Pereira 2019) suggests that translations are in fact thriving in the Brazilian book market.

From our analysis of the collections, we noted that the main translated language was English (40 percent of all translations), followed by Spanish and French (19 percent each). Around 80 percent of translated books were from one of these languages. Other languages represented in the four years that we analyzed included Italian, German, Japanese, Korean and Dutch.

In general terms, translated books in the PNBE are characterized by: (1) a considerable variety of publishing houses; (2) the prevalence of central countries and languages as sources; (3) translators with diverse profiles, including poets, authors, and scholars; (4) the prevalence of prose over poetry; and (5) good literary and visual quality. The quality of the collections was guaranteed, until 2014, by the specialized consulting board of the Center for Literacy, Reading, and Writing of the Federal University of Minas Gerais (Ceale/FaE/UFMG).

Although they represent an important sample of the translations that had been offered to small children until recent years, the PNBE collections do not exactly reflect the Brazilian publishing market. Publishing houses must turn at least a small profit in order to survive, which means they cannot publish without considering commercial issues. The state, however, can prioritize literary quality over marketing appeal. It would be fruitful to evaluate separately the weight of translations in the book market at large, since state schools have always been committed to offering children national literature.

Obviously, we cannot disregard the relations between state and market. Having a book selected for state purchases secures massive sales and prestige. Thus, it is likely that without the state and school institutions, the children's book market would be very different in terms of its pedagogical content, the number of printed books and the rapport between translated and national literature. It will take some time to evaluate the impact of the discontinuation of PNBE on the book market and to insert these first decades of the twenty-first century into the history of BCL.

Final remarks

The aim of this chapter was to examine the role of translations in the historical development of BCL. We have adopted a systemic view, drawing on Antonio Candido and Itamar Even-Zohar, to observe the presence of translations in the constitution of a literary tradition for children in Brazil. Beginning from a historical overview of BCL since the end of the nineteenth century, we drew a line of progress from the first imitations to more recent original creations. It is not possible to fully understand the formation of BCL without considering translations and their interaction with national literature. A literary system demands foreign authors in different degrees, which makes it more or less receptive to imported models (Lefevere 1982). We have seen how this dynamic played out in the beginnings of BCL, and how foreign models were later rejected – although Brazil has never completely freed itself from these models. Whereas the first BCL was committed to local themes and language, it embraced European forms and models. Adaptations, imitations and pastiches worked as accumulation mechanisms in a historical moment in which Brazil still did not hold a tradition of its own. In the case of these first literary manifestations, it was imperative to search for external references.

We recall the association that Candido (2000, 26–28) makes between the formation of the Brazilian literary system and the need to forge a national identity – a question that equally and deeply touches the formation of BCL. The desire to disengage from the colonizers was reflected in BCL in different ways, according to each historical moment. School literature from the early

Republican period represented a cultural continuity with Portugal, although it claimed a Brazilian language. At the beginning of the twentieth century, a home-made, patriotic literature emerged, which adopted national themes and an official and normative Brazilian Portuguese. Romantic ideals and an integrative logic prevailed.

It was from foreign references that BCL was formed, initially by means of literary accumulation and the borrowing of a tradition and, later, by the incorporation and reinterpretation of foreign aesthetic innovations, as we have seen in Lobato. Currently, BCL is consolidated with a consistent local tradition and a set of national authors and works. However, it keeps feeding on translations in a dialectic relation that sometimes inhibits innovation and sometimes encourages it.

As Candido has stated, Brazilian literature is part of Western literature, and we may affirm the same about BCL. Its interaction with central literatures, sometimes taking them as models, sometimes rejecting them, is at the core of its formation. We do not intend to propose a history of translations for children disconnected from the history of BCL but rather to consider translations as a consistent set of works in order to situate translations within BCL and articulate them alongside other elements in the literary polysystem.

Bibliography

Arroyo, Leonardo. 1990. *Literatura infantil brasileira*. São Paulo: Melhoramentos.

Bordini, Ma da Glória. 1998. "A literatura infantil nos anos 80." In *30 anos de literatura para crianças e jovens*, edited by Elizabeth D'Ângelo Serra, 33–46. Campinas: Mercado de Letras.

Busch, Wilhelm. 2012 [1910]. *Juca e Chico: História de dois meninos em sete travessuras*. Translated by Olavo Bilac. São Paulo: Pulo do Gato.

Candido, Antonio. 1989. "Os primeiros baudelairianos." In *A educação pela noite & outros ensaios*, 23–38. São Paulo: Ática.

Candido, Antonio. 2000 [1975]. *Formação da literatura brasileira: Momentos decisivos*. 9th edition. Belo Horizonte: Itatiaia.

Casanova, Pascale. 2007. *The World Republic of Letters*. Translated by Malcolm DeBevoise. Cambridge, MA: Harvard University Press.

Coelho, Nelly N. 2010 [1985]. *Panorama histórico da literatura infantil/juvenil: das origens indo-europeias ao Brasil contemporâneo*. 5th edition. Barueri: Manolo.

Even-Zohar, Itamar. 1990. "Polysystem Studies." *Poetics Today* 11, no. 1: 1–268.

FNDE. "Biblioteca da Escola – Dados estatísticos." Accessed April 20, 2016. http://www.fnde.gov.br/programas/biblioteca-da-escola/biblioteca-da-escola-dados-estatisticos.

Hallewell, Lawrence. 1982. *Books in Brazil: A History of the Publishing Trade.* Metuchen: Scarecrow.

Lajolo, Marisa and Regina Zilberman. 2007 [1984]. *Literatura infantil brasileira: História e Histórias.* 6th edition. São Paulo: Ática.

Lefevere, André. 1982. "Mother Courage's Cucumbers: Text, System and Refraction in a Theory of Literature." *Modern Language Studies* 12: 3–20.

Lefevere, André. 1992. *Translation, Rewriting and the Manipulation of Literary Fame.* London: Routledge.

Lima, Lia A. M. and Germana H. Pereira. 2019. *Traduções para a primeira infância: O livro ilustrado traduzido no Brasil.* Campinas: Pontes.

Lobato, Monteiro. 2010. *A barca de Gleyre.* São Paulo: Globo.

Shavit, Zohar. 1995. "Intercultural Relationships." *Compar(a)ison* 2: 67–80.

Shavit, Zohar. 1996. "Hebrew and Israeli." In *International Companion Encyclopedia of Children's Literature,* edited by Peter Hunt, 783–788. London/New York: Routledge.

Shavit, Zohar. 1997. "Cultural Agents and Cultural Interference." *Target* 9, no. 1: 111–130.

Shavit, Zohar. 2002. "Fabriquer une culture nationale. Le rôle des traductions dans la constitution de la littérature hébraïque." *Actes de la recherche en sciences sociales*, 144, no. 4: 21–32.

Said, spoke, spluttered, spouted

The role of text editors in stylistic shifts in translated children's literature[1]

Marija Zlatnar Moe & Tanja Žigon

Abstract

A published translation into Slovene is always a compromise between everybody involved, most often the translator, the text editor and the book editor. In the case of picture books, text editors' interventions are sometimes such that they change the style, characterization and even meaning of (parts of) the text. The text editor's task is to revise the first translation in terms of orthography, syntax, grammar and style. The latter's level sometimes causes problems in the translation process, as text editors often do not speak the source language, are not familiar with the source culture, and do not use the source text while revising. This is especially true for translations between peripheral languages such as Norwegian and Slovene. Here we survey creators of translated picture books about their experience with editorial interventions in the target texts and present an illustrative case study of such interventions in three translated Norwegian picture books. While the final version is always shaped by the expertise, taste and opinion of at least three people, the translator is nevertheless seen as the author of the target text and can influence the final version to a high degree.

Introduction

Literary translation inevitably brings with it many changes and shifts, small and large. Some are made for linguistic or poetic reasons, others for extratextual reasons. These may involve the relative status of the source and target languages and cultures, the competence of those involved in the translation process, or target culture norms and traditions. Previous research (Zlatnar Moe 2010, 2015, 2017) shows that Slovene translators, editors and publishers generally opt for more foreignizing translations when translating for adults, with the exception

---

1   The authors acknowledge financial support from the Slovenian Research Agency (research core funding No. P6-0265).

of drama translations, which tend to be more domesticating. However, in our work as researchers and translators, we have noticed that Slovene translations of books for children and even young adults often differ significantly in style from their source texts, even if culture-specific elements are retained and the meaning does not change. The most common changes are increased formality, neutralization of language variations, unification of the register, and correction of non-standard language variations. Sometimes those changes are significant enough for the intended audience to change from adults to children (Zlatnar Moe and Žigon 2020). Our own experience and conversations with other translators indicate that these changes often do not occur during the translating itself, but later on, in the process of revision and editing. To determine what is happening and how, we conducted a survey of Slovene literary translators, book editors and text editors and compared our findings with textual analyses of translations of three picture books from Norwegian into Slovene.

Translating picture books

Before we turn to the complexities of translating picture books, let us look at what is considered literature for children in general. There have been many different ways of defining the category. Knowles and Malmkjær (1996, quoted in Lathey 2006) have it as "any narrative written or published for children [including] the 'teen novels' aimed at a 'young adult' or 'late adolescent' reader." Most of us agree, however, that while children's literature is literature that is mainly written by adults for children, it is in fact intended for a dual audience, the primary audience being the child, and the secondary audience being the adults buying and (in the case of pre-readers) reading the book to a child.

Translating for children has traditionally been considered a good way to start one's translating career, as it has been deemed 'easy' (Cerar 1997), mainly because the texts in question are often short and (deceptively) simple, and because the genre of children's literature has often been seen as less prestigious (*ibid.*, see also Shavit 2006). Because of its lower status, literature for children allows the translator greater liberties in dealing with the text: children are mostly seen as young, inexperienced and in need of education (on the subject matter and language among other things), and the translator is seen as the right person to give it to them. Shavit (2006, 26) writes that the translator of children's literature "can permit himself liberties regarding the text as a result of the peripheral position of children's literature within the literary polysystem" and is allowed to manipulate the text in various ways if s/he adheres to two principles: adapting the text to what the target society thinks is good for children, and to what the target society expects the child to understand. Standards of what is good for a child change over time. As López (2006, 41) notes, in the past taboo subjects included divorce, death, and alcoholism, all of which are now frequently discussed in books for children. Meanwhile, Oittinen, Ketola and Garavini (2017) find that taboos, although they have changed, still endure.

Picture books are perhaps the clearest examples of literature for children. The vast majority are intended for young children and their adult purchasers/readers (parents, educators). There is also no question about how experienced the target audience is or whether they need education or not, as they are typically either pre-readers or children learning to read, so not yet either experienced or learned.

Picture books themselves, however, are more complex, as they consist not only of text, but also of pictures, both of which are in constant interaction. Thus Arzipe and Syles (2003, quoted in Oittinen, Ketola and Garavini 2017, 18) define picture books as "books in which the story depends on the interaction between the written text and the image," while Pantaleo (2014, quoted in Oittinen, Ketola and Garavini 2017, 18) defines them as books in which "the total effect depends on the text, the illustrations, and the reciprocity between these two sign systems." While reading a picture book, a reader is asked to undertake a complex activity, consisting of a constant passage from the written text to the images and vice versa, since both expressive means provide readers with different perspectives on the same events (*ibid.*, 22). The readers must therefore interpret both the text and the pictures and must also be able to understand whatever is absent from either the text or the illustrations (*ibid.*). As already mentioned, picture books are often read aloud to the target audience, which also demands some level of interpretation from the reader, as tone, intonation, tempo, and pauses also contribute to the enjoyment of the adult as well as the child (Oittinen, Ketola and Garavini 2017, 69). Like translators of plays or comic books, however, translators of picture books generally only work with one of the multiple channels through which the story reaches the audience, namely the written text.

This situation makes certain demands on the translator, who is faced with deciding the degree to which s/he will take all these considerations into account. Scholars and translators seem to agree that the inexperience of young readers should be considered, but what about the different reading and interpreting competences of their *adult* readers? Should translators adhere to the norm of easy readability? And what about the culture-specific elements in the text and pictures?

All these choices are in principle the translator's to make, but in reality, other participants in the translation process also have their opinions on each of them, based on their own expertise (either in language, visual arts, management, or sales and promotion) and personal taste, and the final result is a compromise between all of them.

Translating for children between peripheral languages

Although most translations into Slovene are made from English and other central languages (see Zlatnar Moe, Žigon and Mikolič Južnič 2019), and most available research to date is either between central languages or in central-peripheral language pairs,[2] books from peripheral languages are also regularly translated into other peripheral languages, for example from Norwegian into Slovene. But the entire translation process is affected in many subtle ways by the involvement of peripheral languages (*ibid.*). In the case of Norwegian books, the translation process is influenced by the fact that there are only a handful of available translators, no bilingual translation tools and no network of experts on the literature and language(s) of Norway.[3] Furthermore, the source country actively participates in the selection of books for translation by generously subsidizing translation of its literature. Another characteristic is that central languages are involved even if the translation itself is done directly from Norwegian, as editors have access to the text in question only through its other translations, and some books are translated via English because of a lack of available translators. This is the case with the recent books (for adults and children) by Jo Nesbø: the publisher used translators from Norwegian for the first few books but has switched to translators from English in order to save time and money.[4] There has been a steady stream of Norwegian literature translated into Slovene in the past two decades. In addition to the (new) translations of the classics, such as Ibsen, Hamsun, and Undset, there have also been translations of modern authors such as Ambjørnsen, Petterson, Knausgård, Ørstavik, Fosse, and Fosnes-Hansen, as well as modern books for children.

Method

We begin with a text analysis of first drafts, edited versions and published versions of three Norwegian picture books, namely *Polenček odpre muzej* (2015) (*Kubbe lager museum* [Kubbe Makes an Art Museum] (K)) by Åshild

---

[2] The terms 'central' and 'peripheral' are here used as defined by Heilbron (1999); see also Heilbron (2000). Peripheral languages are those that contribute no more than 1 percent of the source texts in the global literary translation market.

[3] For details on translators from Norwegian into Slovene, see Zlatnar Moe, Mikolič Južnič and Žigon (2019, 45).

[4] We gathered this information through informal conversations with the translators of Nesbø from Norwegian.

Kanstad Johnsen, *Garmannovo poletje* (2017) (*Garmanns sommer* [Garmann's Summer] (G)) by Stian Hole, and *Čajna ženička* (2018) (*Teskjekjerringa* [The Adventures of Mrs. Pepperpot] (T)) by Alf Prøysen, all translated by one of the authors. All three are originally written in Norwegian Bokmål, one of the two official forms of written Norwegian (the other one being Nynorsk). The first two are more recent, originally published in 2010 and 2006 respectively, while the latter is a Norwegian children's classic from the 1950s. We analyzed corrections and comments by text editors and book editors and compared them to the published versions of the texts. To determine the degree to which those corrections were universal, rather than the preferences of the individuals involved in the translation process, we then turned to other translators and editors, and asked them about their norms, strategies and solutions when translating, editing and publishing picture books by means of an online survey among translators, book editors and text editors. We compared the results of the text analysis with the answers of our respondents to determine how important a role the editors played in producing the final version of the text, and who had the ultimate say.

Text analysis results

In order to see what happens in the process of translating a picture book, we compared first, corrected and final versions of three translations from Norwegian. They were all published by the same publisher (Sodobnost International), but edited by three different book editors and two different text editors.[5] We found that the corrections by the text editors mostly resulted in replacement of non-normative language with normative alternatives, and a more fluent text: thus, on the lexical level, more general words and phrases, such as 'he took a picture,' were changed to the more formal and exact 'he took a photograph' in *Kubbe*; but the text editor decided to simplify 'beetle' to 'ladybird' in *Garmanns sommer*. On the lexical level, the fluency concern was most acute in the translation of *Teskjekjerringa*, where the editors (both the book editor and the text editor) deleted all seemingly superfluous conjunctions which served as markers of spoken language in the source text. Some examples of these kinds of changes are shown in Table 1.

To illustrate how the edits changed the style of the translation, let us take a closer look at *Garmanns sommer*.

---

5 The different roles of book editors and text editors in Slovene publishing are discussed in the section "Text editors" below.

Table 1. Examples of text editors' changes in the analyzed books

Type of change	Translation	Text editor's revision
Deletion of markers of spoken language	**Pa nič**, se bom **pa** sama s sabo pogovarjala [**Alright**, I'll **just** talk to myself **then**] (T)	Se bom **pa** sama s sabo pogovarjala [I'll **just** talk to myself]
Replacement of less formal markers with more formal ones	**Pa ja** ne krevsa naokoli lisjak Miha [**Isn't that** Mike the Fox roaming the woods] (T)	**Menda** ne krevsa naokoli lisjak Miha [**Would that be** Mike the Fox roaming the woods]
Utterance verbs	Je **rekla** [she **said**] (T)	Je **vprašala** [she **asked**]
Lexical changes from less to more formal	**Slike** sva nalepila v album [We glued the **pictures** in an album] (K)	**Fotografije** sva nalepila v album [We glued the **photographs** into an album]
Lexical simplifications	**hrošček** [beetle] (not mentioned before) (G)	**pikapolonica** [ladybird] (mentioned before)
Changes of meaning	Saj vem, **kaj** hočeš [I know **what** you want] (T)	Vem, da **nekaj** hočeš [I know you want **something**]

Case study: *Garmanns sommer* by Stian Hole

Garmanns sommer by Stian Hole was first published in Norway in 2006, and its Slovene translation appeared in 2017. It is the story of a six-year-old boy and takes place on the last day before he starts school. He is nervous and begins exploring other people's fears: his old aunts are afraid of dying, his musician father is afraid of playing too fast, his mother is afraid that Garmann will get hit by a car on his way to school, and so on. The message is that everybody is afraid before a big change and that there is nothing wrong with that. Originally, it was written in standard Norwegian Bokmål, but with the syntax, vocabulary and logic of a six-year-old. This was preserved in the first version of the translation, which was then handed over to the text editor. The text editor made a number of changes, mostly stylistic shifts from non-normative language and style to more normative solutions that made the text seem written by a grown-up, rather than thought by a six-year-old. Most of the changes fall into the categories shown in Table 2, which provides examples of each category.

Table 2. Examples of text editor's changes in *Garmanns sommer*

Type of change	Translation	Text editor's revision
More formal forms of individual words (9 changes)	misli [think]	**po**misli
	pred sto petdeset leti [15 years ago]	pred sto petdeset**imi** leti
More formal words and phrases (18 changes)	**vsi** ljudje [all people]	**vsakdo** [everyone]
	snežena hišica [snow house]	hišica **iz snega** [house made of snow]
	bo **šel** [will go]	bo **odpotoval** [will travel]
	bo **šel čez** [will go across]	bo **prečkal** [will cross]
Lexical changes (5 changes)	zobje [teeth]	proteza [dentures]
	velik [big]	visok [tall]
	hrošček [beetle]	pikapolonica [ladybird]
	mora vaditi [has to go practice]	**odhiti** vadit [hurries off to practice]
Changes of meaning (6 changes)	**Kako pa misliš**, da bo iti v šolo? [How do you feel about starting school?]	**Se že kaj veseliš** šole? [Are you looking forward to starting school?]
	se nima česa **bati** [has nothing to fear]	se ničesar **ne boji** [does not fear anything]
Syntactical changes (11 changes)	preverjal [was checking]	preverjal, **če se zobek maje** [was checking whether the little tooth was moving]
	"Se ti česa bojiš?" **Očka in Garmann sedita...** ["Are you afraid of anything?" Dad and Garmann are sitting...]	"Se ti česa bojiš?" Garmann **vpraša očka, ko** sedita... ["Are you afraid of anything?" Garmann asks his Dad while they are sitting...]

In addition, there are five cases where the typical logic of a six-year-old is changed into grown-up logic. In one example, Garmann links his aunt's need for a *rollator* with his *roller* skates, and offers to give her the roller skates if she ever needs the rollator: "I will soon be needing a rollator to walk," says the aunt, to which Garmann answers, "In that case you can have my roller skates." The text editor deleted 'in that case' and thus all but removed the thought chain that led to Garmann's offer. In another, where Garmann listens to his aunts talking about plants, and muses that flowers have similar names to old ladies, the names of the flowers are capitalized. The text editor removed the capitals, as flower names are not capitalized in Slovene, thus ignoring the context in which they were considered as personal names.

As we can see, most of the text editor's corrections were stylistic. In addition to the changes discussed above, there were also a few changes of the word order, and a few other cases of replacement of a word or phrase with a synonym or a near synonym. In some cases, those stylistic changes were so significant that they influenced the meaning of the text, but even where this did not happen, they did increase the formality and shifted the whole text from the children's spoken register towards neutral standard Slovene.

The revised version of the text normally goes back to the translator, who may either accept or reject the text editor's changes. In this case, the translator deleted most of the stylistic, lexical and semantic changes, sometimes providing explanations in the comments, and also further explanations in the accompanying email. Lastly, the book was edited by the book editor, who accepted all but one of the translator's suggestions, which then appeared in the published version.

The nature and quantity of the editors' changes were not surprising. As our previous research (Zlatnar Moe 2010, 2015; Zlatnar Moe and Žigon 2020) shows, children's language is frequently 'corrected' to standard forms not only in literature for children, but also when children appear as characters or narrators in literature for adults. As our previous research was done on translations from English, we draw on it to assess whether our Norwegian sample shows signs of any source-related bias. For instance, Norwegian children's books sometimes feature content (such as a frank approach to bodily functions) that might be considered too unconventional or unsuitable for children in other cultures. Our sample does not really include any such cases, except perhaps the theme of impending death in *Garmanns sommer*. In any case, we do not find that the possibly more daring content of the books triggered additional editorial interventions beyond what we have found for English books. Nor were there comparatively more changes in translations of Norwegian picture books than in translated English picture books. This strengthens our confidence that our findings here apply to translated children's literature more generally. Rather than between source cultures, the divides were between genres and target audiences; there were relatively more changes in picture books than in novels (translated from either language) for grown-ups, for example. As we shall see later, the answers in our survey to some extent confirm these observations.

Since our text analysis concentrated on a very small sample of three books, one translator, and a handful of editors, we decided to contact other producers of translated picture books and find out what the prevailing norms of the field are.

Survey results

In 2017 and 2018, we carried out a larger study on the division of work and power within the translation process proper, involving the selection, translation and editing of the text. Within this study, we also conducted a survey on the particularities of translating and editing for children. We contacted translators, book editors and text editors. To reach as many potential participants as possible, we contacted the Slovene associations of literary translators, authors and text editors, who forwarded our questions to their members and/or contacts. With their help, we contacted 235 translators, ninety-one text editors, and twenty-six book editors – 351 people altogether. Since we approached respondents through professional societies, we talked to experienced translators, text editors and book editors. To become a member of the Slovene Association of Literary Translators, one has to present a list of published translations. While the Slovene Text Editor Association does not have similar conditions, most of their members are practicing text editors and Slovene language graduates. All of the editors we contacted work for established publishing houses. The survey was open for about a month. In the end, we received sixty answers in total: thirty-two from translators, sixteen from text editors and twelve from book editors. Of these, thirteen translators said they translated picture books (among other things), and two more translated comic books, which are predominantly targeted towards children in the Slovene market (Zlatnar Moe and Žigon 2020). Ten text editors said they edit picture books, as did six book editors, in addition to two who also edit comic books. The questionnaires consisted of two parts: a more general one that was more or less the same for all participants (including questions about experience, working languages, genres, etc.), and a more specific part dealing with the particulars of translating and editing different texts, genres, languages, including collaboration with others. The form of the questionnaire was a combination of multiple-choice questions and open questions where respondents were able to explain their chosen answers if they wished. Afterwards we analyzed the answers from all three groups and compared them to form a picture of how the translation process happens and how the power relations within it work.

Who translates books for children?

All participants in our survey were experienced translators and members of the Slovene Association of Literary Translators, but this is far from usual. When doing our research outside this particular survey, we found that just about anybody who can speak the source language can become a translator of books for children. For example, one owner of a small publishing house freely admitted that she and her son did the translations from English themselves because it was cheaper. One theatre manager said that she translated one of the plays from English herself (and later had it completely rewritten by the text editor). As mentioned, picture books are also often given to beginner translators.

Text editors

Text editors are usually Slovene language and literature graduates who may or may not be fluent in a foreign language,[6] but not necessarily in the source language of the text in question. They work with both translated and original literary and non-literary texts. Their job is to check that the text is adequate in language (by ensuring that punctuation, capitalization and grammar agree with Slovene standard language norms) as well as in style. They also comment on the text's appropriateness for the text type and/or the target public. To achieve this, they correct syntax, structure and word order, and replace words and phrases with others they deem more suitable. While most authors appreciate this stylistic contribution by the text editors, the situation seems to be more complicated in the case of literary translation (for children or otherwise), as translation involves competing cultures, styles, norms of good writing, and language experts, and this can lead to (sometimes heated) disagreements between parties. If a text editor is involved in the process, as is usually the case, the role of the book editor is mostly to choose the translator and the text editor, mediate between them, promote the book, and edit the style to some extent.

---

6   Sometimes in combination with another degree – either in language, literature or another field of the humanities.

The text editors in our survey were all members of the Slovene Text Editor Association, all had more than fifteen years of text-editing experience, and all but one had a degree in Slovene language and literature. They mostly worked with literary as well as non-literary texts (journalistic, technical, promotional and legal). All of them worked with original Slovene texts as well as with translations. All of them also spoke at least one foreign language, most often English and/or one of the South Slavic languages.

The book editors all had a degree in social sciences and/or arts: seven had double degrees in languages and comparative literature, history, or sociology. The majority listed three writing genres as their work fields, and the most common combination was novels, short prose and picture books.

The editing process

The literary translation process in Slovene publishing houses usually begins with the book editor finding and hiring a translator, who then translates the book and sends it to the book editor. The book editor immediately forwards it to the text editor. The edited text then goes back to the translator, with the book editor serving more as a courier between the two than anything else. Lastly, the proofreader reads the formatted text to determine if anything else needs correcting, as does the translator. Because of all this indirect communication, most translators we spoke with usually wrote either an accompanying letter or comments in the text in which they described the style of the text, and what they aimed to do in the translation. The text editors we contacted, however, said that they did not usually receive those comments, or only sometimes received them, and expressed a desire to have more supplemental information from the translator, if not direct contact.

The most common changes by text editors

Text editors only occasionally used the source text in the editing process. They were more likely to do so when editing a text translated from a language they were to some degree proficient in, and mostly used it for clarification, not for complete revision of the translation. As one of the text editors wrote: "My work is with the Slovene text and the Slovene language, its style and norms."

But as we see in Figure 1, most changes the text editors made were – according to translators – on the lexical level, exchanging one Slovene word for another, and not always for a very near synonym. One of our respondents was

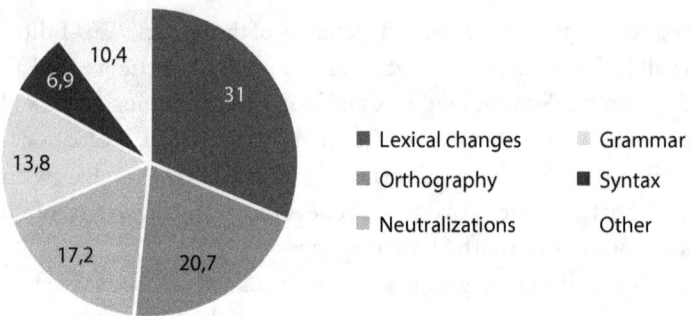

Figure 1. Most common changes by the text editors (answers to a multiple-choice question)

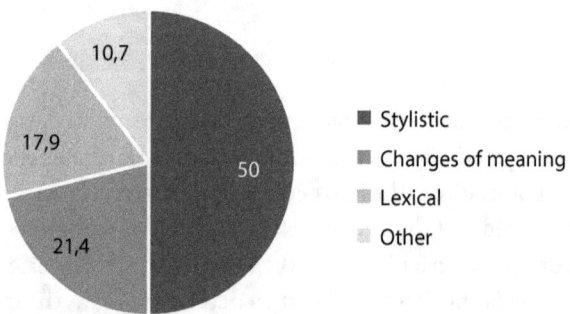

Figure 2. Most common changes by the book editors (answers to a multiple-choice question)

still perceptibly frustrated over a text editor who exchanged all the simple 'buts' for more complicated and formal conjunctions. The large number of orthographical changes is due to different factors, one being the rigidity of the Slovene punctuation system. Stylistic shifts were the third most often-mentioned change. Even after all the translators' efforts to explain the style of the original and the reasons for their choices, the text editors' changes still revolved around replacing non-standard and informal words with more formal ones, and one translator also gave examples of stylistic changes which were so extensive that they completely changed the style of the book. Translators also mentioned the clear preference of the text editors for standard Slovene expressions. Several of the translators also complained about the simplification of the text by the text editor; translators were very opposed to replacing a more advanced word with a simpler one. One third of the translators translating literature for adults as well as literature for children also noticed that there were more corrections in the texts aimed at children (and also, more in the texts from central languages than from the peripheral ones). Only two translators (out of all 32) mentioned having experienced a text editor actually pointing out parts where they thought that the translator had used a word or solution that was too formal for a child (whether too formal for the child character in the book to use, or for the child reading it).

Book editors said that they mostly intervened on the stylistic level, and translators agreed, as Figure 2 shows. This brings with it a whole other set of problems for the translators translating from peripheral languages, such as Norwegian, as the editors most often do not have direct access to the original and are thus correcting the style and meaning of the book based on another translation. Most translators pointed out, however, that the book editors did not intervene much in the text. Unlike their experience with text editors, most translators did not feel that book editors worked differently with books for children and young adults. Only three translators reported that the book editors seemed more involved in those texts.

Our respondents confirmed that the book editor usually was not involved in the discussion between the translator and the text editor. But sometimes, when the text-edited version differed very much from the original, they did express their opinion. One translator said that she got the marked version back with the book editor's instruction not to accept any of the text editor's changes except for commas. Others mentioned that the book editors either left it up to the translators to decide whether they wanted to keep a change or not, or implied that the translators should take the corrections "more as a recommendation, not a rule." Most translators, however, did not experience many contradictions between the book editor and the text editor.

Text editors mostly confirmed that they approached children's texts differently than texts for adults: they concentrated more on the clarity of the text and avoided complex words, phrases and sentences. They also took greater care with the style of the book. Examples of translators' mistakes in literature for children, as reported by text editors, concerned lexical choices and sentence length, and the use of terminology. Text editors also commented on "deleting translator's footnotes as young readers do not know what to make of them." The answers thus confirmed the translators' feeling that the text editors intervened more in texts for children, although there might be some difference of opinion as to the necessity and quality of those interventions. It was also confirmed that the editing is mainly focused on style, keeping the target text within the frame of what is considered 'good writing in Slovene.'

The answers from the book editors confirmed that the translation and editing norms when translating for children are different from the norms governing translation and editing of texts for grown-ups. Domestication of proper names is more prevalent, and the use of non-normative language is unwelcome. Book editors also said that, unlike with literature for adults, they did give some instructions to the translator before they started translating the book. Several respondents felt that children needed to be 'trained' to read in an adult way. Several book editors also felt that text editors adhered more to the norms of standard Slovene in literature for children, while one thought that the text editors were actually more open to the lower registers and non-normative language in such a text than the book editor in question.

The answers in our survey, then, confirm the results of the textual analysis: most of the corrections are stylistic, significant enough to change the register and tone of a text, and often rather unpopular with translators, who seem to choose solutions that are nearer to the source text.

Conclusion

Our textual analysis as well as the answers of professionals we talked to show that while the translator is seen as the ultimate author of a picture book translation, its final version is often heavily influenced by the (text) editors, and a result of negotiations, mostly between the translator and the text editor, with the book editor acting as a mediator between the two. Text editors are often the first (or even only) people who read the target text after the translator, but they mostly work without the source text, and often adapt the target text to the target language and stylistic norms, as well as to their private opinion on what 'sounds better.' This happens even if those norms were violated intentionally in both the source text and the translation. But as they mostly do not have access to the original, do not use it in editing (nor do they use a translation), do not work together with the translator, and do not receive translators' explanations and descriptions, they cannot know this. The changes they make in the text mostly tend towards replacing non-normative language with normative solutions, unconventional messages (e.g. that kids need not always look forward to going to school, as mentioned above) with conventional ones, and informal registers with more formal ones. The appearance of the final version seems to depend very much on three factors: (1) the power relations between the people involved (experienced translators and/or text editors have an advantage, as do translators from peripheral languages); (2) the additional explaining the translator is willing to do; and (3) the book editor's trust in the translator and/or the text editor.

As our textual analysis shows, together with other translators' reports in our survey, the text editor's corrections can change not only the style, but sometimes also the meaning and the message of the text. The reason for this is not only that they mostly work without the source text, but also the beliefs they hold about what is good for children (hence the simplifications and standardization of language). The translator, in our experience, can reject those changes, but not all translators do. As one of our respondents said: "I was too young and too afraid to quarrel with them." The editing is also frequently done in a hurry in order to meet (often unrealistic) deadlines, which limits everybody's time and energy to explain, argue and negotiate. An ideal solution to this problem would be to replace text editing with revision by a person who speaks both languages and can work with the source text, and to give everybody enough time, but that is not possible for the majority of the source languages. A realistic solution, which costs the translator some additional time and frustration, is for the translator to go carefully through all the editors' changes and only include the acceptable ones, or to go through the text together with either the text editor or the book editor, which is the practice of at least one publisher (who has eliminated text editors altogether). Our survey shows that translators, who frequently see themselves as overlooked agents, are nonetheless seen by others involved in the translation process as the main authority on the source and the target texts – even more so when they work with peripheral languages. As such, translators are often able to see their own vision of the target text through to publication.

Bibliography

Arzipe, Evelyn and Morag Styles. 2003. *Children Reading Pictures: Interpreting Visual Texts*. London: Routledge Falmer.
Cerar, Vasja. 1997. "Kako otročje je prevajati za otroke?" ["How childish is it to translate for children?"]. In *Prevajanje otroške in mladinske književnosti*, edited by Vasja Cerar, 5–9. Ljubljana: Društvo slovenskih književnih prevajalcev.
Heilbron, Johan. 1999. "Towards a Sociology of Translation: Book Translations as a Cultural World System." *European Journal of Social Theory* 2, no. 4: 429–444.
Heilbron, Johan. 2000. "Translation as a Cultural World System." *Perspectives: Studies in Translatology* 8, no. 1: 9–26.
Hole, Stian. 2017. *Garmannovo poletje*. Translated by Marija Zlatnar Moe. Ljubljana: KUD Sodobnost International.
Johnsen, Åshild Kanestad. 2015. *Polenček odpre muzej*. Translated by Marija Zlatnar Moe. Ljubljana: KUD Sodobnost International.
Knowles, Murray and Kirsten Malmkjær. 1996. *Language and Control in Children's Literature*. New York: Routledge.

Lathey, Gillian, ed. 2006. *The Translation of Children's Literature: A Reader*. New York: Routledge.

López, Marisa Fernàndez. 2006. "Translation Studies in Contemporary Children's Literature: A Comparison of Intercultural Ideological Factors." In *The Translation of Children's Literature: A Reader*, edited by Gillian Lathey, 41–53. New York: Routledge.

Oittinen, Riitta. 2002. *Translating for Children*. New York/London: Garland Publishing.

Oittinen, Riitta, Anne Ketola and Melissa Garavini. 2017. *Translating Picturebooks: Revoicing the Verbal, the Visual and the Aural for a Child Audience*. New York: Routledge.

Pantaleo, Sylvia. 2014. "Exploring the Artwork in Picture Books with Middle Years Students." *Journal of Children's Literature* 40, no. 1: 5–26.

Prøysen, Alf. 2018. *Čajna ženička*. Translated by Marija Zlatnar Moe. Ljubljana: KUD Sodobnost International.

Shavit, Zohar. 2006. "Translation of Children's Literature." In *The Translation of Children's Literature: A Reader*, edited by Gillian Lathey, 25–40. New York: Routledge.

Zlatnar Moe, Marija. 2010. "Register Shifts in Translations of Popular Fiction from English into Slovene." In *Why Translation Studies Matters*, edited by Daniel Gile, Gyde Hansen and Nike Kocijančič Pokorn, 125–136. Amsterdam/Philadelphia: John Benjamins.

Zlatnar Moe, Marija. 2015. "Stylistic Shifts in Translation of Fiction into Slovene: Is Literary Fiction Translated Differently from Popular Fiction?" In *Contrastive Analysis in Discourse Studies and Translation*, edited by Mojca Schlamberger Brezar, David Limon and Ada Gruntar Jermol, 338–359. Ljubljana: Znanstvena založba Filozofske fakultete Univerze v Ljubljani.

Zlatnar Moe, Marija and Tanja Žigon. 2015. "Comparing National Images in Translations of Popular Fiction." In *Interconnecting Translation Studies and Imagology*, edited by Luc van Doorslaer, Peter Flynn and Joep Leersen, 145–161. Amsterdam/Philadelphia: John Benjamins.

Zlatnar Moe, Marija, Đurđa Strsoglavec and Tanja Žigon. 2017. "How Literature Is Translated between Minor Languages." *mTm – A Translation Journal*, vol. 9: 168–191.

Zlatnar Moe, Marija, Tanja Žigon and Tamara Mikolič Južnič. 2019. *Centre and Periphery: Power Relations in the World of Translation*. Ljubljana: Znanstvena založba Filozofske fakultete.

Zlatnar Moe, Marija and Tanja Žigon. 2020. "When the Audience Changes: Translating Adult Fiction for Young Readers." *Translation and Interpreting Studies*. https://doi.org/10.1075/tis.20015.zla.

Diversity can change the world

Children's literature, translation and images of childhood

Jan Van Coillie

Abstract

That translation is a means of cultural exchange is beyond dispute. The crucial question is what this exchange really amounts to. This is all the more relevant when dealing with children's literature in translation. In an ever more globalized world, the translation of literature for young readers is dominated by commercial factors, creating major imbalances in translation flows worldwide. This begs the question of whether translations may actually limit diversity more than they stimulate it. One can also ask how much of the 'other' culture is or can be preserved in translated children's books. Indeed, cultural context adaptation is one of the most frequently discussed characteristics of children's literature in translation. Addressing these questions, this chapter makes clear how specific translation strategies are determined by images of childhood and by commercial, educational and pedagogical norms. Taking examples from cultures in countries as diverse as India, South Africa and the Netherlands, it shows how the 'foreign' is expressed only selectively and in a reduced form in translated children's books. At the same time, other examples make clear how translated children's books can be truly enriching for young readers. The chapter closes with a discussion of the translation of digital children's books, a medium that offers new possibilities and challenges.

Introduction

Many translators and researchers see translating children's literature as an ideal means to increase intercultural understanding. The French comparatist Paul Hazard saw each translated children's book as "a messenger that goes beyond mountains and rivers, beyond the seas, to the very ends of the world in search of new friendships" (1944, 146). Rosie Webb Joels, who specialized in global perspectives on award-winning children's literature, considered translated children's literature an ideal means for "weaving world understanding" (1999, 65). For Isabel Pascua, a Spanish specialist in translating cultural intertextuality, children's literature in translation helps shape "a new educational policy (...) needed to overcome so much hostility toward the foreign, the strange, 'the other'" (Pascua 2003, 276).

Translated children's books can enrich readers in the target culture in many ways. They can introduce new genres and styles, renew existing genres, and offer an alternative view of the world that challenges dominant ideas, stereotypes, norms or values. One example of this last function of translated children's literature can be found in the work of editor Daniel Goldin Halfon, who stimulated the growth of children's books in Latin America by launching translation-rich children's literature collections for the publishing group Fondo de Cultura Económica. One book from this list that became hugely popular in Mexico was *Willy el tímido* (1991), the translation of Anthony Browne's picture book *Willy the Wimp* (1984).

However, we may ask what this cultural exchange really amounts to. In an ever more globalized world, the translation of literature for young readers is dominated by commercial factors, creating major imbalances in translation flows worldwide. Moreover, one can also ask how much of the 'other' culture is or can be preserved in translated children's books. Indeed, cultural context adaptation is one of the most frequently discussed characteristics of children's literature in translation (Alvstad 2010, 22). This chapter will address these questions, with a special focus on the selection, reduction and revisualization of the 'foreign.'

Selecting the foreign

Much has been written about the 'impenetrable' British and North American book markets. In Great Britain, less than 4 percent of children's books on the market are translations (Donahay 2012; Beauvais 2018, 2). In the US, that figure is less than 2 percent (O'Sullivan 2005, 71). By way of explanation, Elena Abós points to the widespread view among American publishers "that books in translation do not sell" and that "with all the good books already written in English, there is no need to translate more" (Abós 2016, 40).

In most European countries, a substantial proportion of books for children are translations. In the Netherlands and Flanders, approximately one third of the children's books published between 2010 and 2015 were translations (Van Coillie and Aussems 2017). In Sweden this was 45 percent (Alvstad 2018, 173) and in Finland 64 percent (Oittinen, Ketola and Garavini 2017, 3). However, there are limits to this diversity. In Finland, 80 percent of translated children's books in this time period were translated from English; in Sweden, the figure was 70 percent; in the Netherlands it was 62 percent. Other languages lagged far behind. In Dutch, for example, 18 percent of translated children's books was translated from Italian, 10 percent from German, 4 percent from French and 2 percent from Swedish. Other languages constituted under 1 percent. With the exception of Turkish and Russian, no non-Western languages were represented, which is clearly a limitation in an ever more diverse society (Van Coillie and Aussems 2017). How can this limitation be interpreted? That Italian is second on the list of source languages can almost entirely be attributed to one series, the successful *Geronimo Stilton* books, which dominates the seven-to-nine-year-old age group. Among older readers, the impact of bestseller series is significant too: the ten-to-twelve group was dominated in 2015 by *Het leven van een Loser*, the translation of *Diary of a Wimpy Kid* by Jeff Kinney and *De Waanzinnige Boomhut*, the translation of the "Treehouse" series by Andy Griffiths and Terry Denton, both translated from English. For young adults, the selection has been dominated by English translations for some time now, including series such as *Divergent*, *De Labyrintrenner* (translation of *The Maze Runner*), *Twilight* and *De hongerspelen* (translation of *The Hunger Games*).

It is clear that globalization and commercialization (which are closely connected) dominate the translation market for children's literature. This begs the question whether translations limit diversity more than they stimulate it. For small language areas it is incredibly difficult to compete with the marketing apparatuses of the large publishers in the Anglophone world. In her article "How Do Literary Works Cross Borders (or Not)?", Gisèle Sapiro summarizes the impact of this large-scale production thus: "In the era of globalization, the publishing industry has been increasingly dominated by large conglomerates that impose fierce criteria of commercial profitability and operation to the detriment of literary and intellectual criteria" (Sapiro 2016, 87). Moreover, international bestsellers can lead to an impoverishment of the local literature. On the one hand, local titles have a harder time gaining international visibility. On the other, successful series almost always lead to imitation, which means children get more of the same to read.

In areas with emerging children's literatures – Singapore and Indonesia for example – the market is flooded with imported titles from the Western children's literary canon (Miyake 2006). Half of all children's books published in India appear in English, while only 7 percent of children speak English (Khorana 2006). Rita Ghesquiere discovered that school libraries in the Philippines are brimming with American and British books, including authors like Dixon and Blyton, and the *Nancy Drew* series. Teachers had difficulty naming Filipino young adult authors. She also mentions Abu Nasr, who ascribes the late start of Arabic children's literature to the impact of translations from the West (Ghesquiere 2006, 30–31). Emer O'Sullivan has shown that the dominance of Western classics also stymied the development of local children's literature in parts of Africa (O'Sullivan 2000, 138). In her introduction to a special issue on translation in South Africa, Ileana Dimitriu stressed that the subtext behind most articles is "the power of English; the threat to *diversity*" (2002, 1). Haidee Kruger confirmed this, concluding that "the vast majority of books in the African languages in the age group 0 to 12 years are translations, mostly from English originals" (2011, 110).[1] More research on the factors that contribute to this lopsided traffic and the motives behind publishers' selection decisions is urgently needed.

Reducing the foreign

Even when texts *are* selected for translation, it is not always the case that translations actually bring young readers into contact with other cultures. Research shows that translators for children are much more likely than translators for adults to remove foreign elements in a text, or replace them with elements from the target culture (see Shavit 1986; Oittinen 2000; O'Sullivan 2005; Alvstad 2010; Lathey 2010). Most studies focus on translations from English or other Western languages. It is certainly important to investigate whether this strategy occurs more often with texts from other cultures.

Every translator has to make choices about staying close to the source text and adapting the text for a new audience. In other words, does s/he bring readers closer to the original text or does s/he bring the text closer to the readers? This choice between what is often called foreignization or domestication can be made for the text as a whole, but also for specific textual elements. When a translator translates for children, this choice becomes all the more acute. The difference in age and experience between an adult translator and his/her readers causes him/her, consciously or not, to reflect more carefully on the audience. As Emer O'Sullivan (2005, 13) correctly points out, this is true not only for translators but also for publishers, reviewers and other mediators in the field of children's literature.

Throughout the translation process, producers of translated children's literature allow themselves to be led by their own child images, or what I

---

1   Nevertheless, since the 1980s children's literature in the indiginous African languages has been on the rise. See Osayimwense (1985) and Edwards and Ngwaru (2011).

will call images of childhood, which refer to their ideas about how children are, what they like, what they can handle and what is appropriate, good or useful for them. These images are colored by personal experience but also by a particular vision of society, or by an implicit or explicit ideology. The result is that translators for children are guided not only by textual or literary norms, but also by didactic and pedagogic ones (Desmidt 2006, 86).

Specifically, translators who remove the foreignness in their source texts often assume that young readers are not far enough along in their linguistic, literary or cultural development to understand or perceive foreign elements, the principal concern being that foreign elements might keep young readers from fully understanding and identifying with the story and hence diminish the pleasure of reading. Conversely, translators who choose to retain the foreignness in a source text often do so on the conviction that children can handle a bit of strangeness and that encountering the foreign is an enrichment.

In the next two sections, I investigate how translators deal with culture-specific elements in texts. For clarity, I make a distinction between (1) items that have to do with the concrete setting in which the stories take place (culture-specific items or CSIs, such as place names and food items), and (2) customs, behaviors and relationships related to culture-specific norms and values.

Emil or Michiel, trifle or babas?

A common practice in children's books is to replace a foreign name with one from the target culture. Astrid Lingren's 'Emil' is called 'Michel' in the German translation and 'Michiel' in the Dutch translation. This is a practice that appears to follow from the assumption that children identify less easily with someone with a strange name.

Emer O'Sullivan (2000, 230) correctly points out that claims about how many foreign elements young readers can handle are based on assumptions. Studies that look at actual reception by children are scant. The few studies we do have suggest that children either do not notice the cultural other or do not find it important. For instance, Korean children did not appear to find Japanese names any more difficult than Korean names, nor did they have more trouble remembering or identifying them. Adults, on the other hand, responded much more negatively to 'foreign' names, allowing themselves to be led by various stereotypical ideas about the Japanese (Sung, Park and Kim 2016). Haidee Kruger also found differences between adults and children in her study on how both groups process foreign elements in translated South African picture books: "The foreignized effect is sometimes greater for children (as was initially foreseen), but adults at times experience a greater disruption effect as a consequence of the introduction of foreignized elements than children do" (Kruger 2013, 221). However, she warns that "the effects of domesticating and foreignized translation are neither predictable nor one-dimensional" (*ibid.*, 222).

A small-scale reader-response study on the Dutch translation of Sempé and Goscinny's *Le Petit Nicolas* brought to light that children often preferred foreign names and words to local ones because they found them funny-sounding. Kids tended to go on to make their own associations and put their imagination and cultural knowledge to use. For instance, several children found the word 'Marseillaise' funny because it reminded them of 'mayonnaise.' Others liked 'Champagnac' because it reminded them of 'champignon' (Van Coillie and Hellings 2011, 121).

It is no coincidence that these associations refer to food and drink – culture-specific items that, as Gillian Lathey puts it, "matter enormously to young children and constitute an important part of the affective content of any children's book" (Lathey 2016, 41).

Sausages and fried tomatoes, steak-and-kidney pudding and trifle, all served in Harry Potter's world, certainly call to mind different associations for British children than they do for French children. In the French translation, the first two are omitted and trifle is replaced by something thought to call comparable associations to mind: babas (Auvray and Rougier 2001, 76).

When translating culture-specific items related to food and drink, translators' choices can be driven by cultural and, more specifically, religious norms. That is why characters in children's books enjoy a different diet in Iran. As wine is forbidden in Islamic tradition, it is replaced in the Persian translations of *Alice in Wonderland* by soda in a 1928 translation and omitted in a 1965 translation. In a 1995 translation, it is kept as wine, possibly due to a personal choice on the part of the translator (Naghmeh-Abbaspour 2015). Moreover, in many Western translations of children's books, alcoholic beverages are changed to non-alcoholic beverages or omitted altogether.

Such cultural adaptations ensure that children's books can cross borders, be made to suit new contexts and be distributed globally. At the same time, part of the cultural diversity in their content is expunged.

Taboos, norms and values

Even more decisive is the impact of images of childhood in translated passages that touch on sensitive themes such as sex and corporality, cruelty and violence, death, religion, the relation between parent and child, or desirable versus undesirable behavior. I focus here on the first two. Most of the following examples are drawn from translations of fairy tales, probably the most widely distributed literary genre internationally, which makes it particularly interesting for the study of children's literature in translation and the impact of globalization and commercialization.

The most commonly omitted or altered passages are those concerning nudity and sexuality. Studies by Sutton (1996), Dollerup (1999), Kyritsi (2006) and Thomson-Wohlgemuth (2007) offer many examples of how translators adapted and eliminated sexual or scatological references in translations of "Rapunzel," "The Frog-Prince," "Sleeping Beauty," "Little Red Riding Hood" and many other tales.

However, the opposite occurs as well. Depending on his/her image of the child and the sexual norms in a specific society, a translator may exaggerate taboo-breaking elements. In his translation of Andersen's "The Emperor's New Clothes," Jacques Vriens emphasizes the emperor's nudity. In the source text, the little child cries out: "But he hasn't got anything on." In Vriens's version, the boy shouts, "I see his little willie!" and a bit later, "And now I see his buttocks," going on to conclude, "The emperor walks in the altogether" (my translation). Obviously, these additions reveal a different image of the child, responding to children's presumed preference for taboo-breaking humor and adapting vocabulary to children with words such as *piemel* [little willie], *blootje* [nude] and *nakie* [naked] (both informal, 'childish' diminutives).

Alexandra Büchler emphasizes how cultural differences can work in two directions: "The stories that are considered important in European cultures about abuse, bullying, teen pregnancy, drugs, are often considered inappropriate for children by Arab publishers. (…) It works the other way round as well" (Büchler quoted in "Challenges" 2015, n.p.). Once she saw an Arabic children's book on the topic of getting a second mother after the protagonist's father married a second wife. She found it "quite shocking. (…) But they showed reality" (*ibid.*).

Alongside sexuality, violence is also often subject to cultural adaptation. Translators' and publishers' sensitivity concerning violence and cruelty becomes clear from numerous prologues in fairy tale editions in various countries, clarifying that violent passages have been removed (Tatar 1993; Zipes 1991). This also unambiguously exposes their vision of children as vulnerable and in need of protection.

As many of the contributions in this volume show, there is no doubt that the attitude towards violence and the vulnerability of children varies from culture to culture and can change over time. But attitudes can also differ greatly within a specific culture and time, revealing different child images.

That the protective image of childhood continues to influence translations in the twenty-first century becomes clear from the following citation from a 2005 Dutch edition of fairy tales: "Because we tried not to present the events too horribly, we slightly adapted the stories here and there. A little scariness is allowed, but we didn't want to scare our audience too much" (Busser and Schröder 2011, 7; my translation). In the same year, a source-text-oriented translation was published whose prologue betrays a much different image of childhood:

> They reflect a bygone society, in which people thought differently about social relationships, gender and race, and in which, for example, the notion of a stepmother had a different meaning than in the present time. (…) Such cruelty was more normal than nowadays. (…) Experience shows that children have less difficulty with this than adults. (Grimm and Grimm 2005, 7; my translation)

The selection and transformation of foreign or culturally sensitive items is not only done *by* adults (publishers, translators) but also sometimes *for* adult readers, a result of the multiple reader address. In its essence, children's books always address children *and* adults, who, on top of this, can take on different roles as readers (both silent and aloud), listeners and viewers. The Dutch author/translator Jacques Vriens retains the horrifying ending in which Rumpelstiltskin tears himself in two pieces, but he adds some sentences that seem to be mainly aimed at the adult who reads the story aloud, undermining (ironically) a protective image of the child: "Marieke looked in amazement at the two half little men on the floor. 'Come,' she said to her baby, 'we're going. This is nothing for small children'" (Vriens 1996, 22; my translation).

Re-visualizing the foreign

Not only words but also illustrations are sometimes changed to suit the context of the target culture. Illustrations in themselves can be considered as a form of translation, what Jacobson (1959) calls 'intersemiotic translation,' or the conversion of verbal signs into nonverbal signs. This transition from telling to showing necessarily implies interpretation, as illustrators have to fill in the textual gaps (Iser 1974, 280). In doing so, they will always be influenced by what Iser calls "mental images" (*ibid.*, 178) or visions that shape the way we see the world. Moreover, just like translators, illustrators can add, omit, rearrange or substitute elements from the text.

When a children's book is translated into a new language, it is not uncommon to see new illustrations derived from the target culture. This is a cultural modification carried out by the publisher aimed at increasing the book's resonance and recognizability among its target readership. In *Translating Picturebooks: Revoicing the Verbal, the Visual and the Aural for a Child Audience*, Riitta Oittinen, Ane Ketola and Melissa Garavine (2017) show many examples of this practice, particularly in translations from English to Chinese and Arabic.

Fairy tales, for instance, are not only constantly being retranslated and adapted but also re-illustrated. In the past, it was not unusual for such illustrations to be clearly situated in the target culture. In a picture book by the Dutch illustrator Jan Rinke, Cinderella, who is called Ella in the text, wears a typical Dutch cap and clogs (*Asschepoetster* 1909). However, as a result of increasing globalization, fairy tales are less and less likely to be localized. Globalization has gone hand in hand with homogenization. It is well known that the large publishing houses that target the international market explicitly instruct not only authors and translators but also illustrators to avoid culture-specific markers as well as references to sex, violence and anything else that could cause offence. Vanessa Joosen characterizes this trend as follows: "The lowest common denominator of acceptability tends to become the new norm in international co-productions" (Joosen 2010, 108). She gives the example of the Flemish illustrator Ingrid Godon, who was told by her American publisher to draw cows without udders.

The taboo on nudity leads to curious conflicts between text and image in Andersen's "The Emperor's New Clothes." Whereas in most translations, the little boy cries out that the emperor has no clothes on at all, for many illustrators, the nudity of the emperor clearly is a taboo. Many draw the emperor in his underwear or shirt. However, there are versions in which you can admire the naked emperor in all his glory – particularly in translations produced in the Netherlands (Van Coillie 2008, 560).

Lastly, a foreign appearance can also be an obstacle. "In the past, most international publishers would say 'absolutely not' if there was a black character on the cover," according to Adrienne Tang, rights director at Kids Can Press (McMahon 2017, 5). On the other hand, diversity can also be consciously added by illustrators. The Flemish illustrator Sebastiaan Van Doninck depicts Cinderella's prince as a burly man of color, confronting us with our white, Western stereotypes that tend to frame the fairy tale prince as a handsome, slim, white man. This framing is in itself determined by the numerous images we see in books, films and other cultural products.

Going digital

As tablets and smartphones become omnipresent in today's homes and classrooms, children are increasingly coming into contact with digital books. Digitization enriches the classic book with sound and moving images and offers extras like in-story games, reading comprehension exercises and technical reading functionality. Many apps also offer 'hotspots' where children can interact with items and characters from the story.

Worldwide, the number of digital books for young children has increased significantly in recent years, although some markets have developed faster than others. Larger and wealthier language areas have a much larger production than smaller, less wealthy areas (Bus et al. 2019). It is precisely these latter countries that have been inundated with apps from the Anglophone markets. Because these apps are developed by international media companies, they seldom contain localized content (Sari, Takacs and Bus, 2017). In their study of the best-selling apps for young children in Hungary, Turkey, Greece and the Netherlands, Sari, Takacs and Bus (*ibid.*) found that the majority of apps are not available in the local language. Moreover, smaller countries that do produce a relatively large number of digital children's books, like those in the Dutch language area, have seen their 'domestic' production threatened by Anglophone imports. In 2014, 27 percent of the most popular book apps in the iTunes App Store and Google Play Store were books in English, amongst them Disney classics, Dora the Explorer and Dr. Seuss. Fairy tales also figured very prominently. Moreover, most of the digital books in countries and regions with less widely used languages such as Dutch, Catalan, Norwegian and Hebrew offer only restricted animation, with no hotspots (Bus et al. 2019). Because children find interactive apps more attractive, the risk is that the market will be flooded with English-language children's book apps, supplanting apps in the mother tongue.

An added advantage of digital children's books is that they can be easily published in multilingual editions. Take *The Fundels*, a popular collection of digital books in Flanders, which comes with voice-over in Dutch, Turkish and French. However, most children's book apps are published in only one language or with a very restricted choice of translations in major languages. Moreover, the quality of the translations is often questionable (Bus et al. 2019). This is a missed opportunity. Digital books combining international languages with less widely used languages could be a great help for the ever-expanding group of children who receive instruction in a language other than their mother tongue. Digital picture books with sufficient language offerings would enable children to listen to stories independently in the school language or another new language, with visual support and often additional functionality for fostering language acquisition, such as integrated dictionaries and additional language games or exercises.

Conclusion

Whether and the extent to which children come into contact with other cultures through translated children's books depends on a number of factors. In today's globalized world, international market mechanisms play a crucial role. The dominance of Anglophone culture is reflected in the highly uneven translation flows into and out of English. Far fewer books are translated into English than out of English and many markets are flooded with books sourced from the UK and the US. These translation flows are driven both by the needs and requirements of the system itself and by merchandising, which means mainly only those series that were successful in the source culture are selected for translation. Relatedly, the extent to which a book's 'foreignness' is preserved in translation is also partly the result of marketing strategies. Some foreign names are retained precisely because they align with merchandising goals. (Think of Harry Potter.) On the other hand, publishers may also adapt text and illustrations to the target culture if they think doing so will help them reach a larger readership. Internationally oriented publishing conglomerates often adopt a strategy of neutralization, which involves avoiding culture-specific items and culturally sensitive themes.

However, individual intentions and perspectives play a role as well, and these are inseparable from the images of the child as conceived by specific publishers and translators. A publisher or translator may adopt either a strategy of localization in order to increase the recognizability of the story, or a strategy of foreignization aimed at expanding the knowledge of the young reader. Alongside this didactic role is a pedagogic one centered around sharing worldviews about what is 'good' and 'bad' for the education and upbringing of the child. Such worldviews are strongly culturally specific, as we saw in the various approaches to sexuality and violence in the Netherlands, the US and the Arab world. Translators may also let themselves be led by what they think children will *like*. They may change or keep strange-sounding names in order to maintain their 'funniness' or exaggerate or tamper down taboo-laden passages.

Ideas about the acceptability of cultural context adaptation change over time. Since the 1980s, the practice has often been criticized. This criticism was ratcheted up by Lawrence Venuti, who rejected domestication as an "ethnocentric reduction of the foreign text to target-language cultural values" (Venuti 1995, 20). Within the study of translated children's literature, Göte Klingberg (1986) strongly condemned the practice nearly ten years before.

However, more recent research poses the question of whether certain forms of domestication may actually help keep young readers engaged in stories they would otherwise cast aside due, for instance, to an unfamiliar style or uncontextualized norms and values relating to violence or sexuality originating from another culture (see Oittinen 2000; Alvstadt 2018).

Last but not least, the question can be raised of whether the transfer of information about other cultures by means of children's books in translation has received too much attention from translation scholars. Children can gain knowledge about other cultures much more efficiently from other sources, such as reference books, films, documentaries, travel, even short visits. The value of translated children's literature is that it brings young readers into contact with great books, providing unique reading experiences and enhancing literary and thus also cultural 'baggage.'

All great literature gives readers the chance to stand in the shoes of another, to take up residence in their feelings and thoughts. If that other happens to grow up in another culture, it can only be an enrichment to read that, despite their differences, people share many of the same profoundly held human emotions and desires. It is precisely here that the richness of translation resides, and that translators can function as go-betweens for languages and cultures.

Coda

Young people themselves can take up the role of go-betweens, too, by building bridges between languages and cultures, using literary techniques and digital media. The internet makes it possible for young people all over the world to come into contact with each other and share their (reading) experiences. The classroom, which is often a place where children from different cultures mix, plays an important role in this exchange as well. An extraordinary project in an elementary school in Toronto, Canada shows just how well this can work. The children collected clips highlighting qualities shared by all humans and created illustrations for them. Using digital media, they put together a slideshow with voice-overs in more than thirty languages recorded by the children in their native tongue.[2] The title of the montage, "Imagine a World: Celebrating the Differences and Appreciating the Similarities," summarizes what I believe children's literature in translation can do.

---

2   See https://www.youtube.com/watch?v=8zabcX_zoP0.

Bibliography

Abós, Elena. 2016. "Translator: Trafficking between Cultures." *The Horn Book Magazine* 93, no. 3: 35–41.

Alvstad, Cecilia. 2010. "Children's Literature and Translation." In *Handbook of Translation Studies Volume 1*, edited by Yves Gambier and Luc Van Doorslaer, 22–27. Amsterdam/Philadelphia: John Benjamins.

Alvstad, Cecilia. 2019. "Children's Literature." In *The Routledge Handbook of Literary Translation*, edited by Kelly Washbourne and Ben Van Wyke, 159–180. London/New York: Routledge.

Asschepoetster: Een sprookje. 1909. Illustrations by Jan Rinke. Amsterdam: Letteren & Kunst.

Auvray, Ludovic and Marion Rougier. 2001. "Harry Potter: quelques aspects stilistiques et culturels." In *Traduire pour un jeune public*, edited by Fabrice Antoine, 69–79. Lille: Université de Lille III.

Browne, Anthony. 1984. *Willy the Wimp*. London: Julia MacRae Books.

Browne, Anthony. 1991. *Willy el tímido*. Translated by Carmen Esteva. Mexico City: Fondo de Cultura Económica.

Bus, Adriana G., Trude Hoel, Cristina Aliagas Marin, Margrethe Jernes, Ofra Korat, Charles L. Mifsud and Jan van Coillie. 2019. "Availability and Quality of Storybook Apps Across Five Less Widely Used Languages." In *The Routledge Handbook of Digital Literacies in Early Childhood*, edited by Ola Erstad, Rosie Flewitt, Bettina Kümmerling-Meibauer and Íris Susana Pires Pereia, 308–321. New York: Routledge.

Busser, Marianne and Ron Schröder. 2011. *Het grote sprookjesboek voor jong en oud: De mooiste sprookjes opnieuw verteld*. Vianen/Antwerp: The House of Books.

Desmidt, Isabelle. 2006. "A Prototypical Approach within Descriptive Translation Studies? Colliding Norms in Translated Children's Literature." In *Children's Literature in Translation: Challenges and Strategies*, edited by Jan Van Coillie and Walter P. Verschueren, 79–96. Manchester: St. Jerome.

Dimitriu, Ileana. 2002. "Translation, Diversity and Power: An Introduction." *Current Writing* 14, no. 2: 1–14.

Dollerup, Cay. 1999. *Tales and Translation: The Grimm Tales from Pan Germanic Narratives to Shared International Fairytales*. Amsterdam/Philadelphia: John Benjamins.

Donahaye, Jasmine. 2012. *Three Percent? Publishing Data and Statistics on Translated Literature in the United Kingdom and Ireland: Literature across Frontiers*. Aberystwyth: Mercator Institute for Media, Languages and Culture, Aberystwyth University, Wales.

Dutheil de la Rochère, Martine Hennard, Gillian Lathey and Monika Wozniak. 2016. *Cinderella across Cultures: New Directions and Interdisciplinary Perspectives.* Detroit: Wayne State University.

Edwards, Viv and Jacob Marriote Ngwaru. 2011. "African Language Publishing for Children in South Africa: Challenges for Translators." *International Journal of Bilingual Education and Bilingualism* 14, no. 5: 589–602.

Ghesquiere, Rita. 2006. "Why Does Children's Literature Need Translation?" In *Children's Literature in Translation: Challenges and Strategies*, edited by Jan Van Coillie and Walter P. Verschueren, 19–34. Manchester: St. Jerome.

Grimm, Jacob and Wilhelm Grimm. 2005. *Volledige uitgave van de 200 sprookjes verzameld door de gebroeders Grimm.* Rotterdam: Lemniscaat.

Hazard, Paul and Marguerite M. K. Mitchell. 1944. *Books, Children & Men.* Boston: The Horn Book.

Iser, Wolfgang. 1974. *The Implied Reader: Patterns in Communication in Prose Fiction from Bunyan to Beckett.* Baltimore/London: Johns Hopkins University Press.

Jakobson, Roman. 1959. "On Linguistic Aspects of Translation." In *The Translation Studies Reader*, edited by Lawrence Venuti, 113–118. London/New York: Routledge.

Joels, Rosie Webb. 1999. "Weaving World Understanding: The Importance of Translations in International Children's Literature." *Children's Literature in Education* 30, no. 1: 65–81.

Joosen, Vanessa. 2010. "True Love or Just Friends." *Children's Literature in Education* 41, no. 2: 105–117.

Khorana, Meena G. 2006. "India." In *The Oxford Encyclopedia of Children's Literature*, edited by Jack Zipes, 282–285. Oxford: Oxford University Press.

Klingberg, Göte. 1986. *Children's Fiction in the Hands of Translators.* Lund: CWK Gleerup.

Kruger, Haidee. 2011. "Postcolonial Polysystems: The Production and Reception of Translated Children's Literature in South Africa." *The Translator* 17, no. 1: 105–136.

Kruger, Haidee. 2013. "Child and Adult Readers' Processing of Foreignized Elements in Translated South African Picturebooks: An Eye-tracking Study." *Target* 25, no. 2: 180–227.

Kyritsi, M. V. 2006. "Taboo or Not to Be? Adgar Taylor and the First Translations of the Grimms' Kinder- und Hausmärchen." In *Changing Concepts of Childhood and Children's Literature*, edited by Vanessa Joosen and Katrien Vloeberghs, 195–208. Newcastle: Cambridge Scholar Press.

Lathey, Gillian. 2010. *The Role of Translators in Children's Literature.* London/New York: Routledge.

McMahon, Serah-Marie. 2017. "More than Words: Translating a Path to Global Awareness." *Canadian Children's Book News*, Fall: 4–6.

Miyake, Okiko. 2006. "Eastern Asia." In *The Oxford Encyclopedia of Children's Literature*, edited by Jack Zipes, 9–11. Oxford: Oxford University Press.

Naghmeh-Abbaspour, Bita and Tengku Mahadi. 2015. "On Translation of Children's Literature: Characters of Children's Books Enjoy a Different Diet in Iran." *International Journal of Multicultural and Multireligious Understanding* 2, no. 6: 58–67.

Oittinen, Riitta. 2000. *Translating for Children*. New York/London: Garland.

Oittinen, Riitta, Anne Ketola and Melissa Garavine. 2017. *Translating Picturebooks: Revoicing the Verbal, the Visual and the Aural for a Child Audience*. London/New York: Routledge.

Osayinmwense, Osa. 1985. "The Rise of African Children's Literature." *The Reading Teacher* 38, no. 8: 750–759.

O'Sullivan, Emer. 2000. *Kinderliterarisch Komparistik*. Heidelberg: Winter.

O'Sullivan, Emer. 2005. *Comparative Children's Literature*. London/New York: Routledge.

Pascua, Isabel. 2003. "Translation and Intercultural Education." *Meta* 48, no. 1–2: 276–284.

Sapiro, Gisèle. 2016. "How Do Literary Works Cross Borders (or Not)? A Sociological Approach to World Literature." *Journal of World Literature*, no. 1: 81–96.

Sari, Burcu, Zsofia Takacs and Adriana Bus. 2017. "What Are We Downloading for Our Children? Best-selling Children's Apps in Four European Countries." *Journal of Early Childhood Literacy*: 1–18.

Seuss, Dr. 2015. *Aan de andere kant van de heuvels van Horus*. Translated by Bette Westera. Haarlem: Gottmer.

Sung, Seung-Eun, Sook-Jong Park and Kisum Kim. 2016. "Why Not Japanese Names? Reader Response to Character Name Translation." *Neohelicon* 43: 213–231.

Sutton, Martin James. 1996. *The Sin-complex: A Critical Study of English Versions of the Grimms' 'Kinder- und Hausmärchen' in the Nineteenth Century*. Kassel: Brüder Grimm-Gesellschaft.

Tatar, Maria. 1993. *Off with Their Heads: Fairy Tales and the Culture of Childhood*. Princeton: Princeton University Press.

Thomson-Wohlgemut, Gaby. 2007. "…And He Flew out of the Window on a Wooden Spoon." *Meta* 52, no. 2: 173–193.

Van Coillie, Jan. 2008. "The Translator's New Clothes: Translating the Dual Audience in Andersen's *The Emperor's New Clothes*." *Meta* 53, no. 3: 549–568.

Van Coillie, Jan and Marianne Hellings. 2011. "De lach van de vertaler: De vertaling van humor in *Le Petit Nicolas*." *Literatuur zonder leeftijd* 84: 111–134.

Van Coillie, Jan and Inez Aussems. 2017. "Kinder- en jeugdfictie in Vlaanderen en Nederland: een overzicht van het aanbod vertalingen tussen 2010 en 2015." *Filter: Tijdschrift voor vertalen en vertaalwetenschap* 54, no. 3: 57–63.
Venuti, Lawrence. 1995. *The Translator's Invisibility*. London: Routledge.
Vriens, Jacques. 1996. *Grootmoeder, wat heb je grote oren… Klassieke sprookjes, opnieuw verteld*. Houten: Van Holkema en Warendorf.
Zipes, Jack. 1991. *Fairy Tales and the Art of Subversion: The Classical Genre for Children and the Process of Civilization*. New York: Routledge.

Part 2

Text » Context

The creative reinventions of nonsense and domesticating the implied child reader in Hungarian translations of *Alice's Adventures in Wonderland*

Anna Kérchy

Abstract

This chapter conjoins the methodological apparatuses of children's literature studies and translation studies with the aim of exploring the changing meanings of Lewis Carroll's Victorian nonsense fairy-tale fantasy *Alice's Adventures in Wonderland* (1865) throughout its six different Hungarian translations (Carroll 1927, trans. Altay; 1929, trans. Juhász; 1935, trans. Kosztolányi; 1958, trans. Szobotka; 2009, trans. Varró; 2013, trans. Szilágyi). After reflecting on the (un)translatability of the literary nonsense genre and the powerplay involved in language games, I compare domesticating translations bordering on creative adaptations and foreignizing translations intent on respecting criteria of fidelity to the source text. I contend that dominant images of the child and childhood prevailing in the specific sociohistorical cultural context of the target audience addressed inherently influence the translation strategies employed. I examine how this concept of the child – naïve or naughty, innocent or experienced, empathic or rebellious – shapes notions of intended, implied, and ideal child readership. My aim is to explore how the translators' decision to foreground the mature metalinguistic or the infantile trans-verbal registers of Carroll's nonsense wordplay is motivated by their abstract idea of childness that may reconceptualize the source text significations, and eventually contributes to the ludic liberation and/or the discursive discipline of the implied child reader's mutable figure.

Introduction

The puzzlement of Alice, and the triumph of Alice, are attached to her newly acquired skills as a reader. Words spring to life, jostling, unruly, looming, then brilliantly sealed and skeined into ordered sentences. The primary constituency of child readers for the *Alice* books does not imply simplicity – rather, struggle, loneliness, pleasure, and sometimes success, the flair of meaning pinned down, or released. (Beer 2016, 104)

"It seems very pretty, (…) but it's *rather* hard to understand! (…) Somehow it seems to fill my head with ideas – only I don't exactly know what they are!" (Carroll 2001, 156). These thoughts, which Lewis Carroll's Alice formulates upon reading the poem "Jabberwocky" after stepping through the looking glass into a magical dream realm where anything can happen, perfectly encapsulate the cognitive dissonance and affective ambivalence experienced by any audience attempting to make sense of the perplexing genre of literary nonsense. Nonsense literature's ancestral connection with the medieval carnivalesque tradition's transgressive intent, fantastic extravaganza, and grotesque (de)compositions (Heyman and Shortsleeve 2011, 165) can be tracked in the genre's strategic destabilization of coherent meanings, conventional interpretive strategies, and logical reasoning. Nonsense language games force all language users to face their inability to master the consensual sign system that proves to be inherently insufficient to (re)present reality. Yet they also flirt with our communicative compulsion, the human urge to oververbalize the unspeakable, and foreground the ludic potential of discourse. The genre holds a particular appeal for children who enjoy the overturning of disciplinary power structures – literary nonsense mocks educational methods, codes of conduct, scientific classification, and grammar rules alike – and the conjoint problematization of the supremacy of reason over fantasy, of adult over child. Obviously the greatest challenge is that of the translator, who endeavors to reenact in another language how nonsense's semantic and syntactic incongruities embody the ambiguous oscillation "between verbal chaos and verbal constraints, between the need for meaning and the refusal of meaning" (Lecercle 2008, 90), between the experience of readerly incompetence and epiphany.

The very title of Jean-Jacques Lecercle's seminal essay "Translate It, Translate It Not" (2008) foregrounds the ambiguity of making sense of nonsense, the clever combination of creativity with compromises, and the balancing between domestication and foreignization tactics (Venuti 1995) required from translators who venture to adapt into their own language the language-philosophically charged stylistic bravado of literary nonsense. Nonsense is often deemed untranslatable due to its 'meaningless' pseudo-words, which do not belong to a language's vocabulary and often spring from private mythologies, mind games, or *l'art-pour-l'art* rhetorical exercises. Literary nonsense therefore constitutes 'a text that is always already a translation' from an existing source language to a make-believe source language. Another argument *pro* untranslatability is the cultural interdiction imposed by the fact that the genre has canonically acquired, since its Victorian popularization, "the status of a national myth in England" and is permeated by the assumption that "you have to be English to understand nonsense" (Lecercle 1994, 90). Lecercle nevertheless argues for the "total translatability" and international appeal of this apparently untranslatable type of text that flirts with meaninglessness but clearly absorbs sense and invites meaning formations and meaning deconstructions alike. In his view, the primary agenda of translating nonsense is to transpose into another culture the nonsensical *effect* of the original.

I believe that this effect has a lot to do with the sense of absurd humor that has been commonly identified as a specifically British national cultural currency[1] and that gains a crystallized form in literary nonsense's metalinguistic commentary concerning the language user's illusory agency in transmitting the meaning s/he intends to communicate. The transnational excitement of nonsense comes from the tension provoked by the fusion of the necessity of misunderstanding and the impossibility of meaninglessness. On the one hand, we must self-ironically admit that, due to the consensually set, arbitrary relationship between signs and things or actions, we can never really say what we mean: representation entails a loss of immediacy. On the other hand, however, we joyously fill in textual gaps with our own significations, which will necessarily slip, proliferate, change, and generate a plethora of unstable surplus connotations.

The trademark ambiguity of nonsense literature surfaces in its dual address and crossover appeal. It bridges the gap between child and adult audiences by offering the latter a temporary retreat from structures of authority permeating disciplined discourse. It also allows the former a ludic revelry in acoustic registers of signification. It is like a "recess bell that officially freed [youngsters] from the classroom to the playground in their reading" (Darnton quoted in Goldthwaite 1996, 74). At the same time, it allows grown-ups to return to a childhood state, granting them a joyous forgetfulness they wished to understand by rational means. Figuratively speaking, we could easily argue that the two decisive features of literary nonsense represent the infantile and the adult registers of signification. On the one hand, the immersion in a discursively conceived topsy-turvy fictional reality stimulates a mature metalinguistic self-awareness concerning the speaking subject's struggle with

---

1   The *Encyclopedia of Humor Studies* exemplifies particular types of national and ethnic humor with the British penchant for "ridiculing mundane reality by satirically revealing the absurdity of everyday life, relying largely on puns and intellectual humor" (Attardo 2014, 542).

the rule-bound, regulatory limits and transgressive potentials of language in misrepresenting reality (Lecercle 1994). On the other hand, however, nonsense's prioritization of sound over sense also activates the trans-verbal, sensorial, sonoric dimension of discourse, foregrounding the 'revolutionary poeticity' of language use, a lulling repetitive rhythmicality that makes the genre so pleasurable for child readers/listeners dwelling closer to the primal corporeal experience of the 'semiotic realm' preceding the symbolization integral to the disciplinary socialization process (Kristeva 1984).

Out of the myriad choices a translator must make when adapting and reinventing the source text to suit the context of a given target culture, it is important to decide if the mature metalinguistic or the infantile trans-verbal registers of literary nonsense will gain pre-eminence. In this chapter, I aim to explore how dominant images of the child and childhood prevailing in the specific sociohistorical cultural context of the target audience addressed inherently influence the translation strategies employed. Riitta Oittinen (2006) uses the Bakhtinian term "superaddressee" for the abstract notion of the child to whom authors and translators of children's literature are directing their words and images, "whose absolutely just responsive understanding is presumed, either in some metaphysical distance or in distant historical time" (*ibid.*, 96). This concept of Hungarian translations of Alice child, naïve or naughty, innocent or experienced, empathic or rebellious, will influence the way of addressing the target audience, including the flesh-and-blood real child reader who will eventually take up the book to activate occasionally unintended, new meanings. Besides the notion of the intended child reader, I am particularly interested in the figure of the 'implied reader,' which refers in reader response criticism (e.g. Iser 1974) to the author's image of the recipient that is fixed and objectified in the narrative by specific indexical signs. The intended reader superaddressee exists only in the author's imagination, whereas the implied reader is a textual function, a structural position postulated by the narrative. Neither has a real-life existence, yet both will likely end up being customized, updated and modified in translation to meet the preferences of the target cultural context.

It is important to note that the implied reader is not necessarily identical with the 'ideal reader' (Schmid 2013), who willingly adopts the interpretive position and aesthetic standpoint put forward by the work and cooperates in actualizing and bringing to full bloom the 'seeds of meanings' implanted in the text by the authorial intention. This dilemma emerges in the case of children's literary nonsense – a mode of writing that fairy-tale scholar Jack Zipes praises for making youngsters think for themselves (1987, 73). Resisting, rebellious implied child reader figures are reluctant to embrace socially prescribed narrative patterns and revolt against the disciplinary power structures inscribed in language use. Conforming to the illogic of the genre, they self-reflectively destabilize the very process of meaning formation. Paradoxically, though, in literary nonsense, where the only rule is that there are no rules – for "We are all mad here," as the Cheshire Cat puts it in Wonderland – the resisting reader, destabilizing the meanings s/he makes, might eventually emerge as the ideal reader who "understands the work in a way that optimally matches in structure" (Schmid 2013, n.p.).

Lewis Carroll's Alice is a perfect example for this inquisitive implied child reader figure. She questions the sense of the strange speech acts addressed to her: "If any one of them can explain it, I'll give him sixpence. *I* don't believe there's an atom of meaning in it" (Carroll 2001, 128). She frowns upon tyrants who claim mastery over language (like the egg-man Humpty Dumpty), and rebels against meanings imposed on her by grown-ups: "Stuff and nonsense!" she cries at the final trial scene (*ibid.*, 129). She also dares to invent her own interpretations or to shift between languages, aiming to comprehend the curiosities. Her addressing the mouse in the only French sentence she knows, "Où est ma chatte?", is a benevolent attempt at approaching the foreignness of the other. In Carroll's novel, all these odd discursive exchanges are dreamt into being by the sleeping Alice herself. Hence, besides the role of the implied reader, she enacts that of the implied future author who is not driven to despair by all the nonsensical communication acts she gets involved in but decides to write them down, once she grows up, in a book of unprecedented tales of wonder. As Perry Nodelman suggests, the Alice tales metafictionally stage the complex interpretive activity all fictional worlds demand of their readers. The ones designed for children do so emphatically. The intended underage audience can easily identify with the implied reader/co-author adventuress on the grounds of their familiarity with a decisive experience of childhood: the inquisitive questioning of reality. The enquiry about the meaning of things, the relentless quest for explanations, and the attempts at innovative reinterpretations are performed by Alice throughout her search for meaning, logic, and identity. Her struggles to "explore a shadow text larger and more complex than the actual words of the text itself" (Nodelman 2008, 18) neatly resonates with the complex enterprise of the translator's task. Walter Benjamin called this task "a somewhat provisional way of coming to terms with the foreignness of languages" (2005, 23). Eventually, translating the untranslatable might belong to the long list of challenging games Alice attempts to master throughout her fantastic journeys, from chess and card games to the Caucus-race, the lobster quadrille or the queenly croquet game.

My aim in the following is to explore – through the example of Hungarian translations of *Alice's Adventures in Wonderland* – how the image of the child (and the child superaddressee) is rendered by the translator. How the translator domesticates this image to fit the cultural background of the target audience will affect the creative co-authorial agency attributed to the intended and implied child reader figure. His/her decisions are intertwined with the choice about whether rule-bound games (*ludus*) or free instinctive play (*paidia*) that Virginie Iché (2015) called pivotal engines of Carrollian nonsense's ludic aesthetics, should predominate the narrative. Domesticating translations bordering on creative adaptations and foreignizing translations intent on respecting criteria of fidelity to the source text alternately contribute to the ludic liberation and/or the discursive discipline of the implied child reader's mutable figure. These modifications reveal translation as an inventive "act of both inter-cultural and inter-temporal communication" (Bassnett 2002, 9) which allows us to see in different ways the original text that always already bears in itself all possible translations and gets richer with each additional reading–rewriting (Benjamin 2005, 17).

Alice's Journey into Hungarian

Lewis Carroll's Victorian nonsense fairy-tale fantasy *Alice's Adventures in Wonderland* (1865) has six different Hungarian translations published between the 1920s and 2010s (Altay 1927; Juhász 1929; Kosztolányi 1935; Szobotka 1958; Varró 2009; Szilágyi 2013). The book's sequel *Through the Looking Glass* (1871) has only been translated twice into Hungarian (Révbíró and Tótfalusi 1980; Varró and Varró 2009). The first four adopt some ingeniously inventive domesticating solutions but mostly talk down to children and associate childhood with innocent ignorance; the two twenty-first-century translations reclaim for Alice the agency Carroll attributed to his curious and cunning girl child heroine and reader.

As I have pointed out elsewhere (Kérchy 2015), the first Hungarian edition, *Alice a Csodák országában* [Alice in the Land of Wonders] in 1927, was a supplement to the popular children's magazine *Tündérvásár* [Fairy Market]. This abridged version, decorated by some of Tenniel's drawings, was 'retold' by the magazine's editor, Margit Altay, who was in charge of translating several other volumes of the gift-book series for youngsters, including *Robinson*, *Gulliver*, and *Little Lord Fauntleroy*. Warren Weaver assumed – because the Mad Hatter's song mocked the traditional German Christmas carol *O Tannenbaum* – that she likely worked from Antonie Zimmermann's first German translation of 1869 (Weaver 1964, 87). Altay interpreted *Alice* along the line of the docile girls' adventure stories she authored under the pseudonym Aunt Marge. She reproduced Carroll's classic as an innocent piece of children's literature addressing uniquely juvenile audiences; a fairy-tale fantasy about the daydreams of a wealthy, upper-middle-class little girl unburdened by social problems, cultural anxieties, or philosophical dilemmas; a bed-time story devoid of abstractions and ambiguities. She performed a systematic infantilization and idealization of Wonderland. She omitted the death jokes as well as the passages related to identity crisis, and replaced ominous onomatopoeia with more childish, playful ones (the "thump! thump!" of Alice's landing after the fall became *zsupsz, zsupsz,* meaning "oops-a-daisy!"). She harmonized self-contradictions (the "drink me!" bottle offers in the original a gastronomically shocking combination of incompatible flavors whereas its contents here taste uniquely of sweets dear to children) and purified the tale from linguistically challenging puns and wild absurdities (like Alice's footnotes). She consistently turned the remaining nonsense into infantile babble, senseless gibberish far from Carroll's polysemic-polyphonic language games defamiliarizing discourse. ("Curiouser and curiouser" became *kavarcs-quacs, kavarcs-quacs,* in English something like "mixture-quatsch," a coinage similar in sound to the Hungarian equivalent of 'peek-a-boo,' *kukucs* – although the learned reader can recognize the German word for nonsense (*quatsch*) in the final syllable of the compound.) Altay's translation replaced universalizing theoretical speculations about the nature of reality and representation with particularities characteristic of the 'once upon a time' setting of fairy tales. (Tellingly, her Alice only regrets that her sister's specific book lacks pictures, and never ponders about the use and meaning of pictureless books in general.)

The second Hungarian edition, *Alisz kalandjai Csodaországban* [Alisz's Adventures in Wonderland], translated by experimental psychologist and writer Andor Juhász around 1929, was the first to provide Hungarian readers with a full, unabridged text that included all of John Tenniel's original illustrations (even though the artist's name was misspelled as Tenniels). Conforming to the conventional practice of his time, Juhász used Hungarian names and Hungarian phonetic transcripts: Alisz for Alice, Dodó (a diminutive of the male forename Aladár) for the Dodo bird, Mici for Dinah the cat, Hungarian statesman Deák Ferenc for Shakespeare, Lizard Feri for Bill, Tapsifüles [Flopsy Easter bunny] for the March Hare, and Kókusz [coconut] for the Caucus-race (Kérchy 2015). This domesticating strategy was meant to enhance the story's crossover appeal, and contemporary reviews did praise the *Alice* books as the "last reservatories of lost human freedom and innocence, capable of challenging the mainstream juvenile literary trend of aggressive adventure stories of war and colonization, and shedding light on the absurdities of life in a way enjoyable for children and adults alike" (M. M. 1932). Juhász's primary agenda was to embrace the "teach and delight" motto of the children's literary genre, yet the didactic intent was occasionally undermined by the heroine's oscillation between the personas of a brave little adventuress and a lisping little girl.

The third Hungarian edition, translated in 1935 by Hungarian poet Dezső Kosztolányi and illustrated by Dezső Fáy, is the most exciting take on Carroll's classic to date. At that time, the news of the centenary of Carroll's birth and of Alice Liddell's eightieth birthday reached Hungary, and it became clear that the *Alice* books had earned the canonical status of world literary classics. However, Kosztolányi was not so much intrigued by the book's prestigious position as by the challenging "tour de force" implied in translating an untranslatable narrative (Kappanyos 2018, 115). As the title *Évike Tündérországban* [Evie in Fairyland] attests, this is an ingeniously inventive but far-fetched retelling of Carroll's classic. This 'hyperdomesticating' version strategically replaced the linguistic and cultural differences of the foreign source text by narrative solutions more intelligible to the target-language reader. More interested in fluency than faithfulness, it aimed to minimize strangeness and bring the author/text back home to the target audience's comfort zone. It sought to create for contemporary compatriots an *effect* similar to the one produced by the original in its first readers (Kérchy 2015). Interestingly, Kosztolányi's unique linguistic solutions remind us of Caillois' notion of *paidia* surfacing in an imaginative, spontaneous, free play of storytelling. Yet the way this translator positions his child reader is closer to *ludus*, as he frames his target audience within rule-bound, disciplined narrative pleasures.

In his essay on the art of translation,[2] Kosztolányi (1942) repeatedly argued that translation per se is "practically impossible," so instead of the identical reconstruction of the original, the translator should "reimagine" a work of art in its own right, integrated into the cultural context of the recipients. With a cunning (mock) homophony, he called 'translation' 'transmutation' (*fordítás/ferdítés*), a "clever confidence trick." It is practically an "impossible gambit" to faithfully transmit at once the literal meaning of words as well as the "sounds of sentences, the colors of letters," the affective and intellectual charge of all words (*ibid.*, 184). It is challenging to simultaneously satisfy semantic and syntactic requirements dictated by grammatical rules and dictionary definitions and to fulfill musical requirements dictated by the "soul of the literary text" (*ibid.*, 185), to make a compromise between ideal and reality. Therefore, instead of the identical reconstruction of the original,

---

2   The English translations of quotations from Kosztolányi's essay, written originally in Hungarian, are by Anna Kérchy.

the translator should "reimagine" (*ibid.*, 185) a work of art in its own right, integrated into the cultural context of the recipients. The translator must learn how "to gracefully perform a dance while being tied up with ropes in a tight bondage" (*ibid.*, 186). He must transplant into his own mother tongue the verbal traces of another soul's visionary ideas, but he will also necessarily colonize the text he adopts and resuscitate it into a new life, in a reinvented narrative shaped/permeated by his own soul and personality. Hence the translated text is both alien and one's very own familiar. It is radically other yet intimately self-same. It is a work of humble submission and of cunning hijacking. According to Kosztolányi's melancholic, poetic view there is a "metonymical relationship between the source-text and the translation" (Józan 2010, 213) that remains an incomplete fragment of the totality of the initial meaning, a residue that commemorates via its presence what has been lost. Yet paradoxically the translated version's textual gaps turn into a surplus which efface and supersede the original with creative reinvention.

Kosztolányi's domestications in *Alice* include the renaming of the protagonist with the diminutive form of a widespread Hungarian forename, the exchange of plum jam for orange marmalade, coffee and wine for tea, paprika for pepper, a card game called '21' for croquet – all cultural references easily decodable for Hungarian readers. One of the most radical modifications is the elimination of Alice's major adversary, the Red Queen, from the story and her replacement by a schizoid king figure – a modification necessitated by Kosztolányi's decision to use Hungarian playing cards instead of French ones (the Hungarian cards do not have a queen figure). The metaphorical idioms literally embodied by Wonderland's curious characters were domesticated via his ingenious poetic free-play, best exemplified by the transformation of the Cheshire Cat into a Wooden Dog with reference to the Hungarian proverb 'to grin/giggle like a wooden dog' [*vigyorog/vihog mint a fakutya*]. In this idiom of uncertain etymological origin, the wooden dog might be an archaic term for a sledge making a screeching sound on ice evocative of a cackling laughter, or it might refer to a boot-horn shaped like the upward curved lips of a smiling face. Others argue that the grinning dog was an idol decorating pagan sacrificial altars in Ancient Hungarian times. The visualization of the Wooden Dog offers an exciting case of iconotextual dynamics, whereby verbal translation and visual adaptation complement each other, conjointly 'overwriting' the source text. In Tamás Szecskó's two sets of ink drawings for the 1958 and 1974 editions of Kosztolányi's translation revised by Tibor Szobotka, the grinning wooden dog is first depicted in a domesticating style as a hound of the Hungarian *vizsla* breed with bolts at its joints, while in the second round it earns a foreignized hybrid embodiment with a massive

British bulldog head on a patchwork body. This shows that illustration can be interpreted as translation into another medium.

While in Carroll's original *Alice* tale the child reader gains empowerment by being allowed to interactively enter into play with the story, Kosztolányi's domestication of the child reader image entails an infantilization of both the implied and the intended child reader. The translated text seems to play a trick upon its young recipient, who is positioned – along with the protagonist she is invited to identify with – as a mere pawn, a lovely puppet, and a passive listener. Kosztolányi calls Carroll's protagonist Évike, Evie, a diminutive form of a popular Hungarian name. The term of endearment reduces curious Alice to a sweet silly little girl who makes clumsy attempts at finding her way in a fantastic place rearticulated as a Fairyland. This utopian site of ideal happiness is very far from the grotesque absurdities of Carrollian Wonderland but rings familiar to readers of Hungarian folk and fairy tales, which inspired the translation. Kosztolányi intends to integrate his text within the canonized corpus of 1930s Hungarian children's literature. This corpus is largely defined by standards of patriotic and religious moralizing didacticism, and a patronizing, condescending attitude towards juvenile readers, who were meant to be controlled and normativized by the reassertion of dominant values (Kappanyos 2015, 187). Hence, the subversiveness that constitutes the very engine of the Carrollian storyworld became largely eradicated from the translated version. Kosztolányi's agenda is to make a witty 'Hungarian fairy tale,' suggesting this is the only communicative instrument he can truly write, feel, and live in, as a translator allegedly grounded in his own cultural tradition and mother tongue fueled by the nursery room's emotional comfort, flowing in the veins of the native speaker (Kosztolányi 1942).

As I have argued elsewhere (Kérchy 2015), Kosztolányi's greatest poetic feat is his translation of the mock-didactic verse embedded in the prose narrative. He starts out from the assumption that the poems are meant to verify the heroine's true identity through testing her capacity to properly remember poems, well known to Wonderland inhabitants and all readers, who recognize the originals of the parodies and are amused by their distortions. Kosztolányi is not interested in replicating the English originals; he only gains inspiration from the source text to invent his own parodies of popular Hungarian poems, nursery rhymes, folk tales, and songs. The texts he recycles tend to address children younger than Alice's original age (seven and a half). "How doth the little crocodile," initially a twisted rewrite of Isaac Watts's didactic poem for schoolchildren "Against Idleness and Mischief," reads in Hungarian as "Crocodile bathes / In a black lake / To see his mother / In Negro Land. / His skin is rough, / His feet are crooked. / Turn around, turn around, / Iron-nosed witch" with an obvious mocking reference to the lyrics of a singing game popular in kindergarten playgrounds. ("Little duck bathes / In a black lake / To see his mother / In Poland. / His soles are slippery, / His heels are high. / Turn around, turn around, / My golden sweetheart Mary.")[3] It also pokes fun at a monstrous figure of the Eastern European folk tale tradition, the Baba Yaga-like witch with the iron nose (*vasorrú bába*), an early object of infantile phobias as the dark double of the primary caretaker mother figure – embodied in Carroll by the Red Queen, who is missing from Kosztolányi's version.

Throughout the process of domesticating appropriation, many layers of meaning are inevitably lost because the cultural-historical phenomenon of British Victorianism fictionalized in the source text does not have its one-to-one Hungarian equivalent. This necessitated a transnational, cross-cultural reading. Carroll's original Mad Tea Party, where Alice drinks tea in the company of the Hatter and the March Hare, mocks the nineteenth-century bourgeois etiquette expected at the customary, very British five-o'clock tea (and the tea ceremony as a re-socializing therapeutic method employed in Victorian insane asylums (Kohlt 2016)). In Kosztolányi's translation, Evie's companions, the Drunken Brushmaker and April's Fool, are carnivalesque characters reminiscent of folk tales' trickster figures, while the replacement of tea with wine as a Hungarian national drink gains disturbing connotations. Instead of ageless, animalistic fantasy creatures, adult, male, working-class characters seem to deride a bourgeois female child figure, laughing *at* her instead of laughing *with* her. The nonsense around their table is no longer a *l'art-pour-l'art* feat of silly linguistic bravado, but disoriented speech is a symptom of indulging in alcoholic beverages and a manifestation of conflicted class, gender, and age differences. In Tenniel's original illustration to Carroll's text, Alice occupies the most comfortable armchair. In a half-erect, half-reclining posture, she seems slightly bored and bothered, yet defiant and rebellious, willing to put an end to nonsense any time she decides to get up and leave. In Dezső Fáy's image complementing Kosztolányi's text, Evie appears scared and vulnerable, hugging herself for self-protection, a girl child at risk of being victimized by sly-looking adult men. The Hungarian illustration's intersemiotic translation moves the text in the direction of a

---

3   English gloss translations are by the author. In Hungarian the original reads: "Kiskacsa fürdik, / Fekete tóba, / Anyjához készül / Lengyelországba. / Síkos a talpa, / Magas a sarka, / Fordulj ki, fordulj, / aranyos Mariska." In Kosztolányi's translation: "Krokodil fürdik, / Fekete tóba, / Anyjához készül / Négerországba. // Görcsös a bőre, / Görbe a lába, / Fordulj ki, fordulj, / Vasorrú bába" (Carroll 1935, 17, trans. Kosztolányi).

cautionary fairy tale – like that of Little Red Riding Hood threatened by the brute bestiality of the Wolf.

The lyrical prologue to *Wonderland* perfectly illustrates how Kosztolányi distorted the narrative situation to modify the position of the implied child reader from active co-creator to passive listener. In the introductory poem to Alice's adventures, Carroll pays homage to his child-friend muses as co-authors of his novel. He commemorates the birth of his tale on an 1862 boating trip where Alice Liddell and her sisters urged him to entertain them with a story they crafted together throughout an improvisatory oral performance that eventually matured into a book he published with Macmillan in 1865. In Carroll's original, the author puts himself on an equal plane with his child readers: like the anonymous lyrical self, the nameless girl companions are playfully denoted metonymically by their body parts (little arms, little hands, three tongues together, happy voices) and Latin numbers turned with a pun into mock-female names (Prima, Secunda, Tertia), offering easy identificatory positions for child readers whose courage, confidence, and creativity assist in directing the course of the narrative.

Kosztolányi recontextualizes the unmarried mathematics professor's outing with his friends, the dean's daughters, into the much safer frame of family romance where an elderly grandfather figure tells a funny tale to his beloved granddaughters. This storyteller appears in the guise of a wise old man reminiscent of legendary Hungarian folk tale collector and editor Elek Benedek, pennamed Old Father Elek [*Elek apó*], who gathered and reworked for children the marvelous folkloric heritage of his native Transylvania, commonly referred to in the collective Hungarian cultural imagery as Fairyland. Old Father Elek, 'the great storyteller,' was the founding editor of national children's magazines *Az Én Újságom* [My Journal], *Jó Pajtás* [Good Fellow], and *Cimbora* [Chuckaboo]; he took part in the publishing of a book series for youngsters, *Kis Könyvtár* [Small Library]; and he translated and adapted for children tales from the *Arabian Nights* and the Brothers Grimm in *Ezüst Mesekönyv* and *Arany Mesekönyv* [The Golden Book of Fairy Tales, The Silver Book of Fairy Tales] as well as seminal pieces of the Hungarian folk tale tradition. The collection of short tales dedicated to his granddaughter soon became a national classic after its first publication in 1911 under the title *Nagyapó mesél Évikének: Versek, mesék, történetek hat-tizenkétéves gyermekeknek* [Grandpa's Tales for Evie: Poems, Tales, Stories for Children between Six and Twelve]. Kosztolányi's decision to change Alice's name to Evie suggests that the child image he had in mind while performing his translation was determined by the mythified authorial persona of the Old Father storyteller that Benedek earned with his canonically established reworkings of folk and fairy tales.

In Kosztolányi's prefatory poem, instead of the initial version's "merry crew" of co-authors, the Grandfather appears as wise master of storytelling, benevolently superior to his implied and actual child readers. The little ones are reduced to the status of mere listeners who should pay close attention to the "dreams, fantasies, adventures they [the girls and/as intended readers] could never call to life" on their own. The prologue's Grandfather narrator mockingly pretends to subordinate himself to the 'girl power' of Evie, Nelly, and Dora ("I had to tell a tale, what else could I do if they demanded so")[4] but he appropriates the authority of authorship from the loquacious, laughing little girls who took such an admittedly active part in the making up of Carroll's fantastic universe. While wildly imaginative Alice daringly challenges existing norms, restrained Evie is unable to live up to these norms: her nonsense is not admirably revolutionary, but, at most, suffocates in pathetic stupidity. In Carroll the adult male author is simply uttering the words, but the adventures are activated by the child readers, who embark on a journey to pursue in fancy "the dream child moving through a land / Of wonders wild and new, / In friendly chat with bird or beast – / And half believe it true" (Carroll 2001, 7). Creative fantasizing agency is attributed to child audiences in the original (emphasized by verbs like 'fancy,' 'move,' 'chat,' 'half-believe') but is usurped by the fictitious creatures and the author animating them in Kosztolányi, where audiences are marked by ignorance, hesitation, and inhibited imaginative faculties: "the fairy arrives, the wonder appears, both animal and bird – they [the little girls] do not know what it is."[5]

In 1958, Hungarian author and literary translator Tibor Szobotka revised Kosztolányi's translation with the twofold aim to both modernize it and bring it closer to the Carrollian original by polishing many of its poetic liberties he called "beautiful insincerities" (Józan 2010, 216).[6] His version contains some exciting solutions; however, the very idea of creating a foreignizing translation by starting out from a hyperdomesticating one, eradicating some bits and keeping others, seems vitally flawed, as the partial rewriting disrupts the carefully crafted dramaturgy of the earlier translation. As a result, Hungarian readers feel baffled by Alice's pondering, after the recital of her poem, about perhaps "not getting it quite right" and "altering the words" – a reaction they fail to understand because they are unfamiliar with the 'right' version most

---

4   In Hungarian: "Így mesélt a regék / Öreg szerelmese / Ábrándot, kalandot, / Milyent nem tudsz te se," "Három huncut kislány / S vágyuk annyi volt csak, / Hogy meséljek nekik, / Míg libeg a csolnak. / Mi mást tehettem hát, / Ha ők parancsolnak?" (Carroll 1935, n.p., trans. Kosztolányi).
5   In Hungarian: "Egyszerre ámulva / Figyelnek mind oda, / Feltűnik a tündér, / Megjelen a csoda, / Állat is, madár is, / Nem tudni, micsoda" (Carroll 1935, n.p., trans. Kosztolányi).
6   In Hungarian: "szép hűtlenség"

English speakers are aware of, and are thus unaware of a parody taking place. Hence, nonsense risks being transformed into meaninglessness in Szobotka's far too literal translation.

In 2009, when Sziget Publishing House commissioned popular Hungarian children's poet Dániel Varró and children's writer Zsuzsa Varró, his sister, to produce a new Hungarian version under the title *Aliz kalandjai Csodaországban és a tükör másik oldalán* [Alice's Adventures in Wonderland and on the Other Side of the Looking Glass] decorated by Tenniel's original illustrations, their clearly articulated intention was "to make order in the philological chaos" (Hercsel 2010, 3). The Varrós opined that the previous Hungarian adaptations misinterpreted the *Alice* novels as simply sweet, funny, light readings of children's literature, and aimed at reclaiming the books' prestigious status in the Hungarian canon of world literature. Their foreignization was informed by the translators' familiarity with the nineteenth-century English cultural context and with the retrospective mythologization of Carroll's oeuvre. Rejecting simplifications, they insisted on preserving in the target text the original's complex layers of allusions to national, historical and biographical specificities. (Funnily enough, their attempts at fidelity were mingled with fantastification, as the dormouse was turned into a wombat – under the influence of chronologically erroneous speculations in Martin Gardner's annotations – to mockingly refer to the Rossettis' pet Carroll might have encountered.) For the Varrós, Wonderland, far from an easy infantile delight, offers a serious linguistic experiment, a feat in paradoxical logic, complex witticisms, and a grotesque vision of miscommunication with unkind, peevish, pugnacious trickster figures (reflected in the names of the Insane Hatter or Nasty Chubby for Humpty Dumpty [*Undi Dundi*]) who frighten children and amuse only more mature audiences with a taste for the macabre. The choice of words in the Varrós' puns comes from the vocabulary of adolescents rather than children, and their relocating both Alice and her readers as rebellious teenage figures echoes the shift of addressee characteristic of contemporary visual adaptations of Wonderland. Their translation resonates particularly well with Tim Burton's 3D CGI family adventure, a dark Disney production that hit cinemas the same year as the translation and similarly targeted dual or 'crossover' audiences (Beckett 2008). The film turned Alice into a Jeanne d'Arc-like action heroine who rejects repressive social mores and tyrannical regimes to liberate Underland and reclaim a respect for creative fantasists (see Kérchy 2016). Like the Varrós', this is a daring yet self-ironic freedom fighter Alice tailored for trauma-ridden postmillennial times.

As for the prefatory poem's implied reader address, the Varrós adopt a midway solution, where Alice listens in silence yet half-believes, combining passivity and activity. It is only the latest 2013 Hungarian translation by Anikó Szilágyi, a Hungarian scholar working for a PhD in translation studies at Glasgow University, that attempts to reproduce Carroll's original faith invested in the girl child reader's imagination. In Szilágyi's translation, the child audience regains the imaginative agency so characteristic of the original: "They embark on a journey in/on their thoughts / along with the dream-girl / they wrestle with and overcome a multitude of riddles they believe to be true / they converse with animals / they can't even tell how many of them."[7] The girl child reader thus actively initiates adventures, fantasizes, fights, and overcomes obstacles. Her exclamation "Curiouser and curiouser!" signals eager curiosity and excitement. (In Szilágyi's translation it reads, "It is getting ever so exciting!", while in the Varrós' as "Stranger and the strangest!", in Szobotka's as "More or more funny!", and in Kosztolányi's as "Increasingly swell!").[8] The agency attributed to the girl child shows in the omniscient narrator's bracketed comments on soliloquist Alice's psychoanarration: Carroll's original, "(Which was very likely true.)" (Carroll 2001, 13), becomes "(And she was most probably right about this.)" (Carroll 2013, 9, trans. Szilágyi).[9] Szilágyi's is a genuinely contemporary translation: Alice, both implied reader and author, emerges as a self-confident and courageous heroine – like in many contemporary visual adaptations which revive the image-textual significations of Tenniel's original illustrations for Carroll's classic. There, the beamish knight defeating the monstrous Jabberwock is an alter ego of Alice herself, the implied reader/co-author who overcomes textual monstrosity (see Hancher 2019). (Alice never meets the Jabberwock in person. She only encounters a narrative replica of this mythological beast in the form of a nonsensical poem in mirror-writing. Her repeated efforts to decode this key text of Looking-Glass Land's fictitious legendarium represent her relentless imaginative agency.)

Szilágyi, specialized in translating children's literature, combines domesticating familiarization and foreignizing defamiliarization: her text version aims to delight child audiences without assuming that original meanings need to be sanitized, infantilized, or simplified to find their way to the hearts of young readers. Her nonsense strives to stay confusing in a comprehensible manner while

---

7   In Hungarian: "Gondolatban útra kelnek / Ők az álom-lánnyal, / Megbirkóznak igaznak hit / Rengeteg talánnyal, / Állatokkal társalogva– / Azt se tudják, hánnyal" (Carroll 2013, 3, trans. Szilágyi).
8   In Hungarian: "Ez egyre izgisebb!" (Carroll 2013, 16, trans. Szilágyi 16), "Egyre murisabb!" (Carroll 1958, 14, trans. Szobotka), "Egyre klasszabb!" (Carroll 1935, 15, trans. Kosztolányi), "Még furább, legfurább!" (Carroll 2009, 20, trans. Varró).
9   In Hungarian: "(Ebben valószínűleg igaza is volt.)" (Carroll 2013, 9, trans. Szilágyi).

trusting in the creative collaborative capacities of underage booklovers. Her wordplays are multifarious, ranging from cute (Alice mistakes the "antipodes" for "antipathies" in Carroll, and with "antisquirrels" based on an erroneous homonymic identification in Szilágyi (*antipódus/antimókus*)) to the macabre ("Do bats eat cats?" in Alice's monologue reads as "Do bats eat catblood?" grounding a pun in a similarity of sounds: the last syllable of *denevér*, bat in Hungarian, means 'blood,' hence hybrid, possibly horrendous creatures are created with the confusion of the final syllables of cats and bat (*macskák/denevér* becomes *denék/macskavér*)).[10] Of the Hungarian translators of the prologue, Szilágyi is the only female translator and the youngest one, aware of her proximity to Alice the listener and Carroll the storyteller, too. Her translation reminds us of how Columbia University in 1932, at the centennial of Carroll's birth, awarded the eighty-year-old Alice Liddell an honorary doctorate of letters to acknowledge her "noteworthy contribution to English literature" as a co-creator of a national literary treasure for "awaking with her girlhood's charm the ingenious fancy of a mathematician familiar with imaginary quantities, stirring him to reveal his complete understanding of the heart of a child" (Hond 2009, n.p.).

Conclusion

As my brief overview of the Hungarian translation history of the *Alice* books has tried to demonstrate, the dominant images of childhood prevailing in the sociohistorical cultural context of the target audience addressed inherently influence the translation strategies employed and may modify the meanings and overall effects of the storyworld. For example, the translator's choice to infantilize or on the contrary to age the original author's initial concept of the child reader in both the intradiegetic and extradiegetic realms tones down the ambiguous appeal of Carroll's crossover children's book by bringing it closer to a more clear-cut generic category: a pre-readers' picture book in Altay's case, or a young-adult coming-of-age narrative in the Varrós' case. The idea of childness that the translator wishes to convey determines which layer of the source text gains emphasis: Wonderland's fairy-tale enchantment or metalinguistic wit. The former stimulates a more docile affective response of amazement (like Altay or Kosztolányi); the latter demands interactive intellectual agency from readers better versed in textual tricks (as in the Varrós and Szilágyi). Wonderland's verbal exchanges reflect both on the discursive

---

10   In Hungarian: "Esznek a macskák denevért? Esznek a denék macskavért?" (Carroll 2013, 10, trans. Szilágyi).

discipline and the ludic liberation of the child reader, and it is the translator's task to decide to put 'explanations' or 'adventures' first.

Only a careful positioning of the implied and intended reader figure can guarantee that the making of Wonderland remains acknowledged as a collective feat of adult author and child reader. The translator's address of the child reader therefore proves to be more than just an artistic decision. It belongs to what Van Coillie and Verschueren (2016) call the moral, pedagogical responsibilities that translators of children's literature have as "mediators" facilitating the negotiating "dialogue" between source text and a target audience who has no mastery of foreign languages, and for whom "translations are the sole means to enter into genuine contact with foreign languages and cultures," "to step through the magical looking-glass and venture into the beguiling world of Andersen's fairy tales, and Alice's unexpected, mind-boggling Wonderland, or indulge in the charmingly anachronistic fabrications of Pippi Longstocking, and (…) the thrilling, often spine-chilling universe of Harry Potter" (*ibid.*, v).

Bibliography

Attardo, Salvatore. 2014. *Encyclopedia of Humor Studies*. Los Angeles: Sage, Texas A&M.

Bassnett, Susan. 2002. *Translation Studies*. New York: Routledge.

Beckett, Sandra L. 2008. *Crossover Fiction: Global and Historical Perspectives*. New York: Taylor & Francis.

Beer, Gillian. 2016. *Alice in Space: The Sideways Victorian World of Lewis Carroll*. Chicago: University of Chicago Press.

Benedek, Elek. 1987 [1911]. *Nagyapó mesél Évikének: Versek, mesék, történetek hattizenkétéves gyermekeknek*. Budapest: Terra, Kossuth.

Benjamin, Walter. 2005. "The Task of the Translator." In *The Translation Studies Reader*, edited by Lawrence Venuti, 15–23. London: Routledge.

Burton, Tim, dir. 2010. *Alice in Wonderland*. Walt Disney Pictures.

Carroll, Lewis. 1927. *Alice a Csodák országában*. Translated by Margit Altay. Budapest: Pallas.

Carroll, Lewis. 1929. *Alisz kalandjai Csodaországban*. Translated by Andor Juhász. Budapest: Béta Irodalmi Rt.

Carroll, Lewis. 1935. *Évike Tündérországban*. Translated by Dezső Kosztolányi. Budapest: Gergely R.

Carroll, Lewis. 1958. *Alice Csodaországban*. Translated by Dezső Kosztolányi and Tibor Szobotka. Budapest: Móra.

Carroll, Lewis. 2001. *The Annotated Alice: The Definitive Edition. Alice's Adventures in Wonderland* (1865), *Through the Looking Glass* (1871), edited by Martin Gardner. London: Penguin.

Carroll, Lewis. 2009. *Aliz kalandjai Csodaországban és a tükör másik oldalán*. Translated by Zsuzsa and Dániel Varró. Budapest: Sziget.

Carroll, Lewis. 2013. *Aliz Csodaországban*. Translated by Anikó Szilágyi. Cathair na Mart: Everytype.

Goldthwaite, John. 1996. *The Natural History of Make-Believe: A Guide to the Principal Works of Britain, Europe, and America*. Oxford: Oxford University Press.

Hancher, Michael. 2019. *The Tenniel Illustrations to the 'Alice' Books*. Columbus: Ohio State University Press.

Hercsel, Adél. 2010. "Aliz túl a Maszat-hegyen. Varró Zsuzsa és Varró Dániel az Alice fordításáról mesél a Könyvfesztiválon." *Litera*, March 28, 2010.

Heyman, Michael and Kevin Shortsleeve. 2011. "Nonsense." In *Keywords for Children's Literature*, edited by Philip Nel and Lissa Paul, 165–169. New York: New York University Press.

Hond, Paul. 2009. "Alice in Columbialand." *Columbia: The Magazine of Columbia University*. Fall issue. Accessed April 14, 2020. https://magazine.columbia.edu/article/alice-columbialand.

Hunt, Peter. 1999. *Understanding Children's Literature*. New York: Routledge.

Iché, Virginie. 2015. *L'Esthétique du Jeu dans les Alice de Lewis Carroll*. Paris: L'Harmattan.

Iser, Wolfgang. 1978. *The Implied Reader*. Baltimore: Johns Hopkins University Press.

Józan, Ildikó. 2010. "Nyelvek poétikája. Alice, Évike, Kosztolányi meg a szakirodalom és a fordítás." *Filológiai Közlöny* 56, no. 3: 213–238.

Kappanyos, András. 2015. *Bajuszbögre, lefordítatlan: Műfordítás, adaptáció, kulturális transzfer*. Budapest: Balassi.

Kappanyos, András. 2018. "A műfordítás mint extrémsport: *Évike Tündérországban*." *Studia Litteraria*, 1–2: 111–130.

Kérchy, Anna. 2015. "Essay on the Hungarian Translations of Wonderland." In *Alice in a World of Wonderlands: Translations of Lewis Carroll's Masterpiece*, edited by Jon Lindseth and Markus Lang, 294–299. New Castle, Del.: Oak Knoll Press.

Kérchy, Anna. 2016. *Alice in Transmedia Wonderland: Curiouser and Curiouser. New Forms of a Children's Classic*. Jefferson: McFarland.

Kohlt, Franziska. 2016. "Alice in the Asylum." *The Conversation*, May 31, 2016. Accessed April 14, 2020. http://theconversation.com/alice-in-the-asylum-wonderland-and-the-real-mad-tea-parties-of-the-victorians-60136.

Kosztolányi, Dezső. 1942. "Ábécé a fordításról és ferdítésről." In *Ábécé*, 184–191. Budapest: Nyugat.

Kristeva, Julia. 1984. *Revolution in Poetic Language*. Translated by Margaret Waller. New York: Columbia University Press.

Lecercle, Jean Jacques. 1994. *Philosophy of Nonsense: The Intuitions of Victorian Nonsense Literature*. New York: Routledge.

Lecercle, Jean-Jacques. 2008. "Translate It, Translate It Not." *Translation Studies* 1: 90–102.

M. M. (Medve, Miklós). 1932. "A százéves Lewis Carroll." *Korunk* 3 (March): 222–223.

Nodelman, Perry. 2008. *The Hidden Adult: Defining Children's Literature*. Baltimore: John Hopkins University Press.

Oittinnen, Riita. 2006. "The Verbal and the Visual: On the Carnivalism and Dialogics of Translating for Children." In *The Translation of Children's Literature: A Reader*, edited by Gillian Lathey, 84–98. Toronto: Multilingual Matters.

Schmid, Wolf. 2013. "Implied Reader." In *The Living Handbook of Narratology*, edited by Peter Hühn. Hamburg: Hamburg University Press. Online OA E-book. https://www.lhn.uni-hamburg.de/

Van Coillie, Jan and Walter P. Verschueren, eds. 2016. *Children's Literature in Translation: Challenges and Strategies*. New York: Routledge.

Venuti, Lawrence. 1995. *The Translator's Invisibility*. London: Routledge.

Weaver, Warren. 1964. *Alice in Many Tongues: The Translations of Alice in Wonderland*. Madison: The University of Wisconsin Press.

Zipes, Jack. 1987. *Victorian Fairy Tales: The Revolt of the Fairies and Elves*. New York: Routledge.

"Better watch it, mate" and "Listen 'ere, lads"

The cultural specificity of the English translation of Janusz Korczak's classic *Król Maciuś Pierwszy*

Michał Borodo

Abstract

The chapter concentrates on *Król Maciuś Pierwszy* [King Matt the First] (1922), a classic children's book by Polish-Jewish author and pedagogue Janusz Korczak, and its British and American translations, with a special focus on the translation by Adam Czasak published in London in 1990. The chapter demonstrates that the translator culturally assimilated, or, using Venutian terms, domesticated Korczak's classic tale, adapting it, linguistically and culturally, to suit the target-culture context. The translator achieved this by culturally assimilating protagonists' names and using a broad spectrum of lexical items typical of vibrant and colloquial British English. However, instead of making use of standard 'literary' English, the British translation also activates a non-dominant, lower status, 'marginal discourse' as some of the speech patterns used by the translator can be associated with a particular social demographic, that is, the lower middle class and working class. This makes for a rather complex domestication/foreignization dynamic and can be connected to a point that Venuti makes, that foreignization can also be effected by drawing on 'marginal', 'non-standard' and 'heterogeneous' discourse in the target language.

Introduction

This chapter focuses on the cultural specificity of the 1990 translation of *Król Maciuś Pierwszy* [King Matt the First], a classic of Polish children's literature, originally published in 1922 and written by Polish-Jewish author and pedagogue Janusz Korczak. The chapter demonstrates that the English translation, created by Adam Czasak and published in London under the title *Little King Matty*, was linguistically and culturally adapted in order to suit the target-culture context. This was done not only in the more obvious sense of adapting child protagonists' names and culture-specific items but, more interestingly, in the sense of introducing a wide array of lexical items. These include nouns, adjectives, verbs, idioms, sayings and interjections belonging to the colloquial British English commonly attributed to people in the lower middle class or working class. Referring to Lawrence Venuti's (1995, 1998) concepts of domestication and foreignization, the chapter argues that the translator assimilated the Polish classic to the values of the target culture and that the English text may be regarded as a domesticated translation, which resembles and reads like a source text originally written in English, although paradoxically it also exemplifies Venuti's idea of foreignization to some extent.

Cultural specificity and translation

Although every translation is to some extent ethnocentric, as a certain degree of cultural reduction and exclusion is inevitable (Venuti 1995, 310), the translator is often confronted with a choice between two divergent ways of rendering the original in translation. These two disparate strategies include foreignization, the aim of which is "to register the linguistic and cultural difference of the foreign text," and domestication, which involves the "reduction of the foreign text to target-language cultural values" (*ibid.*, 20). A domesticated translation will "conform to values currently dominating the target-language culture, taking a conservative and openly assimilationist approach to the foreign text, appropriating it to support domestic canons, publishing trends, political alignments" (Venuti 1998, 240). It will thus resemble a text originally written in the target culture. A foreignized translation, on the other hand, will counter the ethnocentric tendencies of the receiving culture by foregrounding the values of the source culture or activating marginalized resources in the target language (Venuti 1995, 20), drawing the reader's attention to translation as translation.

Popularized by Venuti, notions of domestication and foreignization are not new in translation theory. Venuti himself draws inspiration from Friedrich Schleiermacher's lecture on translation, published in 1813, in which the German philosopher and translator distinguishes "two roads" open to "the genuine translator," that is, "[e]ither the translator leaves the author in peace, as much as possible, and moves the reader toward him. Or he leaves the reader in peace, as much as possible, and moves the author toward him" (Lefevere 1992, 149). Venuti's other sources of inspiration are Antoine Berman, questioning ethnocentric translation and focusing on translation ethics (Venuti 1995, 20), and Phillip Lewis, with his concept of "abusive fidelity," which resists the values of the target culture through avoiding fluency, favoring linguistic experimentation and foregrounding cultural difference (*ibid.*, 23–24). Venuti also situates himself in direct opposition to the translation tradition epitomized by Eugene Nida, criticizing the notion of "dynamic equivalence" advocated for Bible translation projects, on account of its "ethnocentric violence" and emphasis on "naturalness of expression" (*ibid.*, 21–23). Similar to Schleiermacher, and quite unlike Nida, Venuti is an advocate for moving the reader toward the author, rather than moving the author toward the reader.

Venuti is a prescriptivist and his enterprise, favoring the politico-cultural strategy of foreignization, needs to be understood in that prescriptive context. He was also assuming that his theories would apply to adult literary fiction rather than children's literature and they are based on the assumption of translation of literary, often experimental, fiction from a 'minor' to a 'major' language. Prescriptive approaches to children's literature translation can be found elsewhere, however, and can be traced back to the early days of CLTS (Children's Literature Translation Studies) (Borodo 2017, 36). For example, Carmen Bravo-Villasante (1978, 46) observes that cultural adaptation should generally be avoided in translations for young readers, and Birgit Stolt (1978, 132) points out that translators should not underestimate children's ability to re-experience the foreign and the exotic. Göte Klingberg (1978, 86) similarly suggests that cultural assimilation should not be overused by translators as promoting knowledge about other cultures is one of the major aims of translations for children. A further example of a prescriptive approach is the translation project described by Isabel Pascua (2003), based on the translation into Spanish of multicultural Canadian children's literature reflecting a variety of writers' ethnic backgrounds in order to instill greater tolerance towards other cultures. The assumption behind this project was that the translations should be produced in fluent and accessible Spanish, but with the cultural other in the form of original names and customs consistently retained, as children "should feel that they are reading a translation" (Pascua 2003, 280), which may bring to mind earlier CLTS approaches as well as Venuti.

Earlier CLTS approaches of the 1970s came under criticism from Riitta Oittinen (2000), who advocates a freer and more functionalist translation approach to children's fiction, claiming that the translator should have the right to express the original in novel ways in the new cultural reality, a sign of respect towards both the original author and the reading child. In this context, Maria Nikolajeva (2006) even writes of the Klingberg School and the Oittinen School, the former favoring faithful and literal translation, the latter free and functionalist translation methods. Similar to Oittinen, Nikolajeva (2006, 278) writes in favor of the freer translation approach, which does not refrain from cultural mediation, observing that translations that sound too "strange" may be rejected by young readers. One can also adopt a middle course and a non-prescriptive approach, accepting the value of the arguments of both sides. Gillian Lathey (2016, 38), for example, observes that children's literature may sometimes require a greater degree of cultural assimilation than adult fiction, but also acknowledges that, especially in today's globalized world, children are constantly confronted with new concepts and information anyway and that "adaptation of a foreign milieu removes an element of challenge and excitement."

Many studies on the treatment of cultural specificity in translated children's fiction are descriptive rather than prescriptive in nature. This may be exemplified with various analyses of translators' treatment of culture-specific items (e.g. Mazi-Leskovar 2003; Ippolito 2006) or the influence of national and cultural stereotypes on the selection and translation of books for young readers (e.g. Rudvin 1994; Frank 2007). As the latter two studies demonstrate, translated children's literature seems particularly vulnerable to the perpetuation of stereotypes, with Helen Frank (2007) arguing that French translations of Australian children's books contribute to a stereotypical image of exotic, wild and rural Australia. Similarly, Mette Rudvin (1994, 209) observes that the image of Norway constructed in English translations is predominantly that of a country inseparably related to nature. One of the most popular focuses of children's literature translation criticism in the opening years of the twenty-first century was the treatment of cultural specificity in the translations of *Harry Potter* (e.g. Davies 2003; Valero Garcés 2003; Woźniak 2006), which provided an opportunity to examine translators' preference for either foreignization or domestication in different cultures across the globe. It should also be noted that translations for children will not always necessarily exhibit a clear-cut preference for either of these orientations, but may be characterized by more nuanced and hybrid ways of dealing with cultural specificity, as demonstrated by Haidee Kruger (2013) in her analysis of translators' treatment of proper names, forms of address, loan words, cultural items and idiomatic expressions in the South African context.

The English translation examined in this chapter does exhibit a preference for domestication, although to some degree it also exemplifies Venuti's concept of foreignization. *Little King Matty* was culturally and linguistically adapted by Adam Czasak on various planes with regard to proper names and cultural items but also less obvious markers of culture such as grammatical and lexical patterns. The focus of this chapter will mainly be the latter; that is, the lexical patterns which appear in the English translation and are characteristic of informal British English.

Contextualizing *Little King Matty*

Król Maciuś Pierwszy, published originally in 1922, is the most famous children's novel by Janusz Korczak (the pen name of Henryk Goldszmit), a Polish-Jewish children's writer, educator, social activist, journalist and pediatrician. In pre-war Poland, Korczak was known for his innovative pedagogical methods as the head of a progressive Warsaw orphanage for Jewish children. He also co-established another Warsaw orphanage for Polish children and ran his own radio program about children's rights. He was killed in the Nazi German concentration camp in Treblinka in the summer of 1942, together with his associates and the children from his orphanage, whom he had refused to abandon. Throughout his life, Korczak was a fervent proponent of children's rights. He objected to corporal punishment and subjecting the young to drilling and humiliation (Olczak-Ronikier 2011, 61). In his pioneering work, he advocated showing respect for every child, treating children as partners and equals, engaging in dialogue with them, and acknowledging their needs, rights and dignity (Korczak 1929). Korczak's ideas on children's rights were, according to Moses Stambler, "too avant-garde to develop into a major movement during his lifetime, but they fit in very well with contemporary ideas on human rights and improving the status of disadvantaged groups" (Stambler 1980, 3). Korczak's pedagogical ideas found reflection in the orphanages that he created, which were based on self-government, mutual support, justice, dialogue and democracy. The small children's communities even had their own newspaper, court and parliament (Olczak-Ronikier 2011, 219–221). These ideas can also be found in Korczak's *Król Maciuś Pierwszy*, which narrativizes the idea of granting children autonomy to rule themselves.

A classic of Polish children's literature, *Król Maciuś Pierwszy* is the story of Maciuś, a young prince who after the loss of his parents becomes the king of an imaginary kingdom partly modeled on Korczak's homeland, Poland. Maciuś introduces a number of bold and risky social reforms, such as establishing a children's parliament, which has the authority to decide about the most important matters in his kingdom. Despite having good intentions, he makes numerous mistakes, however. His friends and subjects fail him, his advisors betray him, the country is invaded, and the young king barely escapes death. Eventually he is sent to live in exile on a desert island. The novel is not necessarily widely read by children in Poland today, but both the author and the book are culturally significant, with the story of the orphaned king appearing on the supplementary reading list in primary schools. It was also recently popularized by a TV series and animated film, a Polish–French–German coproduction.

Interestingly, *Król Maciuś Pierwszy* is the most frequently translated children's novel in the history of Polish–English translation. It was first translated in 1945 in New York by Edith and Sidney Sulkin under the title *Matthew the Young King*. The second English translation, *King Matt the First* by Richard Lourie, appeared forty years later, in 1986, also in New York. Adam Czasak's *Little King Matty*, published in London in 1990, was the third translation of Korczak's novel, while the most recent English-language translation was completed by Adam Fisher and Ben Torrent and published in New York in 2014. Three out of four English translations were thus originally published in the US and only one translation, *Little King Matty*, which is the focus of this chapter, was published in Britain.

Its translator, Adam Czasak, was born to Polish parents in north-west England and "studied Polish Philology at the Jagiellonian University, Kraków and English at the University of Ulster and University College London" (Korczak 1990, 1). Apart from his translation of Korczak, Czasak's major achievements in the field of literary translation include his translations of Sławomir Mrożek, Stanisław Ignacy Witkiewicz, Tadeusz Różewicz, Jarosław Iwaszkiewicz, Jerzy Szaniawski and Zbigniew Herbert. A versatile bilingual, professional translator, and interpreter, Adam Czasak also specializes in a number of other fields, such as banking and finance, marketing, legal translation, court interpreting and conference interpreting. He currently lives in Kraków, Poland. His 1990 translation includes not only *Król Maciuś Pierwszy*, but also the sequel *Król Maciuś na wyspie bezludnej* [King Matt on the Desert Island], written by Korczak in 1923. The translation as a whole bears the title *Little King Matty… and the Desert Island*, with the titles of the two novels actually combined into one. Notably, Czasak's translation of the second part of the boy king's adventures is the only English-language version of that novel created to date.

The cultural specificity of *Little King Matty*

Korczak's classic tale was linguistically and culturally adapted by Czasak to the new target context in a number of ways. Czasak adapted child protagonists' names for English readers, rendering Korczak's Maciuś, Felek, Staś, Helenka, Tomek and Antek from the original as Matty, Feldo, Stan, Elly, Tommy and

Andy respectively. Only 'Irenka', which was rendered as 'Irena' rather than the English equivalent 'Irene', diverges from this pattern. Other noteworthy patterns can also be observed with regard to the treatment of culture-specific items related to customs, traditions and food items. For example, Czasak replaces *śmigus*, a traditional Polish Easter festivity involving dousing others with water, with 'Easter-eggs,' certainly a more recognizable tradition in England than the Polish water dousing. On several occasions, he omits references to vodka, replacing it with whisky, and he replaces the characteristically Polish *tłusty czwartek*, or Fat Thursday, the last Thursday of carnival, with the English Pancake Tuesday. As will be demonstrated below, the 1990 translation also contains a wide array of British English expressions, such as 'lads,' 'mates,' 'smashing,' 'brilliant,' 'mingy,' 'peckish,' 'barmy,' 'to nick,' 'to waffle,' 'to take the mickey,' 'righto' and 'blimey,' among others. To better illustrate Adam Czasak's strategy, his 1990 translation will be compared with two other English translations of Korczak's novel – Richard Lourie's *King Matt the First*, from 1986, and Adam Fisher and Ben Torrent's *King Matthew the First*, published in 2014.

"Better watch it, mate" and "Listen 'ere, lads"

The translation by Czasak contains numerous references to people which can be associated with British English, such as the colloquial 'mates' or 'lads.' They appear with a high frequency in the conversations of both adults and children. In Table 1, these forms are compared with the corresponding lines from American translations by Lourie and by Fisher and Torrent.

The first two examples in the table, "Better watch it, mate" and "Hey, mate, heard the news, have you?", both contain the informal interjection 'mate,' the most typical common noun used as a vocative in British English according to Algeo (2006, 210). For comparison, Americans would instead use in this context: 'bro,' 'man,' 'dude,' 'guys,' 'folks' or 'buddy' (*ibid.*), and 'buddy' is indeed used by Fisher and Torrent. Elsewhere in the British translation, the reader will come across other uses of this form such as: "So me and my mates decided to get rid of her" (Korczak 1990, 198), "Watch it, mate!", "Then I started ringing up my mates" (*ibid.*, 215), and "Anyway, there's no telling what he'll do next. Or that Feldo mate of his" (*ibid.*, 248). The next two examples in the table contain the word 'lad,' which appears in American English in the sense of a 'boy' or a 'youth' but is nevertheless used more often in British English (Schur 2001, 182). "Listen 'ere, lads" and "Simmer down, lads," said by the soldiers to little Matty and his friend Feldo travelling to the front, may both be associated with British English.

Table 1. Examples of selected personal references in *Little King Matty*

Korczak (1922)	Lourie (1986)	Czasak (1990)	Fisher & Torrent (2014)
Bądź no ostrożny, synek. (Korczak [1922] 1992, 38)	Better be careful, sonny. (Korczak 1986, 45)	Better watch it, **mate**. (Korczak 1990, 42)	You'd better watch your language. (Korczak 2014, 37)
– Ej, kamrat, a słyszałeś już nowinę? – Jaką? – pyta się Felek. (Korczak [1922] 1992, 234)	"You heard the news?" "No, what?" asked Felek. (Korczak 1986, 311)	"Hey, **mate**, heard the news, have you?" "What news?" Feldo asked. (Korczak 1990, 241)	"Hey buddy, have you heard the news?" "What news?" Felix opened his eyes wide. (Korczak 2014, 251)
Słuchajcie, chłopcy, czy wy naprawdę myślicie wojować? (Korczak [1922] 1992, 40)	Listen, are you boys really thinking of fighting in the war? (Korczak 1986, 48)	Listen 'ere, **lads,** you're not serious about going to war, are you? (Korczak 1990, 45)	Listen, boys, are you really thinking of fighting the enemy? (Korczak 2014, 39)
– No, chłopcy, dajcie pokój – i tak nic nie wymyślimy. Lepiej sobie coś wesołego zaśpiewać. (Korczak [1922] 1992, 41)	"Well, you guys, forget it, there's nothing we can do about it. Better if we sing some happy songs," said one soldier. (Korczak 1986, 50)	"Simmer down, **lads**. No point arguing. How about a song instead?" (Korczak 1990, 46)	"Hey boys, what's the point of this idle talk? We won't reinvent gunpowder. We're better off singing a cheerful song." (Korczak 2014, 41)

These examples are also noteworthy for other reasons. Some of the excerpts in the table contain tag questions ("going to war, are you?", "heard the news, have you?"), which seem to be more frequent in British than in American English. For example, on the basis of their corpus study, Gunnel Tottie and Sebastian Hoffmann (2006, 306) argue that "there are nine times as many tag questions in British English as in similar types of American English," especially in colloquial language. Another characteristic feature of the British translation, which is found in the conversations among children and soldiers, is h-dropping, which may be again illustrated with "Listen 'ere, lads." This has definite class associations, being seen as a marker of working-class speech. As noted by Lynda Mugglestone (2003, 95):

> The use of /h/ in modern English has come to stand as one of the foremost signals of social identity, its presence in initial positions associated almost inevitably with the 'educated' and 'polite' while its loss commonly triggers popular connotations with the 'vulgar', the 'ignorant', and the 'lower class.'

The colloquial references to 'lads' and 'mates,' combined with the use of tag questions and h-dropping, reinforce the colloquial tone of the novel and, in terms of social identity, may be associated with a particular social demographic, that is the lower middle class or working class.

'Nicking,' 'waffling' and 'taking the mickey'

Other British English forms appearing in Czasak's translation include such verb phrases as 'to nick,' 'waffle,' 'buzz off' and 'take the mickey.' Their usage is shown in Table 2.

When the journalist threatens to reveal Matty's friend Feldo's wrongdoings to the king, this is expressed by Czasak with "I'm off to tell the king that you've been nicking parcels." The verb 'to nick,' which means 'to steal' in British English, "has been used in this sense since at least the 1820s," being "rare in the USA" (Thorne 2007, 308), where the informal 'to pinch' would be more common (Schur 2001, 219). Then, when Matty wants the minister of war to inform him about the military potential of his kingdom, he demands, "But quickly – no waffling," using the verb 'to waffle,' a disapproving term for verbosity or for "engaging in silly chatter" (*ibid.*, 356). The third example in the table contains the idiom 'to take the mickey out of someone,' an informal British English expression, "in use since the 1940s" (Thorne 2007, 434), which means to "tease, ridicule, or make fun" of someone (Algeo 2006, 275). For comparison, the American versions simply use the more standard form 'to make fun of someone' instead in this instance. The final example in the table, the informal and chiefly British 'to buzz off' (Schur 2001, 49), is a phrasal verb denoting 'to go away' often used in the imperative. This form is used in reference to Matty's ministers: "They'd better start listening to him now – or buzz off." In the original, Korczak uses informal style which resembles spoken Polish, but, with such examples as 'to nick,' 'waffle,' 'take the mickey' or 'buzz off,' the British translation makes use of even more informal language.

'What a smashing time' and 'brilliant news'

Other instances of typically British English expressions which appear in Czasak's translation are 'brilliant' and 'smashing' (see Table 3). Synonymous with 'excellent,' the informal and slightly old-fashioned 'smashing,' the "colloquialism of the 1950s [which] was revived, often with ironic overtones, after 2000" (Thorne 2007, 403), is used by Czasak to refer to Matty's experience of

Table 2. Examples of British English verb phrases in *Little King Matty*

Korczak (1922)	Lourie (1986)	Czasak (1990)	Fisher & Torrent (2014)
Jak nie, to idę do króla i powiem, że kradniesz paczki i bierzesz łapówki. (Korczak [1922] 1992, 221)	If you don't, I'll go to the king and tell him that you're stealing packages and taking bribes. (Korczak 1986, 293)	In that case I'm off to tell the king that **you've been nicking** parcels and taking bribes. (Korczak 1990, 228)	OK, that's fine; I'll just go and tell the king about the stolen parcels and the bribes. (Korczak 2014, 236)
– Panie ministrze wojny, co pan powie? Krótko – bez wstępów. Bo i ja wiem wiele. (Korczak [1922] 1992, 221)	Mr. Minister of War, tell me everything you know. But be quick and don't beat around the bush, because I know a lot myself already. (Korczak 1986, 293)	Minister, tell me what you know. But quickly – **no waffling** – because I've already heard a lot myself. (Korczak 1990, 229)	Minister of War, tell me what you know. Briefly, quickly and without a lengthy introduction if you please; I just want the gist of it. I think I have a pretty sound grasp of the situation. (Korczak 2014, 237)
Maciuś z nich zażartował. (Korczak [1922] 1992, 171)	Matt was making fun of them. (Korczak 1986, 225)	Matty was **taking the mickey out of them**. (Korczak 1990, 178)	Matthew was making fun of them. (Korczak 2014, 182)
Dość tych ministerialnych rządów. Albo się muszą słuchać, albo – fora ze dwora. (Korczak [1922] 1992, 71)	The ministers had ruled long enough. Either they obey him or out they go. (Korczak 1986, 90)	Enough of their messing! They'd better start listening to him now – or **buzz off**. (Korczak 1990, 78)	"Enough is enough!" he determined. "It's about time I put a stop to the rule of ministers in my kingdom. Either you listen to me, or get lost, dear ministers. (Korczak 2014, 75)

playing with other children in the garden. Thus, King Matty had "a smashing time" in Czasak's translation, but he had "a wonderful time" and "a great time" in the American versions. 'Smashing' might have been a little *passé* in 1990, but the fact that the context is literary might make it more acceptable. Perhaps the fact that Korczak's text was written many years before Czasak's translation, and because the world described in the book is a bygone world, old-fashioned language was sometimes deliberately used by the translator.

In Czasak, the reader will also encounter 'brilliant,' a word which "in all of its uses, is more frequent in British English than in American" (Algeo 2006, 208). Consequently, when Lourie's translation observes that "things were far

Table 3. Examples of 'brilliant' and 'smashing' in *Little King Matty*

Korczak (1922)	Lourie (1986)	Czasak (1990)	Fisher & Torrent (2014)
Król Maciuś bawił się doskonale. (Korczak [1922] 1992, 15)	King Matt had a wonderful time. (Korczak 1986, 14)	And what a **smashing** time Matty had! (Korczak 1990, 18)	King Matthew was having a great time. (Korczak 2014, 13)
Gazeta przyznawała, że jeszcze nie ma wielkiego porządku… (Korczak [1922] 1992, 209)	The article admitted that things were far from running smoothly… (Korczak 1986, 275)	The paper admitted that it hadn't been a **brilliant** start… (Korczak 1990, 217)	The paper admitted that there were some hiccups… (Korczak 2014, 223)
– Nowina, zgadnij, co się stało? (Korczak [1922] 1992, 210)	"Guess what just happened." (Korczak 1986, 277)	"**Brilliant** news! Guess what's happened?" (Korczak 1990, 217)	"Guess what has happened?" (Korczak 2014, 223)
A to niespodzianka. Doskonale! (Korczak [1922] 1992, 67)	What a surprise! Wonderful! (Korczak 1986, 83)	Well, how about that! **Brilliant**, eh? (Korczak 1990, 73)	"That's great! The sooner the better!" (Korczak 2014, 70)

from running smoothly" and Fisher and Torrent's version notes that "there were some hiccups," referring to one of Matty's controversial reforms, the British translation notes that "it hadn't been a brilliant start." In a similar vein, when overjoyed Klu-Klu, Matty's African friend, runs in clapping her hands and exclaiming, "Guess what just happened" and "Guess what has happened?" in the American versions, in the British translation she exclaims, "Brilliant news! Guess what's happened?"

Finally, when Matty mentions the battle that will take place on the following day, the overjoyed officers use different words in the American ("Wonderful!" and "The sooner the better!") translations and in the British ("Brilliant, eh?") version. The latter is, incidentally, followed with the following string of words: "We can tell our lads that the king's alive and that he'll lead the attack himself" (Korczak 1990, 73), in which the soldiers are again referred to with the British form 'lads.'

'Mingy,' 'peckish' and 'barmy'

Further examples of distinctively British English adjectives used by Czasak include 'mingy,' 'peckish' and 'barmy,' which are presented in Table 4. 'Barmy' relates to someone behaving in a very silly or strange way or someone who is

Table 4. Examples of 'barmy', 'peckish' and 'mingy' in *Little King Matty*

Korczak (1922)	Lourie (1986)	Czasak (1990)	Fisher & Torrent (2014)
zawsze musieli być cicho. A teraz zupełnie jak wariaci... (Korczak [1922] 1992, 220)	They've had to be quiet and obedient all their lives. And so now they're running wild. (Korczak 1986, 292)	So they've always had to be quiet. That's why they've gone a bit **barmy** now... (Korczak 1990, 228)	and they always had to keep quiet. And now, just like madmen or savages... (Korczak 2014, 236)
Kiedy już posłowie się zmęczyli i byli głodni, Felek oddał pod głosowanie projekt. (Korczak [1922] 1992, 202)	When the delegates were tired and hungry, Felek put the proposal to a vote. (Korczak 1986, 269)	When everyone had finished complaining and started feeling a bit **peckish**, Feldo decided to call a vote. (Korczak 1990, 211)	When the deputies got tired and hungry, Felix put the bill to the vote. (Korczak 2014, 217)
Bardzo skąpi są wasi królowie. (Korczak [1922] 1992, 245)	Your kings are awfully stingy. (Korczak 1986, 327)	What **mingy** kings! (Korczak 1990, 254)	Your kings are rather on the mean side, aren't they? (Korczak 2014, 263)
„Skąpy czy co?" – pomyślał Maciuś. (Korczak [1922] 1992, 91)	Is he stingy or what? thought Matt. (Korczak 1986, 118)	"Must be a bit **mingy** him," Matty thought. (Korczak 1990, 99)	*Are you a miser or what?* Thought Matthew. (Korczak 2014, 97, original italics)

crazy (Schur 2001, 21). The adjective is used to refer to the unruly footmen who are "running wild" in Lourie and are behaving "like madmen or savages" in Fisher and Torrent, but who "have gone a bit barmy" in Czasak's translation.

The adjective 'peckish,' which means 'hungry,' 'wanting a snack' or "hankering after a little something to fill the void" (Schur 2001, 242), is used by Czasak to refer to the members of the children's parliament, which was established by Matty. After a turbulent committee session devoted to education reform, they become "hungry" in the American translations but "a bit peckish" in the British version. Czasak also uses the portmanteau adjective 'mingy,' "a term of childish criticism or abuse which is a blend of 'mean' and 'stingy' with which it rhymes" (Thorne 2007, 292). It appears in the British translation when Matty, having lost the war with three other kings and been placed in a cell where he is not fed particularly well, observes, in a mocking tone, "What mingy kings!" Similarly, earlier on, when Matty is visiting one of the three kings for the first time, he is surprised at the modesty of the reception and thinks to

Table 5. Examples of 'flipping heck', 'righto' and 'blimey' in *Little King Matty*

Korczak (1922)	Lourie (1986)	Czasak (1990)	Fisher & Torrent (2014)
Patrz, co ty za milicjant. (Korczak [1922] 1992, 206)	What kind of policeman are you, anyway! (Korczak 1986, 274)	**Flippin' 'eck**, what a hopeless **copper**. (Korczak 1990, 215)	Some policeman you are! (Korczak 2014, 221)
Dobrze, niech będzie wojna… (Korczak [1922] 1992, 11, original italics)	"Fine, let there be war"… (Korczak 1986, 5)	*Righto*, let's have war… (Korczak 1990, 14, original italics)	Then let there be war… (Korczak 2014, 8)
Jak oni się biją! I to chłopcy. Niezdary, niedołęgi, fujary. Biją się już dziesięć minut, a nikt nie zwyciężył. (Korczak [1922] 1992, 193)	And those boys, just look how they fought. The clumsy ninnies, the boobs. They had already been fighting for ten minutes, and nobody had won yet. (Korczak 1986, 256)	**But blimey!** They were hopeless at it. Should've seen them boys. Load of pansies. Ten minutes' hard slog and still no winner. (Korczak 1990, 203)	Oh boy, they cannot fight! thought Clue-Clue. Some boys they are! Klutzes, baboons, lubbers! They've been fighting for ten minutes and neither side has won. (Korczak 2014, 206, original italics)

himself, "Must be a bit mingy him." Syntactically, the personal pronoun at the end can be associated with British English, and such elliptical sentences with emphatic syntactic constructions, which abound in the translation by Czasak, contribute to the more colloquial and conversational tone of the text. By using such forms as "a bit barmy," "a bit peckish" or "Must be a bit mingy him," the translator may be credited with breathing new life into Korczak's classic, using lively, colloquial and conversational language as it is spoken in Britain.

'Flippin' 'eck,' 'righto' and 'blimey'

Czasak's readers will also encounter such expressions as "righto," "blimey" and "flippin' 'eck" (see Table 5). In the first example in the table, the translator introduces the distinctively British and euphemistic qualifier 'flipping' (Algeo 2006, 155), used in a pejorative sense similar to 'bloody' (Schur 2001, 123) and mainly used as a mild intensifier in such expressions as 'flipping hell' or 'flipping heck' (Thorne 2007, 165). This is one of the best examples in the 1990 translation of a British English colloquialism that is linked to class. "Flippin' 'eck" suggests that the speaker is lower middle class or working class, which may be even more apparent because of g-dropping and h-dropping found in this expression. It should also be noted that a qualifier such as 'flipping' is now somewhat dated as English has changed in the three decades since Czasak's translation was published. Apart from the contracted form of 'flipping heck,' the first example in the table also contains the informal British 'copper,' which contrasts with 'policeman' used in the American translations.

Then, Korczak's *Dobrze, niech będzie wojna*, which could be rendered as "All right, let there be war," is translated by Czasak as "Righto, let's have war," with 'righto' being classified as a characteristically British interjection by Algeo (2006, 212). The final example in Table 5 is a passage describing a fight during a session of children's parliament and contains the old-fashioned interjection 'blimey,' referred to as a typically British form by Algeo (2006, 207). This final excerpt is also noteworthy for other reasons. It contains several other colloquial forms, such as the determiner 'load of' and the non-standard use of 'them' as a determiner in "them boys." Employing the personal pronoun 'them' as a demonstrative pronoun is a common feature of non-standard modern English dialects (Trudgill 1990, 79), and the colloquial determiners 'loads of' and 'a load of' are more common in British than in American English (Algeo 2006, 65).

Conclusion

Adam Czasak culturally assimilated, or, using Venutian terms, domesticated Korczak's classic tale in translation. He did that not only in the sense of adapting culture-specific items and protagonists' names but also in terms of introducing a number of lexical items characteristic of the variety of the English language as it is, or at least was, spoken in Britain. The translator's decisions can also be seen in political terms. Some of the speech patterns Czasak uses may be associated with a particular social demographic, that is, the lower middle class and working class, and he uses such patterns for narration as well as for the language of children. Consider the translator's use of such expressions as 'lads,' 'mates,' 'mingy,' 'barmy,' 'to nick,' 'to take the mickey,' 'righto,' 'blimey' and 'flippin' 'eck,' or the informal phonetic and grammatical patterns, such as h-dropping ("Listen 'ere lads"), tag questions ("Hey, mate, heard the news, have you?") and syntactic patterns used for adding emphasis and focusing information in a sentence ("Must be a bit mingy him"). This makes the comparison of the British and American translations in terms of domestication and foreignization slightly more complex. On the one hand, Czasak's is a domesticated translation: it reads fluently, it does not register the cultural and linguistic difference and it does reduce the foreign text to target-language cultural values. However, instead of using standard 'literary' English, Czasak's translation also activates a non-dominant, lower status, 'marginal discourse.' This makes for a rather complex domestication/ foreignization dynamic and can be connected to a point that Venuti makes, that foreignization can also be effected by drawing on 'marginal' and 'non-standard' discourse in the target language. Czasak's 1990 translation may be a noteworthy example of a text largely unaffected by the standardizing role played by translation conventions favoring neutral and 'proper' linguistic forms over non-standard, marginal, regional and heterogeneous language varieties. Lathey points to a tendency in the UK, especially in the first half of the twentieth century, but also beyond, "to choose a higher social register in translation than that used in the source text" (2016, 77). She illustrates this with the British translation of Erich Kästner's classic *Emil and the Detectives*, in which the "stylized Berlin street slang" was transformed by Margaret Goldsmith, in accordance with the literary and sociocultural conventions of the day, into "the dialogue of the English boarding-school story" (*ibid.*, 76). As a result, the original sociolect of the lower middle class was replaced with that of the upper middle class. Czasak did the opposite: he chose a lower social register than that used in the source text, sometimes replacing Korczak's simple and colloquial language with lower middle class and working class English. As a result, Czasak's translation is more colloquial in tone and uses a lower social register than the American translations, but also Korczak's original. The colloquial and distinctively British character of Adam Czasak's translation is not simply a matter of the intrinsic qualities of the target language, but also the result of the translator's decisions and his artistic vision.

Bibliography

Algeo, John. 2006. *British or American English? A Handbook of Word and Grammar Patterns*. Cambridge: Cambridge University Press.

Borodo, Michał. 2017. *Translation, Globalization and Younger Audiences: The Situation in Poland*. Oxford: Peter Lang.

Bravo-Villasante, Carmen. 1978. "Translation Problems in My Experience as a Translator." In *Children's Books in Translation: The Situation and the Problems*, edited by Göte Klingberg, Mary Orvig and Stuart Amor, 46–50. Stockholm: Almqvist & Wiksell.

Davies, Eirlys E. 2003. "A Goblin or a Dirty Nose? The Treatment of Culture-Specific References in Translations of Harry Potter Books." *The Translator* 9, no. 1: 65–100.

Frank, Helen. 2007. *Cultural Encounters in Translated Children's Literature: Images of Australia in French Translation*. Manchester: St. Jerome.

Ippolito, Margherita. 2006. "Translation of Culture-Specific Items in Children's Literature: The Case of Beatrix Potter." In *No Child Is an Island: The Case for Children's Literature in Translation*, edited by Pat Pinsent, 107–118. Lichfield: Pied Piper.

Klingberg, Göte. 1978. "The Different Aspects of Research into the Translation of Children's Books and Its Practical Application." In *Children's Books in Translation: The Situation and the Problems*, edited by Göte Klingberg, Mary Orvig and Stuart Amor, 84–89. Stockholm: Almqvist & Wiksel.

Korczak, Janusz. 1929. *Prawo dziecka do szacunku*. Warszawa: Wydawnictwo Jakuba Mortkowicza.

Korczak, Janusz. 1986. *King Matt the First*. Translated by Richard Lourie. New York: Farrar, Straus and Giroux.

Korczak, Janusz. 1990. *Little King Matty... and the Desert Island*. Translated by Adam Czasak. London: Joanna Pinewood Enterprises.

Korczak, Janusz. 1992 [1922]. *Król Maciuś Pierwszy. Król Maciuś na wyspie bezludnej*. Warszawa: Latona.

Kruger, Haidee. 2013. "The Translation of Cultural Aspects in South African Children's Literature in Afrikaans and English: A Micro-Analysis." *Perspectives: Studies in Translatology* 21, no. 2: 156–181.

Lathey, Gillian. 2016. *Translating Children's Literature*. New York: Routledge.

Mazi-Leskovar, Darja. 2003. "Domestication and Foreignization in Translating American Prose for Slovenian Children." *Meta* 48, no. 1–2: 250–265.

Mugglestone, Lynda. 2003. *'Talking Proper': The Rise of Accent as Social Symbol*. Oxford: Oxford University Press.

Nikolajeva, Maria. 2006. "What Do We Do When We Translate Children's Literature." In *Beyond Babar: The European Tradition in Children's Literature*, edited by Sandra Beckett and Maria Nikolajeva, 277–297. Lanham: The Scarecrow Press.

Oittinen, Riitta. 2000. *Translating for Children*. London: Garland Publishing.

Olczak-Ronikier, Joanna. 2011. *Korczak. Próba biografii*. Warszawa: WAB.

Pascua, Isabel. 2003. "Translation and Intercultural Education." *Meta* 48, no. 1–2: 276–284.

Rudvin, Mette. 1994. "Translation and 'Myth': Norwegian Children's Literature in English." *Perspectives: Studies in Translatology* 2, no. 2: 199–211.

Schleiermacher, Friedrich. 1992. "On the Different Methods of Translating." In *Translation/History/Culture: A Sourcebook*, edited by André Lefevere, 141–166. London/New York: Routledge.

Schur, W. Norman. 2001. *British English A to Zed*. Revised by Eugene Ehrlich. New York: Facts on File.

Stambler, Moses. 1980. "Janusz Korczak: His Perspectives on the Child." *The Polish Review* 25, no. 1: 3–33.

Stolt, Birgit. 1978. "How Emil Becomes Michel – On the Translation of Children's Books." In *Children's Books in Translation: The Situation and the Problems*, edited by Göte Klingberg, Mary Orvig and Stuart Amor, 130–146. Stockholm: Almqvist & Wiksell.

Thorne, Tony. 2007. *Dictionary of Contemporary Slang*. 3rd edition. London: A&C Black.

Tottie, Gunnel and Sebastian Hoffmann. 2006. "Tag Questions in British and American English." *Journal of English Linguistics* 34, no. 4: 283–311.

Trudgill, Peter. 1990. *The Dialects of England*. Oxford: Blackwell.

Valero Garcés, Carmen. 2003. "Translating the Imaginary World in the *Harry Potter* Series or How *Muggles, Quaffles, Snitches,* and *Nickles* Travel to Other Cultures." *Quaderns: Revista de traduccion* 9: 121–134.

Venuti, Lawrence. 1995. *The Translator's Invisibility: A History of Translation*. London: Routledge.

Venuti, Lawrence. 1998. "Strategies of Translation." In *Routledge Encyclopedia of Translation Studies*, edited by Mona Baker, 240–244. London: Routledge.

Woźniak, Monika. 2006. "Czy Harry Potter pod inną nazwą nie mniej by pachniał?" *Przekładaniec* 16, no. 1: 171–192.

Brazilian rewritings of Perrault's short stories

Nineteenth- and twentieth-century versus twenty-first-century retellings and consequences for the moral message

Anna Olga Prudente de Oliveira

Abstract

This chapter analyzes Brazilian rewritings of Charles Perrault's tales from the book *Histoires ou contes du temps passé, avec des moralités or Contes de ma mère l'Oye* (*Stories or Tales from Past Times, with Morals or Mother Goose Tales*) from a diachronic and synchronic perspective with the aim of comprehending the different forms in which the seventeenth-century French writer's stories have been rewritten in the Brazilian literary system. Informed by Descriptive Translation Studies and based on André Lefevere's theoretical work on *rewriting* and *patronage*, it is suggested that rewritings (translations, adaptations, etc.) exert a central role in establishing or maintaining literary canons and project new or distinct images of works and authors. These images align with the poetological and ideological conceptions of rewriters and their editors. Two time periods reflecting different perspectives are observed: from the end of the nineteenth century throughout most of the twentieth century, and from the 1990s into the twenty-first century. In the first period, the prevailing conceptions of literature and translation allowed Perrault's tales to be retold with many kinds of modifications. However, from the 1990s to the mid-2010s, new editions have been published that give these stories a literary and authorial perspective by maintaining the full text, including the morals in verse, which were previously suppressed.

Introduction

Containing the tales "The Beauty in the Sleeping Forest," "Little Red Riding Hood," "Bluebeard," "The Capable Cat or Puss in Boots," "The Fairies," "Cinderella or The Little Glass Slipper," "Riquet with the Tuft" and "Little Thumb," the book *Stories or Tales from Past Times, with Morals or Mother Goose*

Tales, by the seventeenth-century French writer Charles Perrault, went on to become one of the most famous works for children and young people. It was at its time of writing that the French term *contes de fées* [fairy tales] began to designate the literary genre in vogue in the salons of the Louis XIV court, which consisted of narratives made up and retold by women in the main, but also by men, like Perrault himself. As Jack Zipes explains:

> The French writers created an institution, that is, the genre of literary fairy tale was institutionalized as an aesthetic and social means through which questions and issues of *civilité*, proper behavior and demeanor in all types of situations, were mapped out as narrative strategies for literary socialization, and in many cases, as symbolic gestures of subversion to question the ruling standards of taste and behavior. (Zipes 1999, 334)

In other words, while Perrault's literary fairy tales may have gone on to attain the status of timeless classics, they were elaborated according to specific literary conceptions in a particular setting. It is in this way that the peculiarities of each of the eight tales from his book can be comprehended: stories told in prose followed by a moral in verse, in which the writer expresses – sometimes with a critical perspective, other times with irony – his own conclusions about the story told.

Informed by Descriptive Translation Studies, the theoretical perspective adopted here approaches the various rewritings of Perrault's short stories as cultural artifacts belonging to different times and literary systems. These artifacts reflect the specific worldviews and literary conceptions of their rewriters (translators, adaptors, etc.) and their editors (as agents of patronage). *Rewriting* is understood here using André Lefevere's concept, who defines rewriters thus:

> Whether they produce translations, literary histories or their more compact spin-offs, reference works, anthologies, criticism, or editions, rewriters adapt, manipulate the originals they work with to some extent, usually to make them fit in with the dominant, or one of the dominant ideological and poetological currents of their time. (Lefevere 1992, 8)

To study a foreign literature in a specific literary system, it is therefore necessary to analyze what I call the *rewriting factor*. This entails turning attention to the actual translations, adaptations, and other types of rewritings that exist in the literary system in question. If, as Donald Haase states, fairy tales are products of their time, with "specific sociocultural roots (…) [and] historically determined values" (Haase 1999, 359), when rewritten as translations or adaptations, these tales will also express different ideological and poetological conceptions (Lefevere 1992, 5). As such, they may significantly alter or transform how the target audience reads them. As this study will discuss, Perrault's tales were first presented to the Brazilian readership at the end of the nineteenth century and continue to be present in different kinds of rewritings to the present day. However, the significance ascribed to Perrault's tales will differ significantly according to the time and the rewriters' perspectives on literature for children and young people. Perrault's tales exist in their own context, as do the other (re)writings, such as those by the Brothers Grimm in the nineteenth century. Similarly, when a work is rewritten in another literary system, this new rewriting is permeated by the values of its culture and time, reflecting its own relations of patronage and the particular perspectives of its rewriters.

The role of rewriting in the development of Brazilian children's literature

In Brazil, the development of a national literature aimed at children dates back to the nineteenth century, with writers such as Figueiredo Pimentel (1869–1914). It then reaches a striking and decisive moment in the early twentieth century with the writer Monteiro Lobato (1882–1948). (See Lima and Pereira's contribution in this volume for more on the development of Brazilian children's literature.) We can observe that rewritings exert a significant influence on this incipient literature, as Nelly Novaes Coelho points out:

> The first literary books for children (…) appeared at the same time as forms of teaching designed to bring Brazilian culture into line with that of [so-called] civilized nations. These books were evidently not originals, but translations or adaptations of works that were popular amongst children in Europe.[1] (Coelho 2006, 18)

One of the first literary children's book published in Brazil was an anthology of tales called *Contos da Carochinha* [Old Wives' Tales], by Figueiredo Pimentel.

---

1   Unless otherwise stated, all translations are by the author. In Portuguese: "os primeiros livros literários infantis (…) surgiram simultaneamente às formas do ensino que procuravam adequar a cultura brasileira à das [assim chamadas] nações civilizadas. Tais livros, evidentemente, não eram originais, mas traduções ou adaptações de obras que, na Europa, faziam sucesso entre os pequenos."

Published by Livraria Quaresma in 1896,[2] it contained sixty-one stories and was presented as a "book for children containing a wonderful collection of popular, moral and useful tales from various countries, some translated and others collected from the oral tradition" (Pimentel 1911, cover).[3] Pedro Quaresma, the owner of the bookshop and publishing house, exerted an important role as an agent of patronage for Brazilian children's literature. He published translations and adaptations into Portuguese and children's books by Brazilian authors at a time when Brazilian children's literature was still in its infancy. Quaresma subverted the prevailing order in the publishing market, which was dominated by foreign books and publishers based in Europe, such that many Brazilian writers had no choice but to publish abroad. In the Livraria Quaresma catalogue, alongside the aforementioned anthology of fables, there are other books published for children at the time, such as *Histórias da Baratinha* [The Cockroach's Stories], *Histórias do Arco da Velha* [Amazing Stories], *O Castigo de um Anjo* [The Punishment of an Angel] and *Histórias da Avozinha* [Granny's Stories], the last of which is presented as

> a very fine volume containing 50 stories of the most varied kind, humorous, serious, happy and sad, which speak of werewolves, saints, miracles and fairies, *all, however, very moral, in order to teach children to love their neighbor, to care for animals, to do good deeds and be virtuous*; in short *kind and good sentiments*.[4] (Pimentel 1911, 12; emphasis added)

By the end of the nineteenth century, there was already a need in Brazil for literature aimed at children. These tales were thus (re)written as children's literature, based on the understanding that books for children should not only entertain, but must also have an educational and moral function, as can be seen from the paratexts of the editions. (Re)writing for children should exert its function of pedagogical art. This is made explicit in the text by the editors of the new book in the Livraria Quaresma catalogue:

---

2   There is a previous edition (1894), which "was a small 200-page brochure, containing [only] forty stories" ("Preface to the 17th edition." In Pimentel 1911, ix).
3   In Portuguese: "Livro para crianças contendo maravilhosa coleção de contos populares, morais e proveitosos de vários países, traduzidos uns, e outros apanhados da tradição oral" (original with updated spelling).
4   In Portuguese: "Lindíssimo volume contendo 50 histórias das mais variadas, sérias, humorísticas, alegres e tristes, onde se fala em lobisomens, em santos, em milagres e em fadas, todas, porém, muito morais, de modo a ensinar às crianças o amor do próximo, o afeto aos animais, a prática do bem e da virtude; em suma sentimentos generosos e bons" (original with updated spelling).

Written in simple language, as befits children, *Contos da Carochinha* is a valuable book, an eternal book, because in Brazil to this day nothing to equal [these tales] has been published; they are eternal, they date from centuries past and will last for centuries yet. To mothers, teachers and people in general, *we recommend this precious book, the only one capable of leading children towards good and virtue, delighting and entertaining at the same time.*[5] (Pimentel 1911, 11; emphasis added)

The above paratexts about these two very popular books, *Histórias da Avozinha* and *Contos da Carochinha*, reveal some of the prevailing ideological conceptions concerning literature for children in late-nineteenth-century Brazil: moralism combined with an educational purpose. As Leonardo Arroyo states in *Literatura Infantil Brasileira* [Brazilian Children's Literature], "tales with a moral basis [were] in accordance with the conceptions of the time about what children should read" (Arroyo 2011, 236).[6] A review in the newspaper *Diário de Notícias* about *Contos da Carochinha* corroborates this perspective, considering it an

excellent work of great usefulness for schools, because, at the same time that it delights children, interesting them in the narration of very well delineated moral tales, it arouses in them sentiments of good, of religion, and of charity, major elements of children's education.[7] (Sandroni 2011, 38)

As Coelho observes, the sixty-one stories in the book consisted of "tales by Perrault, Grimm and Andersen, fables, apologues, allegories, cautionary tales, legends, parables, proverbs, playful tales, etc." (Coelho 2006, 30).[8] These rewritings, however, were not related to their sources, as the edition contains no mention of the authorship or origins of each story. Figueiredo Pimentel

---

5   In Portuguese: "escritos em linguagem fácil, como convém às crianças, os *Contos da Carochinha* são, pois, um livro valioso, um livro eterno, porque no Brasil até hoje nada se tem publicado que os iguale; eles são eternos, datam de séculos e séculos durarão ainda. Às mães de família, aos educadores e ao povo em geral, recomendamos este precioso livro, único que pode guiar as crianças no caminho do bem e da virtude, alegrando e divertindo ao mesmo tempo" (original with updated spelling).
6   In Portuguese: "contos de fundo moral [estavam] de acordo com os conceitos da época em matéria de leituras para crianças."
7   In Portuguese: "excelente trabalho de grande utilidade para as escolas, porque, ao mesmo tempo que deleita as crianças, interessando-as com a narração de contos morais muito bem-traçados, lhes desperta os sentimentos do bem, da religião e da caridade, principais elementos da educação da infância."
8   In Portuguese: "contos de Perrault, de Grimm e de Andersen, fábulas, apólogos, alegorias, contos exemplares, lendas, parábolas, provérbios, contos jocosos etc."

made use of existing models in foreign cultures – fairy tales, folk tales from oral traditions, and other sources – in order to elaborate versions that he considered appropriate for Brazilian children. Without any identification of the source texts, Pimentel's anthology would appear to contain six stories whose titles suggest they came from Perrault. However, after a textual analysis (Oliveira 2018, 124–126), it was found that only three can be regarded as rewritings of Perrault's tales on the basis of plot similarities: "The Beauty in the Sleeping Forest," "Bluebeard," and "Puss in Boots." A general feature of Pimentel's tales is the absence of the moral in verse and the exclusion of the line "once upon a time," typically used to open fairy tales by Perrault. Likewise, the stories are relocated, situated in specific times and places, and the characters are personalized and given proper names, which is not very common in fairy tales.

It is interesting to observe that the modifications made by Pimentel often do not bring the text any closer to the Brazilian reality; on the contrary, they introduce images of worlds distant from the readership's reality, such as the 'Orient,' as we see in "The Beauty in the Sleeping Forest," whose father is introduced as "The Emperor of the Turks, Tamerlão I" (Pimentel 2006, 112).[9] The values the rewriter inscribes on the text can be seen from the gifts the fairies bestow on the princess: "On the day of the baptism, all [the fairies] appeared and prophesied great happiness for the young Iris, wishing her *comeliness, beauty, fortune, kindness, talent, and a rich fiancé*" (ibid., emphasis added).[10] At the end of the story, the princess and the prince, who have proper names (Iris and Heitor), get married "with such bounty that no longer exists, even in countries of the Orient" (ibid., 114).[11] In this tale, Pimentel evokes a culture considered distant and exotic at the time, which provided an imagery of exuberance and opulence. *Contos da Carochinha*, published in the late nineteenth century, was a landmark in Brazilian children's literature and was passed down through the generations, influencing readers throughout the twentieth century. Even in contemporary times, a new edition of the book was brought out by the publishing house Villa Rica (2006).

As one of the pioneers of Brazilian children's literature, Figueiredo Pimentel played an important role in bringing literary models from the oral tradition and the foreign children's literature canon to the national literary system and making these works fit for the purpose of the moral education of Brazilian children. However, it was with Monteiro Lobato that the development of a literature aimed at children gained more substance. A writer, translator, editor-in-chief and

---

9 In Portuguese: "O imperador dos turcos, Tamerlão I."
10 In Portuguese: "No dia do batizado compareceram todas [as fadas], e vaticinaram à jovem Iris todas as felicidades, desejando-lhe formosura, beleza, fortuna, bondade, talento, e um noivo rico."
11 In Portuguese: "com um brilhantismo que hoje não existe, nem mesmo nos países do Oriente."

owner of a publishing house, Lobato was already "concerned with innovating and expanding the Brazilian publishing market, which was then very precarious" (Coelho 2006, 639).[12] Although Pimentel's and Lobato's rewritings may have been produced at relatively similar times and driven by comparable beliefs about the existence of a child audience with specific demands, they differ in terms of their objectives and, as a consequence, the literature they produced.

While Pimentel's work was guided by conceptions of an educational and moralizing function for children's literature, Lobato planned to create a Brazilian children's literature guided by the tastes and interests of children. With Lobato, Brazilian children's literature gained a strong enough impetus to push the balance between art and education more towards art, toning down or making less explicit the didactic or educational intent. At the time, the incipient publishing market was restricted to a very few publishing houses, which focused on established authors. So it was that in 1919, Lobato founded Monteiro Lobato & Cia, later renamed Companhia Editora Nacional, and "introduce[d] totally new processes to the publishing market: open[ed] space for new writers; modernize[d] not only the books' graphic design, but also the sales and commercial distribution processes" (Coelho 2006, 637).[13] In his plans to develop Brazilian literature, Lobato the editor became an important agent of patronage, while as a writer and translator he inaugurated a new literature for children.

Lobato worked to translate many authors of adult and children's literature, believing that the existing Portuguese translations (Brazilian readers' main way of accessing foreign literature) were hard to understand. He felt that the structure and vocabulary used were anachronistic. In the letters he wrote to his friend and translator Godofredo Rangel, published in the book *A Barca de Gleyre* [Gleyre's Boat], Lobato set out his thoughts about translation and his general editorial approach. He treated all the works he intended to translate in a similar way; he did not regard them as 'untouchable,' but as works that should be translated in such a manner that the Brazilian audience could come to like and appreciate them. In a letter dated 1925, he therefore made Rangel a proposal:

> I am sending the songs taken from Shakespeare's plays so you can choose some of the most interesting ones to translate into quite singular language; I want to turn each song into a short book for children. Translate about

---

12 In Portuguese: "preocupado em inovar e expandir o campo editorial brasileiro, então precaríssimo."
13 In Portuguese: "introduz[iu] no mercado editorial processos totalmente novos: abr[iu] espaço para escritores inéditos; moderniz[ou] não só o tratamento gráfico dos livros como também os processos de venda e distribuição comercial."

three of your own choice and send us them with the original; I want to use the prints. Keep the style straightforward, OK? And feel free to improve on the original wherever you want. (Lobato 2018, 100, trans. Atkinson)

Lobato's aim was to render the works accessible, transforming them to language that could be easily comprehended by everyone, and thereby making them pleasing to the audience. Writing against a hermetic literature, he finished the letter with a cry from the heart and a call to arms: "I'm taking a look at the tales by Grimm that Garnier gave me. Poor Brazilian children! What a Portuguese accent these translations have! We really must redo them all – make the language sound Brazilian" (Lobato 2018, 101, trans. Atkinson). Lobato imposed on his translation process – and also on the translators from his publishing house – the task of helping to constitute and fortify the nation's incipient children's literature. Rather than just translate, he wanted to "make the language sound Brazilian," and he was not afraid of taking radical measures in the process, such as cutting out sections of the works, as we can see in a letter from 1924 (in this excerpt, talking about literature for adults):

Do not be in a hurry with Michelet. Take your time. I think it is a great book, even if it is quite big. We could abridge it by cutting the introduction. If you put some alum in the ink, you could shorten it by some fifty pages in the translation. (Lobato 2018, 100, trans. Atkinson)

Translation strategies that drastically alter the source text (severely abridging it, for example) can be seen as adapting this source text, taking into account a certain target literary system and a certain target audience, even if the publishers of such rewritings present them as translations. Concerning the development of works aimed at children, a letter from 1916 reveals how Lobato was already reflecting on his proposal to transform foreign stories into Brazilian ones, as well as his desire to create a new literature for this audience. Having published his first book for children in 1920, *A Menina do Narizinho Arrebitado* [The Girl with Little Nose Turned Up], he had already acted on behalf of a Brazilian children's literature in his work as an editor/translator. Commenting on the reception of the stories told for children, Lobato shows his perception that the morals of the fables were not suitable for such readers and reveals how free he felt to make whatever transformations that he found necessary for his project, as we can see in another letter to Rangel:

I have many ideas in mind. One: to garb the old fables by Aesop and La Fontaine in national dress, using only prose and reworking the morals.

> Something for children. It came to me when I noticed how engrossed my little ones are by the fables Purezinha tells them. They remember them and retell them to their friends – but without paying the least attention to the morality, as is normal. Morality stays in our subconscious to reveal itself later on as our understanding grows. It strikes me that a collection of fables with animals from here rather than from abroad, if it were done artfully and skillfully, would be an absolute gem. The fables in Portuguese that I know, normally translations of La Fontaine, are clumps of brambles in the forest – prickly and impenetrable. What can our children read? I haven't a clue. Fables like that would be a first step in the literature that we lack. As I have something of a knack for pulling the wool over people's eyes, so that they take my skill for actual talent, I am toying with the idea of starting something. Our children's literature is so limited and stupid that I cannot find anything for my children's early years. (Lobato 2018, 99–100, trans. Atkinson)

As part of this bid to bring out works that could be understood and appreciated by Brazilian children, Companhia Editora Nacional [1934] published Lobato's translation of Perrault's *Tales*, containing "Little Red Riding Hood," "The Fairies," "Bluebeard," "Puss in Boots," "Donkey Skin," "Cinderella," "Riquet with the Tuft," "The Sleeping Beauty" and "Little Thumb." The only one not from *Tales of Mother Goose* was "Donkey Skin." This tale, originally written in verse, was presented in prose by Lobato. He translated the eight tales of *Mother Goose*, excluding the morals, and although he did not make any great alterations to the prose, he adopted a markedly colloquial style designed to give the effect of orality, with idioms, onomatopoeia and explanations of difficult or unknown terms – elements that were not present in the source text. An emblematic example is the term 'ogre,' used by Perrault in tales such as "The Beauty in the Sleeping Forest," which Lobato translated as *papão* (masculine) and *papona* (feminine), a word that is very familiar to Brazilian children because of the expression *bicho papão* [bogeyman], a monster that would come out at night and eat little children. There is a passage in Perrault's text with the following description: "La reine-mère envoya sa bru et ses enfants à une maison de campagne dans le bois, pour pouvoir plus aisément assouvir son horrible envie" (Perrault 2002, 126). ("The queen mother sent her daughter-in-law and her children to a country house in the woods, in order to assuage her unspeakable desire more easily" (Perrault 2002, 127, trans. Appelbaum).) Lobato translates this passage with an explanation:

> a rainha-mãe enviou a nora e os meninos para uma casa de campo situada no meio da floresta, bem longe, onde ela, rainha, pudesse dar largas ao seu

apetite de bruxa, filha de ogro comedor de crianças, ou papão. Era papona, a diaba.

The queen-mother sent her daughter-in-law and the children to a country house far away in the middle of the forest, where she, the queen, could unleash her *witch's appetite, as she was the daughter of a child-eating ogre, a bogeyman. She was a bogeywoman, a she-devil.* (Perrault 2007, 72, my translation, emphasis added)

In this short passage, Lobato inserts an explanation of the term, putting it in a way that would be familiar to his target audience: children.

In translating Perrault, Lobato introduced Brazilian children living in the early 1900s to the famous fairy tales of world literature that were not yet available in translation in Brazil. Unlike his precursor, Pimentel, whose *Contos da Carochinha* gave no indication of the source authors used and were essentially free adaptations of tales from many origins, Lobato's rewritings, despite dropping the morals in verse, gave Brazilian readers access to Perrault's prose.

After these two books, which marked the early development of Brazilian children's literature, other editions of Perrault's tales were published in Brazil. These included the rewritings by Olívia Krähenbühl (Círculo do Livro 19--), Ariadne Oliveira (Melhoramentos 1983/1987), Maria Cimolino and Grazia Parodi (Rideel 1993), and also an edition by the publishing house Paulinas, from 1962, whose rewriter is not identified. All of these texts have one thing in common: the exclusion of the morals in verse. Some of them also abridge or significantly alter parts of the narratives, adjusting the text with their target audience in mind (Oliveira 2018). Even the edition by the translator Olívia Krähenbühl, which is presented as a "complete edition" of Perrault's work, excludes the morals and gives no explanation for this in any of the book's paratexts. Of the editions analyzed in my research, only at the end of the twentieth century, in the 1990s, did rewritings of Perrault's tales begin to be published with the morals, as in the case of the rewriting by Ruth Rocha, a prominent name in Brazilian children's literature. In her book *Contos de Perrault* [Perrault's Tales], published for the first time in 1988, with the latest edition in 2010, Rocha announced in the Introduction that she was keen to "maintain the narratives of these tales totally faithful to their originals" (Rocha 2010, 5).[14] Aimed at children, Rocha's rewriting includes not only Perrault's prose but also some of his verses.

---

14   In Portuguese: "manter as narrativas destes contos de Perrault inteiramente fiéis aos seus originais."

Rewritings in the twenty-first century

Since 2005, many new rewritings of the work of the French author have been published in Brazil. The perspective envisioned in Ruth Rocha's translation project is the dominant characteristic of contemporary rewritings. The rewriters tend to be well-known writers for children or literary translators: Ana Maria Machado (Global 2005), Rosa Freire d'Aguiar (Companhia das Letrinhas 2005/2012), Katia Canton (DCL 2005), Mário Laranjeira (Iluminuras 2007), Fernanda Lopes de Almeida (Ática 2008), Hildegard Feist (Companhia das Letrinhas 2009), Walcyr Carrasco (Manole 2009; Moderna 2013), Maria Luiza Borges (Zahar 2010), Ivone Benedetti (L&PM 2012), Leonardo Fróes (Cosac Naify 2015) and Eliana Bueno-Ribeiro (Paulinas 2016). Most of the rewritings are presented as translations, but there are some presented as adaptations or retellings. All of them, with the exception of Walcyr Carrasco's rewriting, maintain the morals in verse and set about maintaining and/or recreating literary elements of Perrault's text (writing style, vocabulary, plot, etc.).

Three books that exemplify this new approach, in which the literary elements of Perrault's tales are reworked without any major cuts or radical alterations, are the recent translations by Rosa Freire d'Aguiar and Hildegard Feist. Published under the children's literature imprint Companhia das Letrinhas of the publishing house Companhia das Letras, the books *Chapeuzinho Vermelho* [Little Red Riding Hood] and *O Pequeno Polegar* [Little Thumb], by Freire, and *O Barba-Azul* [Bluebeard], by Feist, contain just one tale each, large illustrations and paratexts aimed at children. Their purpose is announced for children in the introduction to the story of Little Thumb: "We think many of you will have already heard it, in all sorts of versions and adaptations – but never told as well as in this beautiful book, by the original 'voice' of Mother Goose" (Perrault 2005, 6).[15]

In "Little Thumb," just as Perrault tells it, we read about the drama of the children living in extreme poverty who are abandoned not once but twice by their parents. In "Little Red Riding Hood," we have the tragic end of the main character and her grandma, devoured by the wolf. Rosa Freire seeks to preserve the literary characteristics of Perrault's tales: the plot, the pace of the narrative (with its repetitions, for instance), its structure and the moral in verse. The same applies to Hildegard Feist's translation, which maintains

---

15   In Portuguese: "Apesar de acreditar que muitos de vocês já a ouviram, em toda sorte de versões e adaptações – mas nunca tão bem contada como neste livro bonito, pela 'voz' original da Mamãe Gansa."

the original structure of the tale without significantly altering the phrasal constructions of the narrative, working on the literary aspects of the text, the rhythm and style of Perrault's writing, and maintaining the moral at the end. Below are examples of each of the translators' work to illustrate their strategies.

In the translation of "Little Red Riding Hood," Freire maintains the repetitions of sentences, such as are seen in the source text. In Perrault's tale, some of the dialogues are repeated word for word, like the initial conversation between the grandmother and the wolf (pretending to be the girl), and then the one between the wolf (pretending to be the grandmother) and the girl. Such mirroring is present in Freire's translation, with the repetition of almost every word in the dialogues; there is just the smallest of differences in the verbal form of the girl's answer in the second dialogue, which is presented in brackets below.

> Toc, toc.
> Grand-mère/Loup: – Qui est là ?
> Loup/Le Petit Chaperon rouge: – C'est votre fille le Petit Chaperon Rouge (…) qui vous apporte une galette et un petit pot de beurre que ma mère vous envoie.
> Grand-mère/Loup: – Tire la chevillette, la bobinette cherra.
> (Perrault 2002, 132–134)

> "Rap, rap."
> Grandma/Wolf: "Who is it?"
> Wolf/Little Red Riding Hood: "It's your granddaughter, Little Red Riding Hood, (…) bringing you a biscuit and a little pot of butter that my mother is sending you."
> Grandma/Wolf: "Pull the little peg, and the little latch will open."
> (Perrault 2002, 133–135, trans. Appelbaum)

> toc, toc.
> Vovozinha/Lobo: – Quem está aí?
> Lobo/Chapeuzinho Vermelho: – É a sua netinha, Chapeuzinho Vermelho, (…) que está lhe trazendo um bolinho e um potinho de manteiga mandados pela mamãe. (É a sua netinha, Chapeuzinho Vermelho, que lhe traz um bolinho e um potinho de manteiga que a mamãe mandou).
> Vovozinha/Lobo: – Puxe o pino, e o trinco abrirá.
> (Perrault 2012, 10–17, trans. Freire)

English backtranslation of the Portuguese:
knock, knock.
Grandma/Wolf: "Who's there?"
Wolf/Little Red Riding Hood: "It's your little granddaughter, Little Red Riding Hood, (...) who is bringing you a cake and a little pot of butter sent by mother." (It's your little granddaughter, Little Red Riding Hood, (...) who brings you a cake and a little pot of butter that mother sent).
Grandma/Wolf: "Pull the peg, and the latch will open."

This textual strategy demonstrates attention to the author's style, which in this case plays with identical dialogues in the two situations of the arrival of the girl (the false and the real one) at her grandmother's home. Another quite significant example concerning the translator's textual choices can be observed in Feist's translation of "Bluebeard," in the scene where the wife is about to be murdered by her husband. Desperate, she urges her sister to go to the top of the tower and look out to see if their brothers are coming to save her. Repetition is used as a strategy to build expectations about the brothers' arrival. In Perrault, there is a sequence of four repetitions of identical questions by the desperate wife, intensifying the suspense and expectations about what will happen next. The translator Hildegard Feist maintains the same structure, introducing just one small difference: in French, each question mentions the sister's name twice, but in the translation only in the first question is her name repeated. In the dialogue between the sisters, the first two answers by the sister Anne are identical. The same occurs in Feist's translation.

– Anne, ma soeur Anne, ne vois-tu rien venir? (4x)
– Je ne vois rien que le Soleil qui poudroie, et l'herbe qui verdoie. (2x)
(Perrault 2002, 144)

"Anne, sister Anne, don't you see anything coming?"
"All I see is the sun raising dust and the grass growing green."
(Perrault 2002, 145, trans. Appelbaum)

– Ana, minha irmã Ana, está vendo alguém?
– Estou vendo apenas o sol que reluz e a relva que verdeja.
(Perrault 2009, 19–21, trans. Feist)

English backtranslation of the Portuguese:
"Ana, my sister Ana, do you see anyone?"
"I see only the sun that shines and the grass that grows green."

Such characteristics are important when thinking about the motivations of rewriters and their conceptions of literature for children. Whereas in the past the morals in verse and other parts of the stories or specific scenes were often cut or altered because they were deemed unfit for children, in the three new rewritings from the early years of the twenty-first century (as well as in the other new rewritings mentioned above), new perspectives have emerged. Freire's and Feist's rewritings do not propose a new or contemporary view of Perrault's tales. However, by introducing children to stories that used to be abridged or adapted, they present the possibility of knowing the Mother Goose tales in their literary versions, as Perrault proposed in seventeenth-century France. As Jack Zipes points out, with regard to "Little Red Hood", the French author changed many elements of an existing oral version by "refin[ing] and polish[ing] it according to his own taste and the conventions of French high society in King Louis XIV's time" (Zipes 1993, 346). For that matter, "Perrault revised the oral tale to make it the literary standardbearer for good Christian upbringing" (*ibid.*, 348).

The contemporary translators' motivations and their strategies for dealing with the text are not restricted to telling the story (the events). They also have bearing on how the literary characteristics of Perrault's tales are presented (such as the repetitions, as we saw, or the moral in verse, which was omitted by previous rewriters). Freire's and Feist's books are examples of how the plot, the structure and the rhythm of the author can be translated to another language and culture in works aimed at children, without the need to add explanations or abridge the text. The rewritings are published in formats that are easily handled by children, with large illustrations, and yet they can be read as literary tales, such as Perrault intended: a conjunction of a 'story of the olden days' and the author's perspective on specific situations or realities, even if these realities are depicted in fairy tales.

Moral

As part of the children's literary canon, Perrault's tales rose to the status of timeless classics, while also hiding in the shadows of memory, disguising themselves as part of the collective or individual unconscious (Calvino 2007, 10). These are stories that everyone knows or has heard of. However, from the perspective adopted here, Perrault's literature, like the literature of any author, is constituted through particular retellings, through rewritings, and thus in new or distinct ways of signification or interpretation. Retellings are contingent, cultural and historical, and a study of literary works can shed light on the visions of (re)writers and agents of patronage in relation to an author or a literary work.

From a diachronic perspective, two time periods were observed: from the end of the nineteenth century throughout most of the twentieth century, and from the 1990s into the twenty-first century. In the first period, the conceptions of literature and of translation allowed Perrault's tales to be retold with many kinds of modifications, the most common being to cut the moral in verse. Such alterations were not explained in the paratexts of the editions; indeed, they were sometimes presented as 'complete translations' of the work. In the twenty-first century, however, new editions have been published giving these well-known yet not always so widely read stories a literary and authorial perspective. They are presented in their full versions with the morals in verse and emphasize the name of Perrault as their author. Yet there is a critical perspective that argues against the adequacy of the morals, especially when the work is aimed at children, as exemplified by Maria Tatar:

> Those morals often did not square with the events in the story and sometimes offered nothing more than an opportunity for random social commentary and digressions on character. The explicit behavioral directives added by Perrault and others also have a tendency to misfire when they are aimed at children. (Tatar 2002, xv)

Curiously, most of the tales published in book form in contemporary times have included the morals in verse, as well as the complete text in prose. Unlike their predecessors, these new rewritings are consistent with the dominant ideological and poetological currents, namely, a tendency on the part of publishers to value direct and complete translations of literary works, whether for adults or for young readers. It could be speculated that two factors are at play here: the prevailing trend against the censorship or significant manipulation of literary works (such as limitations on the number of pages, on themes, etc.), strategies that were common at other times, such as during the military dictatorship; and the development of Brazilian children's literature itself, with the emergence of well-known and respected writers for this age group. Children's literature has essentially gained recognition as literature in its own right, which means that translations of works such as the classics tend to respect the authors' literary choices. All of this is, of course, contingent and related to the perspectives of the agents responsible for setting the path taken by literature: (re)writers, editors, critics, researchers.

In this sense, by maintaining certain previously overlooked elements, the contemporary rewritings of Perrault's tales give Brazilian readers access to a new way of knowing Perrault and thus a new image of the author and his work, since the tales had not been published in their entirety either for adult readers or for children until the end of the twentieth century.

We have seen how Perrault's tales have been an almost constant presence in Brazilian literature since its inception. This is thanks in the first instance to Figueiredo Pimentel and Monteiro Lobato. The tales have since been published over the years as translations, adaptations, and retellings rendered by translators or writers of prestige in the Brazilian literary system. Likewise, we have seen that the tales have taken root in the target culture according to the poetological and ideological conceptions of the rewriters and agents of patronage involved in their (re)production. They have appeared in many different guises: in books for children; with parts of Perrault's texts abridged or cut out altogether; in dated and updated versions; and with greater or lesser regard for the source texts' literary virtues, to mention just some of the many strategies employed. This means that any study of the transmission of the tales in Brazil, and particularly studies focused on rewritings, will have to put translation at the heart of the analysis. The works studied here clearly propose specific interpretations of Perrault's tales – interpretations that reflect the prevailing ideological and poetological conceptions (Lefevere, 1992) of their time of production and publication.

It therefore follows that the recent rewritings, which have reproduced the tales in their entirety, not cutting any of the scenes or lexical items that have previously been regarded as inappropriate for children, are also indicative of a prevailing ideological trend: that the author and his work deserve the utmost respect. This does not preclude the existence of other perspectives, which may, for example, give rise to re-creations that subvert the way these and other popular or fairy tales, such as those by the Brothers Grimm, have traditionally been portrayed. Interestingly, however, this kind of transgression was not present in the rewritings analyzed here.

Just as the motivations and strategies of rewriters change over time, so too do the analytical perspectives used by researchers to understand them. Some contemporary rewritings have given fairy tales a feminist slant, constituting rich material for new research. The present study focused on rewritings as a means to examine how Perrault's tales functioned in Brazil at various times throughout the history of its literary history. Surely, there are as many other ways to approach Perrault's tales and their rewritings as there are ways of rewriting them.

Bibliography

Arroyo, Leonardo. 2011. *Literatura infantil brasileira*. 3rd edition. São Paulo: Unesp.

Calvino, Italo. 2007. *Por Que Ler os Clássicos*. Translated by Nilson Moulin. São Paulo: Companhia das Letras.

Coelho, Nelly Novaes. 2006. *Dicionário Crítico da Literatura Infantil e Juvenil Brasileira*. 5th edition. São Paulo: Companhia Editora Nacional.

Haase, Donald. 1999. "Yours, Mine, or Ours? Perrault, Brothers Grimm, and the Ownership of Fairy Tales." In *The Classic Fairy Tales*, edited by Maria Tatar, 353–364. New York/London: Norton.

Lefevere, André. 1992. *Translation, Rewriting, and the Manipulation of Literary Fame*. London: Routledge.

Lobato, Monteiro. 2018. "Letters (extracts)." Translated by Rebecca Frances Atkinson. In *Palavra de Tradutor: Reflexões sobre tradução por tradutores brasileiros* [The Translator's Word: Reflections on Translation by Brazilian Translators], edited by Marcia A. P. Martins and Andréia Guerini, 99–103. Florianópolis: Editora UFSC.

Oliveira, Anna Olga Prudente de. 2018. "Histórias do Tempo Antigo com Moralidades: Uma Análise Diacrônica e Sincrônica das Reescritas da Obra de Charles Perrault no Brasil / Stories of Bygone Times with Morals: A Diachronic and Synchronic Analysis of Rewritings of the Work of Charles Perrault in Brazil." PhD diss., Pontifical Catholic University of Rio de Janeiro.

Perrault, Charles. 2002. *The Complete Fairy Tales in Verse and Prose: A Dual Language Book / L'intégrale des contes en vers et en prose*. Edited and translated by Stanley Appelbaum. Mineola, NY: Dover Publications.

Perrault, Charles. 2005. *O Pequeno Polegar*. Introduction by Tatiana Belinky. Translated by Rosa Freire d'Aguiar. Illustrations by Clotilde Perrin. São Paulo: Companhia das Letrinhas.

Perrault, Charles. 2007. *Contos de Fadas*. Translated by Monteiro Lobato. 2nd edition. São Paulo: Companhia Editora Nacional.

Perrault, Charles. 2009. *O Barba-Azul*. Translated by Hildegard Feist. 1st edition. São Paulo: Companhia das Letrinhas.

Perrault, Charles. 2012. *Chapeuzinho Vermelho*. Translated by Rosa Freire d'Aguiar. Illustrated by Georg Hallensleben. 4th reprint. São Paulo: Companhia das Letrinhas.

Pimentel, Figueiredo. 1911. *Contos da Carochinha*. Rio de Janeiro: Quaresma & CIA Livreiros Editores.

Pimentel, Figueiredo. 2006. *Contos da Carochinha*. Belo Horizonte: Villa Rica.

Rocha, Ruth. 2010. *Contos de Perrault*. São Paulo: Moderna.

Sandroni, Laura. 2011. *De Lobato a Bojunga: As reinações renovadas*. 2nd edition. Rio de Janeiro: Nova Fronteira.

Tatar, Maria, ed. 2002. *The Annotated Classic Fairy Tales*. New York/London: Norton.
Zipes, Jack, ed. 1993. *The Trials and Tribulations of Little Red Riding Hood*. New York/Abingdon: Routledge.
Zipes, Jack. 1999. "Breaking the Disney Spell." In *The Classic Fairy Tales*, edited by Maria Tatar, 332–352. New York/London: Norton.

Translating crossover picture books

The Italian translations of *Bear Hunt* by Anthony Browne

Annalisa Sezzi

Abstract

This chapter sets out to explore the challenges posed by the translation of crossover picture books, that is, works addressing the child and the adult alike. Building on recent research on the translation of picture books and on the aspects related to performativity and read-aloudability in children's literature, the investigation focuses on the Italian translation (1990) and retranslation (1999) of *Bear Hunt* (1979) by Anthony Browne. The case study shows how the two translators adopted different solutions when tackling the relationship between visual and verbal, the read-aloud situation put on by the adult reading aloud, and the different layers of meaning of Browne's picture book. Grounded on O'Sullivan's scheme on narrative communication for translation, the comparative analysis also attempts to account for the differences between the implied child reader and the implied adult reading aloud in the source text and in the target texts.

Introduction

Picture books for preschoolers are complex, multimodal literary artifacts in which pictures and words intertwine to create meaning. This collaboration between two semiotic codes is fundamental because these books are designed to be read aloud: the adult reads the words aloud while the illiterate child looks at the images and listens to the story. Crossover picture books exploit this multiple addressee because they simultaneously address the child and the adult alike, offering manifold levels of meaning. As Beckett points out, "[c]rossover picture books are multileveled works that are suitable for all ages because they invite different forms of reading, depending on the age and experience of the reader" (Beckett 2012, 16). They include a "dual addressee" since both "small children and sophisticated adults" are equally positioned as co-readers (Nikolajeva and Scott 2006, 21). As crossover picture books also appeal to grown-up readers, they are characterized by intertextual references, complex visual and verbal interplay, genre blending, and often deal with challenging adult themes such as death (Beckett 2012). Needless to say, their translation poses many challenges.

The present chapter investigates the Italian translation and retranslation of *Bear Hunt*, a crossover picture book by the British author and illustrator Anthony Browne.[1] The book narrates the story of a bear with a magic pencil who draws his way out of dangerous situations being caused by two hunters chasing him. *Bear Hunt* was first published in 1979 and was translated into Italian in 1990. A retranslation then appeared in 1999.[2]

The analysis sets out to explore the differences between the translation strategies adopted in the Italian translation and retranslation of this crossover picture book, and to better understand how its performative aspect and its multi-layered meanings are rendered. The investigation will also try to account for the possible different images of the child and of the adult in the source and target texts.

Picture book translation

Picture books for preschoolers rely on the simultaneous presence of two semiotic systems, the verbal and the visual. Their interaction is the *conditio sine qua non* for the construction of the narrative meaning and for the fruition and enjoyment of the genre (see Moebius 1986; Nodelman 1998; Nikolajeva and Scott 2006). As previously mentioned, picture books are intended to be read aloud. Therefore, Painter, Martin and Unsworth (2012, 5) observe that their meaning is also negotiated orally. In this regard, Spitz (1999) emphasizes how the adult reading aloud becomes a sort of mediator and performer. Given this shared 'collaborative' reading experience, Spitz goes even further by stating that picture books are similar to scripts or musical scores (*ibid*., 16) because of the intrinsic potential dramatization the adult adds during narration.

Besides providing pleasure in reading, picture books are also connected with emergent literacy: not only do children come into contact with the book as an object, its reading direction and order, but also with the codes that structure the world of children (Stephens 1992, 8), as well as models of behavior and experiences from the society in which they live (Cardarello 1995, 9). Indeed, as Shavit points out, society requires children's book writers to be more attentive to their readers than writers for adults, as both the literary and

---

1   On the translations of Anthony Browne's Bear series, see also Pedrelli (2015).
2   The editions used for the analysis are: Anthony Browne. 1994. *Bear Hunt*. London: Puffin Books; Anthony Browne. 1990. *Orsetto e i cacciatori*. Milan: Ugo Mursia Editore; Anthony Browne. 1999. *Caccia all'Orsetto*. In *Orsetto e matita*, trans. Giulio Lughi. Turin: Einaudi.

the educational system place constraints upon them (Shavit 1983). Society's notion of childhood – that is, what is believed to be suitable for children – is closely interrelated with the image of the child. As Oittinen claims, "child image is a complex issue: on the one hand, it is something unique, based on each individual personal history; on the other hand, it is something collectivized in all society" (2000, 4). Thus, like all children's literature, picture books convey a specific notion of childhood, and a related image of the child, which might diverge over time and according to where a certain book is produced (see Shavit 1982; Oittinen 2000; O'Sullivan 2005). Translations are particularly revealing of the differences between the varying images of the child since, as Shavit observes, adjustments in characterization, plot, and language in translations are made "in accordance with what society regards (at a certain point in time) as educationally 'good for the child'" (Shavit 1986, 171–172).

With regard to the reading-aloud context, the translation of picture books is similar to theatre translation or dubbing (Oittinen 2000). The translator's intervention is limited to the verbal code because pictures – either a support or a strong paratextual constraint – cannot usually be modified. Likewise, the translator must be aware that the words to be translated are meant to be read aloud and the whole text is somehow meant to be acted as in theatre or film translation. All its oral and aural features, such as songs, alliterations, onomatopoeias, and the overall rhythm have to be taken into account. As Oittinen highlights, "[t]ranslators of picture books translate whole situations including the words, the illustrations, and the whole (imagined) reading-aloud situation" (*ibid.*, 75). Moreover, in crossover picture books, the adult not only plays the role of performer but is also an endorsed addressee together with the child, thus challenging the translator even further.

The implied aloud-reader

O'Sullivan's theoretical framework (2005) provides a basis for identifying diverging child images and translating strategies related to reading-aloud qualities. It stems from Chatman's scheme of narrative communication (1998) and the further amendments brought about by Schiavi (1996) and Hermans (1996) in order to broaden the picture to include translations. In particular, a real translator – positioned outside the text – establishes the communication between the real author of the source text and the real reader of the target text, transferring the source message thanks to the implied translator, an agency which is encoded in the text. During the translation process, the translator first acts at an extratextual level by becoming the real reader of the source text because of his/her double competence in the source and target language and culture. S/he identifies the implied reader of the target text and takes on its role so as to decipher and re-transmit the message for the new target readers. By so doing, s/he creates an extra intratextual agency (or TL author), the 'implied translator,' who constructs a new implied target reader. Therefore, a new relationship between the readers and the text is created, given the different *Weltanshauung* and cultural encyclopedia of the author and of the target addressees. Additionally, the author's voice and the translator's voice do not always correspond, such that the translator's voice can reveal itself, for example, in footnotes or in other paratextual elements. According to O'Sullivan, who applies the model to children's literature, the translator's voice can also be detected at the narrative level when it does not duplicate the voice of the narrator (2005, 109). Moreover, in children's literature, which is characterized by asymmetrical communication and influenced by society's idea of the child, the translator's conception of the reading child may differ from the author's supposed child audience, thus leading to amplifying or reductive narration, or to drowning out the voice of the narrator of the source text (*ibid.*, 114–118).

The implied adult reading aloud

Translating picture books is more challenging when the implied reader is what Nodelman (1988) calls an "implied viewer." The intended child reader is also an implied listener of the adult's narration, whose performance is also inscribed in the text. Read-aloudability is crucial in many genres of children's literature and has to be considered when translating, as underlined by Dollerup (2003), Van Coillie (2014a), and Lathey (2006). In particular, Oittinen (2018) stresses its importance in picture books where the adult is expected to perform the text. She also observes that in translated picture books characters are often 'revoiced.'

Still, if the dual addressee is in fact inherent to picture books, O'Sullivan's model has to incorporate an implied adult reading aloud (the implied aloud-reader), since the author of the text is aware of the necessity of the adult's voice. This agency is construed as both an oral performer in charge of staging a dramatization of the text and as an unavoidable mediator with regard to its comprehension and the ideological content expressed in the text. Its intratextual agency obviously acts at the extratextual level, in the voice of the person who reads the story.

The discursive presence of the implied adult reading aloud can be inferred from textual traces, whose function is to render the reading fun and comprehensible. These stage directions can be visual, determined by the picture/layout, the typography or the punctuation, or they can be verbal, such as lexical, syntactic, phonosymbolic or direct speech instructions (Sezzi 2009). Furthermore, some strategies facilitating the adult mediation are sometimes added in the translation: for example, explicative and cultural facilitations, and reassuring or ideological interventions (*ibid.*). Hence, the implied adult reading aloud, like the child implied reader, might be different in the source text and the target text, thus conveying not only a different image of the child but also a different image of adulthood.

The analysis of the translations of Anthony Browne's crossover picture book *Bear Hunt* gives some hints on how the two types of audiences are dealt with in the two target texts. Because one of the picture books under scrutiny is a retranslation, it might shed some light on how the performative aspect is perceived ten years later. As Cabaret (2014, 14) points out: "Retranslations enable a variety of options and experiences as far as orality is concerned, especially with picture books which may also resort to typography, colours and layout to visually guide readers in their reading and (re)interpretation of a text." The retranslation of fairy tales has pinpointed the importance of this component for texts meant to be read aloud (Van Coillie 2014b). It is thus necessary to investigate the issue of read-aloudability and performance, whilst including those additions that may facilitate the adult in his/her role.

The Italian translations of *Bear Hunt*: *Orsetto e i cacciatori* and *Caccia all'Orsetto*

In *Bear Hunt*, published originally in 1979, Anthony Browne elaborates and pays tribute to Crockett Johnson's *Harold and the Purple Crayon* (Doonan 1996, 232): all the books of the series (*Bear Hunt, A Bear-y Tale, Bear Goes to Town*) revolve around the adventures of a little white bear who has a magic pencil that draws him out of problematic situations and incidents, as everything he draws comes into existence. They are instances of a narrative metalepsis or metafictive picture book, where

> Bear functions as both a character constructed within the text and as an authorial figure who actively creates and changes the discourse of the text. By transgressing his narrative function, Bear disrupts the conventional hierarchy of relations between character, narrator and author. (McCallum 1996, 592)

Bear goes back and forth between the fictional world and the author's world every time a problem arises, breaking the boundaries between the two dimensions (Lewis 2001, 85). Furthermore, the picture book also serves "socio-political ends" (Doonan 1996, 232) addressed to the adult (aloud) reader. Besides the more evident criticism of hunting, *Bear Hunt* also shows Browne's criticism of war. His pacifist message is to be found at a visual level, where there are clear references to World War II. Two hunters, Bear's antagonists, are driving a green jeep, typical of World War II. On close inspection, we can see that the wheels of the jeep do not touch the ground, as if flying. Also, the symbol of the Japanese flag (the red rising sun) can be seen on the car doors: the hunters' car hence resembles a World War II Japanese fighter aircraft. Similarly, close to the front wheel, we can see the shark mouth of the US 'Warhawk' fighter aircraft. That is, the two hunters are associated and concurrently represent two main World War II opponents. Since the two symbols are depicted on the same vehicle, it can be inferred that there is no good side in a war. The allusion to the war is finally confirmed at the end of the picture book when the protagonist flies away on a white dove.

The setting of the story is a jungle as suggested by the palm trees and the exotic flowers in the background. This jungle is composed of surrealistic details typical of Browne' style: "plants are wearing white collars and colourful ties, a blob has eyeglasses, fish are swimming through the jungle, and a flower has tennis shoes for leaves" (Cullinan and Person 2005, 123).

In the first Italian translation (henceforth referred to as TT1), published by Mursia Editore as *Orsetto e i cacciatori* [Little Bear and the Hunters] eleven years after the source text, the name of the translator is not mentioned. The title in Italian diverges from the English. The diminutive/affectionate form *-etto* in Italian is added to make a noun sound smaller or sweeter and it is a typical feature of Italian children's literature. In this case, the word *Orsetto* evokes a teddy bear. This change makes the protagonist closer to something all children are familiar with, namely toys, thus associating him with positive experiences and sensations. Interestingly, the focus is different too. In the Italian title, there is no reference made to the fact that the protagonist is the victim of the hunt.

On the other hand, the target title of the 1999 translation, *Caccia all'Orsetto* [Little Bear Hunt] (henceforth referred to as TT2), adheres more closely to the source title even if the name of the protagonist is still translated into the diminutive *Orsetto*. The book was translated by Giulio Lughi for Einaudi Ragazzi and appeared in a collection of the three books of Bear's adventures entitled *Orsetto e matita* [Little Bear and the Pencil]. The format is also different from the original: it does not have the square format and the full-page images of the original. In fact, it is rectangular, thereby affecting the layout in that the images are smaller and framed by the white page.

With regard to the narration, as Lewis points out, Bear continuously crosses the borders between the fictional and the author's realms (Lewis 2001, 85). Accordingly, at a visual level,

> [to] hamper this slippage between realms, whenever his Bear is in the act of drawing, Browne strips away the colourful, surreal jungle that acts as a backdrop to most of the scenes and places the character against a blank, white surface. He thus appears to float in the ether, somewhere alongside his own creator. (*ibid*.)

Similarly, the verbal narration alternates the simple past account of a third person narrator with its own intrusions by directly addressing the protagonist. For example, the narrator warns him with remarks such as "Look out! Look out, Bear!" or by commenting on his clever solutions to escape the hunters' traps, such as "Well done, Bear!", yet without being visually signaled by the traditional quotation marks. When seen within the perspective of the performance and of the reading-aloud situation involved in the genre, these incursions are performance (lexical) instructions that stage-direct the adult aloud-reader and which, together with the pictures, create the reading-aloud situation.

As observed by Toolan, the verbal text for *Bear Goes to Town* is made of short sentences and is greatly "dependent (…) on the pictures to articulate developments and connections that the text does not spell out. Consequently, a rather high degree of inference-making is required from the reader/listener" (Toolan 2001, 201). Toolan also suggests that this is not generally a problem for children, who love the book despite its difficulties.

When analyzing TT1, this seems to present an enormous challenge – both for the child and especially for the adult reading aloud. This difficulty is detected in the Italian translation when suspension points are added in the very first pages.

> ST: One day Bear went for a walk. / Two hunters were hunting. / They saw Bear.

> TT1: Un giorno Orsetto stava passeggiando… / Due cacciatori, che stavano cacciando… / …videro Orsetto.

> Backtranslation: One day Little Bear was walking… / Two hunters, who were hunting… / …they saw Bear.

Besides the change in the paratactic structure, the Italian translation warns the adult reader that something is to be expected, adding further punctuation instructions and giving the adult aloud-reader clear advice on the text structure. S/he has to build up suspense because the sentence does not end until the following page.

TT2 adopts other strategies:

TT2: Un bel giorno, Orsetto esce a passeggiare. / Ad un tratto arrivano due cacciatori. / I cacciatori vedono Orsetto che passeggia.

Backtranslation: One fine day, Orsetto goes for a walk. / All of a sudden two hunters arrive. / The hunters see Little Bear who is walking.

The concise source text is expanded in TT2 with typical narrative formulas such as *Un bel giorno* [One fine day] and an adverbial phrase, *Ad un tratto* [All of a sudden]. This addition makes the clausal relations clearer. This can be ascribed to one of the hypothesized universals of translation, that is, 'explicitation,' or the tendency to "spell things out rather than leave them implicit" (Baker 1996, 180; with regard to children's literature see also Puurtinen 2004 and Ippolito 2013). A subordinate sentence specifying the picture is also added (*I cacciatori vedono Orsetto che passeggia* [The hunters see Little Bear who is walking]). This is a "verbalization of the pictorial information" (O'Sullivan 2005, 103), which has an explicative function. All of these changes help the adult reader in his/her mediation of the text by providing him/her with a more accessible and livelier text.

The need to support the adult's performance and enliven the text can also be detected in the fact that the past tense is replaced by the present tense in TT2. As noted by Lathey, "[it is precisely] the visual attributes of the present tense, together with the nature of the interaction between adult reader and child listener, [that] are particularly relevant to the picture book" (Lathey 2006, 136).

The original text moves on by showing one of the hunters' first attempts to trap Bear in a big butterfly net and Bear starting to draw a stumbling wire to escape. The verbal text reads:

ST: Look out! Look out Bear! / Quickly Bear began to draw.

The two Italian translations are very similar except for the present tense used in TT2. They are, to different degrees, adherent to the ST. Both TT1 and TT2 maintain the recurrent structure of the narrator's warnings to Bear, exclamatives directly addressing the protagonist ("Run, Bear, run!"; "Look up, Bear!"; "Clever Bear!"; "Do something Bear!"). Both of them exploit one of the figures of speech typical of children's literature, the epizeuxis, or the immediate repetition of a word, in this instance for emphasis:

> TT1: Attento! Attento, Orsetto! / Svelto svelto, Orsetto si mise a disegnare.
>
> Backtranslation: Careful! Careful, Little Bear! / Quick quick, Little Bear began to draw.
>
> TT2: Attento! Attento Orsetto! Orsetto comincia a disegnare…
>
> Backtranslation: Careful! Careful, Little Bear! Little Bear begins to draw.

The double spread that follows shows the hunter who has just stumbled on Bear's wire. The voice of the narrator intervenes again. In this case, both translations diverge from the original:

> ST: Well done, Bear!
>
> TT1: Ah! Ah! Ben fatto Orsetto!
>
> Backtranslation: Ah! Ah! Well done Little Bear!
>
> TT2: Sistemato il cacciatore!
>
> Backtranslation: The hunter is dealt with!

In TT1 two interjections (phonosymbolic instructions indicating triumph and laughter) are added to enliven the text, whereas TT2 opts for an informal expression. The hunters' second attempt at catching Bear is with a lace, as depicted in the next double spread. Again, the narrator advises Bear ("Run, Bear, run!") and he holds his pen to draw a rhinoceros in order to escape.

The fact that the pen is magic is never stated in the ST. Its magic properties and the subsequent solution deriving from Bear using his pen are only inferred. However, in TT1 the inference-making process is assumed to be too challenging for the child to comprehend and too challenging for the adult reader to mediate. The 'magic' property of the pencil is hence made explicit in the translation. It is an explicative facilitation accompanied by the addition of the conjunction 'but.' As such this is another example of explicitation.

This does not occur in TT2, which opts for the repetition of the sentence as in the first attempt, still with a view to making the text more enjoyable for the children.

> ST: Out came Bear's pencil.
>
> TT1: Ma ecco la matita magica di Orsetto.
>
> Backtranslation: But here comes Little Bear's magic pencil.
>
> TT2: Orsetto comincia a disegnare…
>
> Backtranslation: Little Bear begins to draw…

Next, one of the hunters tries to catch Bear, pointing a rifle at him. This is depicted in the illustration. The ST seems to create a type of dialogic situation in which it is not the narrator who intervenes within the narration but one of the hunters, who shouts, "Stop!" As in the cases of the narrator's interventions, there are neither quotation marks nor the name of the speaker. It is also somewhat ambiguous since the only voice heard up to this moment was that of the narrator. However, this exclamative does not have the same repetitive structure as the other narrator's warnings, in which Bear is always openly addressed. TT1 prefers to translate it as a narrator's comment. In this way, the translator of TT1 helps the adult reading aloud in the oral rendition of the story by making the narrator speak instead of the hunter, using the interjection *Uffa!* [What a nuisance!] and commenting: "The hunter again!!". TT1 opts for a recursive structure without requiring the adult reader to mime a dialogue.

> ST: Stop! The hunter's back…
>
> TT1: Uffa! Di nuovo il cacciatore!!
>
> Backtranslation: What a nuisance! The hunter again!!
>
> TT2: Altolà! Di nuovo il cacciatore!

The second translation replicates this sort of dialogic situation, so that the 'Stop' of the hunter is translated with *Altolà* [Halt], evoking military vocabulary. As TT1, it substitutes the suspension points with exclamation marks.

The next page shows a picture without any verbal text. It depicts the solution drawn by Bear when the hunter points the rifle at him: he folds the barrel of the rifle. Since this cannot be immediately evident and amounts to a relatively long pause for the adult reader, the sort of formula used when Bear is thinking up solutions is repeated in TT1, together with a warning for the hunter.

ST: ⊘

TT1: Ben fatto! Attento, cacciatore!

Backtranslation: Well done! Be careful, hunter!

TT2 follows the source text and no verbal text is inserted.

The hunters' last attempt is made with a cage and Bear is finally caught. Yet Bear draws a saw, cuts the bars of the cage and escapes. The verbal text of the original repeats the same structure of the narrator's comments. The two Italian translations enrich the ST with two informal expressions that emphasize Bear's ability and two interjections. TT2 also involves the child readers with the appellative 'friend' for Bear.

ST: Clever Bear!

TT1: Ah, che furbacchione!

Backtranslation: Ah, what an old fox!

TT2: In gamba, eh, l'amico Orsetto!

Backtranslation: On the ball, eh, our friend Orsetto!

In the next double spread, Bear falls down a hole in the ground. He shouts, "HELP," written in capital letters in the ST. The capital letters, employed to mark the salience of the words and a different pronunciation, are neutralized in TT1. This might be due to the fact that the Italian publisher does not deem the capital letters important (either on account of inaccuracy or inexperience). The dash, which leaves the image to recount the event indicating a pause, is also omitted, being uncommon in Italian. This suggests that probably the adult reader is not thought able to read it properly. Capital letters are kept in TT2, but still without a dash.

ST: HELP – !

TT1: Aiuto!

TT2: AIUTO!

As usual, Bear finds a solution. He draws a dove and flies away:

ST: So Bear escaped… / …and the hunters were left far, far behind.

TT1: E così Orsetto se ne scappò via… / lontano, molto lontano dai cacciatori.

Backtranslation: And so Little Bear ran away… / far, very far from the hunters.

TT2: Così Orsetto se ne va… /…e i cacciatori restano là!

Backtranslation: So Little Bear ran away… / and the hunters stay there.

TT1 is very close to the ST while TT2 adds a final rhyme, perhaps signally a more performance-oriented translation strategy.

Conclusions

Picture books have an intrinsic dual audience. Crossover picture books in particular exploit these different readerships by addressing both the child and adult readers. Thus, two implied readers are created by the author, simultaneously conveying a specific image of the child but also a specific image of the adult. These two images may differ when picture books are translated. This is all the more the case in crossover picture books, which reveal themselves to be fruitful *loci* for detecting and investigating these changes.

Bear Hunt by Anthony Browne and its Italian translations are a case in point. Contrary to Berman's "retranslation hypothesis" (1990), which states that the first translation is usually more target-oriented than retranslations, the first Italian translation shows a more apparent adherence to the source text. (The past tense of the original text is retained, for example.) However, the seemingly simple short text of the original is considered too difficult for the Italian child. At one point, Bear's pen is explicitly identified as magic in the Italian TT1. Later, a dialogue is modified to make the reading of the text more comprehensible. This type of intervention also suggests that the adult reading aloud is not considered capable of coping with this complex situation and of mediating it for the child reader. Similarly, the analysis shows that s/he is also thought not to be able to deal with Browne's minimal text; it is therefore enlivened with exclamation marks and interjections. That is, the adult is assisted with performing his/her task by using strategies that contribute to a more readable and enjoyable text. Yet, the challenging contrast between the somewhat dry verbal text and the rich pictures of Anthony Browne's original text – which is instrumental in presenting the theme of the war – is toned down so that even the message for the adult loses its strength.

The second translation is even more performance-oriented while at the same time more trusting of both the adult and child readers' interpretive skills. Even if there is a verbalization of the visual text at the very beginning, the use of capital letters and the interpretation of the difficult dialogical exchanges between the different voices, as well as the maintenance of the primary inference on which the source text is based, reflect an increasing genre awareness and a confidence in the adult reading aloud. The translator of TT2 is so aware of the reading aloud situation that both rhymes and the present tense are used to make the adult's reading more vivid. As for TT1, the translator's choices tended to make the text more traditional for children, once again mitigating the message for the adult.

To conclude, the diverse solutions in the two Italian translations reveal different images of the child and of the adult reading aloud compared to the source text. Both target texts, in different ways and to different degrees, help the adult reader in his/her reading performance of the text for the child. Translation decisions made in TT1 and TT2 suggest efforts to liven up an apparently dry text. However, TT1 also tended to mediate the content, adding a fundamental explicitation that suggested its dual audience was not thought to be capable of dealing with the implicitness of the source text. The strategies aimed at making the text more fun and exciting also appear to have a lightening intent, as they mitigate the disquieting but central theme of war. This calls into question not whether children can deal with such themes, but rather whether adults can.

Bibliography

Anstey, Michèle and Geoff Bull. 2004. "The Picture Book: Modern and Postmodern." In *International Encyclopedia of Children's Literature*, edited by Peter Hunt, 329–339. New York: Routledge.

Baker, Mona. 1996. "Corpus-based Translation Studies: The Challenges That Lie Ahead." In *Terminology, LSP and Translation*, edited by Harold Somers, 175–118. Amsterdam: John Benjamins.

Beckett, Sandra. 2012. *Crossover Picturebooks: A Genre for All Ages*. London: Routledge.

Berman, Antoine. 1990. "La retraduction comme espace de la traduction." In *Palimpsestes*, no. 1, edited by Bensimon Paul and Coupaye Didier, 1–7. Paris: Presses de la Sorbonne Nouvelle.

Browne, Anthony. 1990. *Orsetto e i cacciatori*. Milan: Ugo Mursia Editore.

Browne, Anthony. 1994. *Bear Hunt*. London: Puffin Books.

Browne, Anthony. 1999. *Caccia all'Orsetto*. In *Orsetto e matita*. Translated by Giulio Lughi. Turin: Einaudi.

Cabaret, Florence. 2014. "Introduction." In *La Retraduction en littérature de jeunesse. Retranslating Children's Literature*, edited by Virginie Douglas and Florence Cabaret, 11–19. Oxford: Peter Lang.

Cardarello, Roberta. 1995. *Libri e bambini: La prima formazione del lettore*. Firenze: La Nuova Italia.

Chatman, Seymour. 1998. *Storia e discors: La struttura narrativa nel romanzo e nel film*. Translated by Elisabetta Graziosi. Piacenza: Pratiche.

Cullinan, Bernice E. B. and Diane Goetz Person. 2005. *Continuum Encyclopedia of Children's Literature*. New York: Continuum.

Dollerup, Cay. 2003. "Translating for Reading Aloud." *Meta* 48, no. 1–2: 81–103.

Doonan, Jane. 1996. "The Modern Picturebook." In *International Companion Encyclopedia of Children's Literature*, edited by Peter Hunt, 231–241. London/New York: Routledge.

Hermans, Theo. 1996. "The Translator's Voice in Translated Narrative." *Target* 8, no. 1: 23–48.

Ippolito, Margherita. 2013. *Simplification, Explicitation and Normalization: Corpus-based Research into English to Italian Translations of Children's Classics*. Newcastle upon Tyne: Cambridge Scholars Publishing.

Lathey, Gillian. 2006. "Translating Sound in Children's Literature." In *No Child Is an Island: The Case of Children's Literature in Translation*, edited by Pat Pinsent, 182–186. Lichfield Staffordshire: Pied Piper Publishing.

Lewis, Davis. 2001. *Reading Contemporary Picturebooks: Picturing Text*. New York/Abingdon: Routledge.

McCallum, Robyn. 1996. "Metafictions and Experimental Work." In *International Companion Encyclopedia of Children's Literature*, edited by Peter Hunt, 587–598. London/New York: Routledge.

Moebius, William. 1986. "Introduction to Picturebook Codes." *Word & Image: A Journal of Verbal/Visual Enquiry* 2, no. 2: 141–158.

Nikolajeva, Maria. 2005. *Aesthetic Approaches to Children's Literature*. Lanham: Scarecrow Press.

Nikolajeva, Maria and Carole Scott. 2006. *How Picturebooks Work*. London: Routledge.

Nodelman, Perry. 1988. *Words about Pictures: The Narrative Art of Children's Picture Books*. Athens: University of Georgia Press.

Oittinen, Riitta. 2000. *Translating for Children*. New York: Garland Publishing.

Oittinen, Riitta, Anne Ketola and Melissa Garavini. 2018. *Translating Picturebooks: Revoicing the Verbal, the Visual and the Aural for a Child Audience*. London: Routledge.

O'Sullivan, Emer. 2005. *Comparative Children's Literature*. Translated by Anthea Bell. London/New York: Routledge.

Painter, Clare, Jim R. Martin and Len Unsworth. 2012. *Reading Visual Narratives: Image Analysis in Children's Picturebooks*. Sheffield: Equinox Publishing.

Pedrelli, Debora. 2015. "Translating Anthony Browne's Picture Books: Bear and His Adventures in Italian – Tradurre gli albi illustrati di Anthony Browne: Orsetto e le sue avventure in italiano." Unpublished BA diss., University of Modena and Reggio Emilia.

Puurtinen, Tiina. 2004. "Explicitation of Clausal Relations: A Corpus-based Analysis of Clause Connectives in Translated and Non-translated Finnish Children's Literature." In *Translation Universals: Do They Exist?*, edited by Anna Mauranen and Pekka Kujamäki, 165–176. Amsterdam: John Benjamins.

Schiavi, Giuliana. 1996. "There is Always a Teller in a Tale." *Target* 8, no. 1: 1–21.

Scott, Carole. 1999. "Dual Audience in Picturebooks." In *Transcending Boundaries: Writing for a Dual Audience of Children and Adults*, edited by Sandra Beckett, 99–110. New York/London: Garland Publishing.

Sezzi, Annalisa. 2009. "The Translation of Pre-school Picturebooks: Towards a Different Child Image and of a Different Voice of the Adult Aloud Reader." In *Proceedings of the 23rd AIA Conference – Forms of Migration/Migration of Forms*, edited by Domenico Torretta, Marina Dossena and Annamaria Sportelli, 352–368. Bari: Progedit.

Sezzi, Annalisa. 2010. "Bariery literatury dla dzieci. Recepcja ksiazek obrazkowych we wloszech a kwestia glosnej lektury", *Przekładaniec. Półrocznik Katedry UNESCO do Badań nad Przekładem i Komunikacja Miedzykulturowa UJ* 2–1, no. 22–23: 226–244. Kraków: Wydawnictwo Uniwersytetu Jagielloń.

Shavit, Zohar. 1983. "The Notion of Childhood and the Child (Test Case: Little Red Riding Hood)." *Journal of Research and Development in Education* 16, no. 3: 60–67.

Shavit, Zohar. 1986. *Poetics of Children's Literature*. Athens, GA/London: The University of Georgia Press.

Spitz, Ellen H. 1999. *Inside Picture Books*. New Haven: Yale University Press.

Stephens, John. 1992. *Language and Ideology in Children's Fiction*. London: Longman.

Toolan, Michael. 2001. *Narrative: A Critical Linguistic Introduction*. London/New York: Routledge.

Van Coillie, Jan. 2014a. "How Hard It Is to Play the Translator's Game." *Marvels and Tales* 2: 346–365.

Van Coillie, Jan. 2014b. "Nibble, Nibble Like a Mouse/Who is Nibbling at the Source Text's House. Retranslating Fairy Tales: Untangling the Web of Causation." In *La Retraduction en littérature de jeunesse. Retranslating Children's Literature*, edited by Virginie Douglas and Florence Cabaret, 39–52. Oxford: Peter Lang.

Pettson and Findus go glocal

Recontextualization of images and multimodal analysis of simultaneous action in Dutch and French translations

Sara Van Meerbergen & Charlotte Lindgren

Abstract

This chapter focuses on the recontextualization of images and the translation of simultaneous action expressed multimodally in picture book translations. It analyzes several spreads from the globally translated and distributed picture books about Grandpa Pettson and Findus by Swedish author-illustrator Sven Nordqvist and compares their French and Dutch translations using a social semiotic multimodal text analysis examining both words and images. Within the theoretical framework of social semiotics, but also drawing on central thoughts within Descriptive Translation Studies, the authors see translation and the act of translating as motivated by and within its specific social and situational context, depending on the signs that are culturally available within this context. The results of the analyses show that the translated picture books about Pettson and Findus can be described as 'glocal' artefacts, combining globally spread images with new meaning depending on the local choices made in the different translations, in this case as expressed through the depiction of simultaneous action.

Introduction

The concept of globalization and its impact on today's society and cultural production have been discussed widely within several research disciplines, including the humanities. Globalization is often connected to political, economic and cultural dimensions (see Coupland 2013, 3) or more specifically to economic liberalization and Americanization (see Ricento 2013, 123). In connection to the translation of children's literature and globalization, Borodo (2017, 8) states:

> [Globalization] is thus identified with the spread of sameness, the erasure of genuinely local and national cultural practices and referred to as Westernization, Americanization, cultural imperialism, or, to use popular neologisms, the Coca-colonization, Disneyfication and McDonaldization of the world.

These words reflect the ongoing discussion over the last two decades about the influence of globalization on children's media (see also Davies 2004; O'Sullivan 2005). While some critics initially argued that we are moving towards a more global culture (for children), which threatens cultural diversity, more recent research has focused on the growing countermovement of local forces and so-called 'localization' of global media, resulting in 'glocal products' (see Borodo 2017; Machin and van Leeuwen 2007). At the same time, an urgent need is expressed for more thorough analysis of the complexity of the relationship between the local and the global in given situations rather than subscribing to "sweeping generalizations" (van Leeuwen and Suleiman 2013, 232).

Against this background our chapter considers some features in the Dutch and French translations of the picture books about Grandpa Pettson and his cat Findus by picture book artist Sven Nordqvist. Originally Swedish, these picture books achieved global circulation (over six continents) and have now been translated for fifty-five different target cultures.[1] Although the pictures in the books depict a typical 'idyllic,' quiet and peaceful local Swedish countryside setting, including red wooden cottages (see Källström 2011), a previous study by Gossas et al. (2015) has shown that the Swedishness of the books has been dealt with in various ways in different European target cultures. This earlier study for the most part focused on publishing processes and translation strategies in connection with the translation of cultural specifics in the written text. In our current study, we want to shift the focus to a multimodal approach where meanings created by both words and images can be taken into account (see Kress and van Leeuwen 2006; Van Meerbergen 2010; Painter, et al. 2013; Oittinen, Ketola and Garavini 2017).

---

1 According to details provided by the publisher Opal after email contact (August 29, 2018), these target cultures include languages from around the globe such as Arabic, Chinese, Persian, Portuguese, Spanish, Somali, Russian and Thai, and several English translations for different target cultures. In this respect, it must be noted that the term 'target culture' does not fully coincide with 'language.' There are, for example, several English translations of the Pettson and Findus books that are area-specific and also published by different publishers, for New Zealand, the US and the UK.

In contrast to other multimodal studies on picture books and their translation, such as Oittinen et al. (2017), our analytical method is directly inspired by the model for multimodal text analysis proposed by Kress and van Leeuwen (2006) within the theoretical framework of social semiotics and systemic functional linguistics (see van Leeuwen 2005; Halliday and Matthiessen 2004). This implies that we see all signs and forms of communication, including translation and the act of translating, as *motivated* by and within the social and situational context surrounding it (see Kress 2010; Van Meerbergen 2010, 2014). This social semiotic approach, in its turn, correlates well with the central tenets of Descriptive Translation Studies (DTS), where translational behavior is seen as shaped by social and cultural norms within the context of the target culture (see Toury 1995; Hermans 1999). In line with Toury (1995) and DTS, in our analysis, we will first be looking at the context surrounding and initiating the translation (Toury's so-called 'preliminary norms'), before moving on to a comparative multimodal analysis of source and target text (Toury's 'operational norms'). Our reason for subscribing to the multimodal text analysis proposed by Kress and van Leeuwen (2006) is that it provides us with tools to analyze both the visual and verbal depiction of characters and their actions, which will be the main focus of our analysis.

While other studies of (translated) children's literature using a social semiotic model of multimodal analysis have focused on ideological dimensions related to how picture book characters are depicted by words and images (see Unsworth 2005; Moya and Pinar 2008; Painter et al. 2013; Van Meerbergen 2010, 2014; Lindgren 2016), our present analysis focuses on the depiction of simultaneous action and movement in images and words, being a key feature in the picture books about Pettson and Findus. One of the central questions in our analysis relates to the concept of 'recontextualization,' which Bezemer and Kress (2016, 75) in relation to Bernstein (1996) describe as "literally, moving 'meaning-material' from one context, with its social organization of participants and its modal ensembles, to another, with its different social organization and modal ensembles." We will use this concept to describe and analyze what happens with images and their relationship to words when they are re-used within a different context – in other words, within the context of a translated or 'manipulated' text (see Lefevere 1992), which in turn is shaped and formed by the social and cultural context of the target culture (see Toury 1995; Hermans 1999). More specifically, we ask: will a recontextualization of images depicting characters performing certain actions give rise to possible new interpretations of these images and will new potential meanings be connected to them within the context of a target text?

Before moving on to the comparative multimodal analysis of simultaneous actions in the Dutch and French translations of some sequences from two books about Pettson and Findus, we will first discuss the publishing context of the books.

Pettson and Findus go global

The first book about Pettson and Findus, *Pannkakstårtan*, was published in Swedish in 1984. Over the subsequent years, several books followed, and this series of picture books came to consist of nine titles, the last of which was published in Swedish in 2012. As well as the 'original' series, other books and products related to the main characters were produced, such as cardboard books, activity books and audio books. The success and popularity of the series and characters also led to the production of other media, such as theatre performances, songs, (animated) films, computer games, and other typical merchandise products for children. Many of these entered international markets (see also Gossas et al. 2015). These marketing and production strategies can be seen in the light of what Borodo (2017, 11) refers to as a "Total Product," where characters from children's literature or other media, such as animated films, are distributed and promoted globally by way of a range of texts and products. Against this background, where global 'sameness' seems to be a key factor, we find it interesting to look more closely at the dynamics between the global spreading of images and their local recontextualization and how translated multimodal texts can subsequently be characterized as 'glocal' artifacts, in other words artifacts resulting from a process where an internationally distributed product is made suitable and acceptable for its specific local target culture (see Robertson 1995; Roudometof 2016), depending on the choices made by the translator in the translation process.

In their study on the translation of Pettson and Findus, Gossas et al. (2015, 76) have shown that there is a difference in publishing patterns and translation strategies in the Germanic and Romance target cultures included in their study, namely Dutch, French, German, Norwegian and Spanish (all within a European context). Whereas the publication of the translations into Dutch, German and Norwegian followed relatively quickly after the publication of the originals, the French and Spanish translations were published and republished in different translation waves at (often) later points in time and by different publishers (see also Lindgren 2015).

In France, the first Pettson and Findus book to be translated was *Pannkakstårtan* in 1985, one year after the publication of the Swedish original. Since then, three different French publishers (Centurion, Autrement and Plume de carotte) have been involved in the translation and publication of the books. The books' success was not immediate, and it took several years and different publishers for the entire series to be translated. Earlier studies have shown that this was partly because the written text parts in the books were deemed too long for a modern French picture book audience, resulting in the shortening of the written text parts in the later French translations (Andersson and Lindgren 2008; Gossas et al. 2015; Lindgren 2015, 2016).

Similarly, in Dutch, the first book to be translated was *Pannkakstårtan*, which was published two years after the Swedish original, in 1986. Contrary to the French translations, over the following years all the other books were translated and published in close succession to their original text. In several cases, translations were even published in co-production the same year as the originals. An interesting aspect of the publication of the Dutch translation of the series is that it was published by the Flemish publishing house Davidsfonds Infodok in Belgium. This is notable because Flanders constitutes only a small part of the Dutch language area, where the literary field has traditionally been dominated by publishers in the Netherlands. While Pettson and Findus, according to the Flemish publisher, are more popular in Flanders, the translated books are also distributed and sold in the Netherlands (personal correspondence with Veerle Moureau, October 22, 2018).

Gossas et al. (2015) connect the differences on the level of the publishing context for the Dutch and French translations to differences in translation strategies on a textual level. Their analysis shows that, when it comes to the translation of cultural specifics, the Dutch translations have kept more closely to the original texts, preserving characters' names, for example, and thereby adhering to a source-text or adequacy-oriented translation strategy (see Toury 1995). In the French translation, character names were adapted and transformed into more French-sounding names, thus opting for a target-culture or acceptability-oriented strategy (*ibid.*). When it comes to the study of cultural specifics in translation, DTS offers a well-suited method for analyzing translational shifts and relating them to target text cultural norms. However, when dealing with the translation of multimodal texts, where both words and images create meaning together, it becomes clear that the traditional models for translation analysis within DTS do not always suffice because they are primarily concerned with texts where the verbal mode is seen as the prominent one (see Díaz-Cintas 2004, 22; Van Meerbergen 2014, 99; Dicerto 2018, 4–8). By using parts from the model for multimodal text analysis proposed by Kress and van Leeuwen (2006), we will thus analyze depictions of simultaneous action expressed through *both* words and images in the

Pettson and Findus books and their translations. Our methodology for this is discussed in a more precise manner in the next part of our chapter, where we also present our analysis.

A multimodal analysis of simultaneous action

When Sven Nordqvist first wrote his books about Pettson and Findus in the 1980s, he did so within the context of a long but also changing tradition within Swedish children's literature. In Nordqvist's books, we detect elements of nostalgia for Swedish nature and the countryside, thus hinting at the older romantic traditions in children's literature by Elsa Beskow (Kåreland 1998, 278). At the same time, there is a clear focus on fantasy and the imagination in the humoristic and detailed visual storylines that can be explored freely by readers, as they are not always mentioned or commented on in the verbal storyline. In this sense, the picture books by Nordqvist can be compared to what Rémi (2011) describes as 'wimmelbooks,' books crawling with visual details that invite and challenge the reader to engage actively while enhancing cognitive learning at the level of (visual) literacy and language development. Nordqvist's style can be described as being (early) postmodern, as it uses elements of play, intertextuality (e.g. the use of romantic and stereotypical Scandinavian imagery) and the interactive potential of the pictures, which points readers to forms of creative involvement (see Sipe and Pantaleo 2010; Van Meerbergen 2012).

Sven Nordqvist has often been praised for his (at the time of publication) innovative use of interplay between words and images, and for a visual language that has been described as dynamic, full of pictorial detail, chaotic-like, playful and full of action (see Gossas et al. 2015). Some more specific pictorial elements that are discussed by Nikolajeva and Scott (2001, 143) are the ever-present use of multiple visual side-narratives (i.e. narratives expressed only visually, not verbally) and the frequent use of so-called "simultaneous succession," where one character is depicted multiple times on one spread in a succession of different actions (Nikolajeva 2000, 204; Lindgren 2015, 97). Originally used in medieval hagiographies depicting the lives of saints, the use of simultaneous succession is something that we nowadays also typically find in comic books (see McCloud 1994).

As these instances of simultaneous succession are a typical visual feature in the books about Pettson and Findus, adding to the playful and dynamic character of the imagery in the books (see Nikolajeva and Scott 2001), we decided to focus on this specific feature in our translation analysis. When looking more closely at the written text in the Swedish source texts, we noticed an extensive use of verb constructions expressing so-called coordinating actions, when two (or more) verbs are linked together by the Swedish coordinating conjunction *och* [and], expressing several, sometimes ongoing actions performed in close succession or even simultaneously (see Kvist Darnell 2008). An example of this could be: *Han står och tittar på trädgården*, which can be translated literally as: "He is standing and looking [at] the garden" thus expressing that the subject in question is performing both actions simultaneously and continuously. In other words, it seems that forms of simultaneous actions are expressed through both words and images in the picture books about Pettson and Findus. Before moving on to the translation analysis, we first briefly explain some of the terminology that will be used in the analysis drawing on the model for multimodal text analysis proposed by Kress and van Leeuwen (2006).

In the analysis of multimodal texts such as picture books, the verbal mode is typically described as temporally structured, while the visual mode relies on spatially manifested resources to create meaning (Kress 2003, 1–4). In the verbal mode, actions in time are often expressed through the use of 'processes' realized by verbs connected to certain participants (Kress and van Leeuwen 2006; Painter et al. 2013, 53–89). Processes can also be expressed visually through the use of visual depictions of participants engaging in actions indicated by vectors or bodily movements (*ibid.*). One participant can be depicted performing several processes simultaneously or at the same time. For example, a character can be shown walking while looking at something or talking to somebody via speech bubbles (Kress and van Leeuwen 2006, 59–113). In cases of 'simultaneous succession,' one participant is depicted several times within the same picture book spread engaging in several processes and thus performing several actions in close succession.

Keeping in mind the main goal of our analysis (studying the recontextualization of images in translation), we now present some examples of specific instances in the text where characters are depicted as performing several actions simultaneously or in close succession, and where visual depictions are combined with *different* verbal processes when the written text parts are translated into Dutch and French. At this point it is also important to highlight that our analysis is qualitative, and that we do not have any quantitative ambitions in this study. In our analysis we have chosen to focus on some examples taken from the books *Kackel i grönsakslandet* (1990) and *Rävjakten* (1986). Both books were translated into Dutch by Griet van Raemdonck under the titles *Gekakel in de moestuin* (2003) and *Vossenjacht* (2005), published by

Figure 1. Spread with simultaneous succession of gardening actions in *Kackel i grönsakslandet* (1990), © Bokförlaget Opal AB and Sven Nordqvist

Davidsfonds Infodok. In French, the first book was translated as *Grabuge au potager* (2014) by Camille Gautier and the other one as *Pettson piège le renard* (2008) by Paul Paludis, both published by Autrement.[2]

Figure 1 shows Grandpa Pettson engaging in several visual processes.[3] On the left side of the spread he is performing several visual actions simultaneously: he is standing in the garden holding what looks like a shovel. He is also holding something in his other hand and is looking at it. On the right side of the spread we see Pettson performing a series of gardening actions in close succession to each other. The actions can be described as: digging the garden, loosening or leveling the soil with a rake and planting some seeds.

The visual depictions of Pettson are combined with slightly different descriptions of action in the verbal text components in the Swedish, Dutch and French texts. Table 1 shows excerpts from the Swedish source text (hereafter referred to as ST) and the Dutch and French target texts (hereafter referred to as TTnl and TTfr). For the sake of clarity, each of the excerpts is provided

---

[2] In the course of finalizing this chapter, a new translation appeared in French published by Plume de Carotte. Unfortunately, we were not able to include this new translation in our analysis.
[3] We want to express our gratitude to the publisher Opal AB and Sven Nordqvist for granting us the permission to publish the images in Figures 1 and 2.

Table 1. Parallel extracts from Swedish, Dutch and French texts (Example 1)

	Text	Backtranslation
ST	Gubben Pettson stod i grönsakslandet och tittade och kände på jorden.	Grandpa Pettson stood in the vegetable garden and looked (at) and felt the soil.
TTnl	Opa Pettson keek naar zijn moestuin. Hij voelde eens aan de aarde.	Grandpa Pettson looked at his vegetable garden. He quickly felt the soil.
TTfr	Pettson se tenait là, au milieu du jardin, à observer le sol.	Pettson was standing there, in the middle of the garden, while observing the soil.

with our own English backtranslation. In Table 1, we can see the written text parts in ST, TTnl and TTfr that accompany the visuals on the left side of the spread where the simultaneous processes of 'standing,' 'holding a shovel,' 'holding something in the other hand' and 'looking at the hand' are depicted (see Figure 1).

Table 1 shows that the written text part in the ST expresses three coordinated actions, which can be directly related to the visual depiction of Pettson: "stood," "looked" and "felt." ST thus creates a specific form of what Van Meerbergen (2010, 86; 2014) has referred to as "referential interplay" between words and images, meaning that certain of the visually depicted objects, in our case depicted actions, are picked up on and referred to directly in the written text. The only process that is not directly picked up on in the verbal text of ST in Example 1 is the visual process of 'holding a shovel.' On a verbal level, the three processes are all coordinated and connected by the Swedish conjunction *och* and are presented as ongoing actions succeeding each other closely in time. In connection to the visual depiction of Grandpa Pettson, these actions are even likely to be interpreted as happening simultaneously, as we can clearly see Pettson depicted as performing these three actions at the same time.

Looking at TTnl and TTfr in Example 1, we can notice some differences in the written text when it comes to the rendering of the verbal processes, which subsequently also influence the referential interplay with the visuals when it comes to the depiction of action. In TTnl, the number of processes in the written text is reduced from three to two: 'looked' and 'felt.' The process of standing is thus not picked up on explicitly in the verbal text and is therefore only expressed visually in TTnl. An observant reader will also notice that Pettson is described as looking at his *vegetable garden*, not at the soil in his hand, as is the case in ST. This thus creates a partly different interpretation of the visual depiction of Pettson where we can see him looking at something dark in his hand, or it might suggest a different action that is not depicted visually. Interestingly, too, the coordinated aspect of the actions is not present at all in the written text part of TTnl, where the processes of 'looking' and 'feeling' are presented without any coordination, nor as ongoing actions. Instead of choosing a possibly more complicated syntactic construction to render the ongoing aspect in the actions (in Dutch this would be an infinitive construction with an auxiliary), the processes are split up and divided over different sentences in TTnl, which also gives them a less close connection in time to each other. Altogether, it seems as if closely coordinated and ongoing aspects of actions are neutralized in the written text where only the process of 'feeling the soil' has a direct connection to the visually depicted processes in TTnl.

Contrary to TTnl, the translator of TTfr clearly opts for a rendering of the ongoing and simultaneous aspect of the processes and actions in the written text part. Here a rather complex construction can be found where a position verb *tenait* [stood] is used as auxiliary in an infinitive construction with *à observer* [to observe] expressing a simultaneous and ongoing action (see Kortteinen 2005): "He was standing there (…) while observing." In relation to the visual depiction and the processes that Pettson is engaged in, the process of 'standing' is picked up on in the written text part of TTfr while the processes of 'looking' and 'feeling' are summarized and rendered together through one more general process 'to observe' (*à observer*), which can be interpreted as rather referring to 'looking' than to 'feeling.' This makes the referential interplay to the images partly different from the ST, as the visually depicted actions of 'looking' and 'feeling/holding something' are referred to in a more general way in TTfr rather than named specifically.

Table 2 shows the descriptions in the written text in ST, TTnl and TTfr accompanying the simultaneous succession of Pettson's gardening actions depicted visually on the right side of the spread in Figure 1. On a visual level, a succession of three actions following closely after each other in time is depicted: 'to dig up,' 'to rake' and 'to plant.'

The written text of ST rendered in Table 2 starts by referring to two of the visually depicted actions: 'dig' and 'rake,' before then moving on to describe each of the actions separately in direct reference to the visual depiction: *grävde upp* [dug], *jämnade till* [levelled out] and *sådde* [planted]. This same structure is followed closely by TTnl, although here more specific temporal markers ('first (…) and then') are added in order to depict the actions in a clearer temporal order in line with the order in which the actions are presented visually. This

Table 2. Parallel extracts from Swedish, Dutch and French texts (Example 2)

	Text	Backtranslation
ST	–... Men först ska vi gräva och kratta. ... Pettson grävde upp grönsakslandet och jämnade till jorden. Han sådde fröna i raka fina rader. Morötter och lök, ärtor och bönor.	–... But first we have to dig and rake. ... Pettson dug the vegetable garden and levelled out the ground. He planted the seeds in well-formed straight lines. Carrots and onions, peas and beans.
TTnl	'... Maar eerst moeten we alles omspitten en harken.' ... Pettson spitte eerst de moestuin om en dan harkte hij de aarde. Hij zaaide de zaden in mooie, rechte lijnen. Wortels en uien, erwten en bonen.	'... But first we have to dig up (break up) everything and rake.' ... Pettson first dug (up) the vegetable garden and then he raked the ground. He planted the seeds in well-formed straight lines. Carrots and onions, peas and beans.
TTfr	'... Mais d'abord, au travail'. ... Pettson sarcla et ratissa la terre. Il planta les graines, bien alignées en rangs: carottes, oignons, petits pois et haricots verts.	'... But first, (let's get) to work'. ... Pettson weeded and raked the ground. He planted the seeds, well aligned in lines: carrots, onions, peas and beans.

adheres to a Western reading tradition from left to right (see Kress and van Leeuwen 2006, 179–185). In contrast to ST and TTnl, the written text in TTfr does not include any direct initial references to the depicted actions. Instead the actions are initially referred to on a more general level with the words *au travail* [let's get to work]. After this there is also a succession of gardening verbs. An interesting choice is made in the first verb describing the series of gardening actions in French where *sarcler*, meaning 'to weed,' is used while ST and TTnl describe this action as 'to dig up.' Here one could argue that the TTfr names and interprets the visually depicted action of 'digging' in a different way. Overall, we can thus see that the depiction of verbal action in TTnl is following the ST rather closely in Example 2, whereas TTfr makes some different choices creating a partly different referential interplay with the images and providing a different interpretation for one of the visually depicted gardening actions.

In Figure 2, a spread with a visual depiction of simultaneous succession from the book *Rävjakten* (1986) is shown. On the right side of the spread we can see Grandpa Pettson as a participant in three visual processes depicting typical thinking behavior marked by his specific body language. The last action suggests an expression of shock, where Pettson's feet are up in the air and his hands are in a cramped position, also combined with an invisible speech bubble rendering the exclamation "UH?".

Figure 2. Spread with simultaneous succession from *Rävjakten* (1986), © Bokförlaget Opal AB and Sven Nordqvist

In Table 3 the written text parts from ST, TTnl and TTfr describing the simultaneous succession of actions on the right side of the spread in Figure 2 are displayed. While the ST names each visual action separately as a coordinated series of processes ('think and ponder and reflect'), these three processes are reduced to one process summarizing all three in both TTnl and TTfr ('think for a long time/deeply') as is shown in Table 3. Hereby, again an element of repetition is reduced and neutralized, and the written text is also shortened. The last line in ST describes the fourth visual depiction of Pettson with an instance of three simultaneously performed processes: *bet i luften* [grabbing for air], *morrade* [groaned], and *sen ett förskräckt "Uh?"* [then (producing) a startled "Uh?"]. TTnl only includes the first two processes and does not mention the exclamation which is also removed visually from the picture in TTnl. TTfr reduces this last sequence entirely, shortening the text even more, and also here the exclamation is omitted from the image. To conclude, also in Example 3 we find different forms of referential interplay between actions depicted in words and images in the instance of simultaneous succession depicted in Figure 2. Again, it seems as if the target texts, in these instances, have chosen to avoid repetition and to reduce the written text.

Table 3. Parallel extracts from Swedish, Dutch and French texts (Example 3)

	Text	Backtranslation
ST	Och Pettson började tänka och grubbla och fundera. Ibland hördes en del ljud från honom, när han kom på något bra, eller när han kom på att det inte var så bra, det som han just hade kommit på. Till slut bet han i luften och morrade, sen ett förskräckt "Uh?" sen skrattade han ett tyst gnäggande och sa: ...	And Pettson started to think and ponder and reflect. Sometimes some sounds could be heard coming from him, when he came up with something good, or when he came up with something that was not so good. At last he grabbed for air and groaned, then (he produced) a startled "Uh?" then he laughed a whinnying laugh and said: ...
TTnl	Pettson dacht lang na. Soms mompelde hij wat als hij iets goeds gevonden had of als hij datgene dat hij net bedacht had, toch niet zo goed vond. Tenslotte hapte hij naar lucht, gromde en grinnikte dan stilletjes.	Pettson was thinking for a long time. Sometimes he mumbled a bit when he came up with something good or when he did not like the thing that he just came up with after all. At last he grabbed for air, grumbled and then chuckled quietly.
TTfr	Pettson se mit à réfléchir profondément. Puis il grogna. C'est ce qu'il faisait à chaque fois qu'il était persuadé d'avoir une idée géniale. C'est aussi ce qu'il faisait lorsqu'il se rendait compte que son idée n'était finalement pas si géniale que ça.	Pettson started to think deeply. Then he groaned. That was what he did every time he was convinced that he had a genius idea. That was also what he did when he realized that his idea was not so great after all.

Results and conclusion

In this chapter we investigated the recontextualization of images when globally distributed picture books displaying seeming 'sameness' through their visual make up are translated and when certain choices are made in the local versions of the written text in the picture book. Using parts of the model for multimodal text analysis proposed by Kress and van Leeuwen (2006), we looked more specifically at the depiction of simultaneous action through words and images in some of the picture books about Pettson and Findus and their Dutch and French translations. Although the idyllic pictures of the Swedish countryside and its many aspects remain physically the same (apart from, for example, speech bubbles), our analysis clearly shows that these pictures are used and referred to in different ways in the ST and the TTs. In line with earlier research, we notice some reductions in the written text of the TTs when it comes to repetition and the depiction of action, creating different forms of referential interplay between words and images in the ST and the TTs. In some cases, this leads to different possible interpretations and potential meanings of images.

Some interesting differences between TTnl and TTfr are evident when it comes to the rendering of ongoing and simultaneous actions in the written text. Here the examples from TTnl show a tendency towards neutralizing and reducing ongoing simultaneous actions, reformulating these instead into actions performed one after the other, but also splitting up and dividing the actions over different sentences. This results in less complex verb structures compared to the option of rendering the actions as simultaneous and ongoing, which could be achieved using a more complex Dutch infinitive structure with an auxiliary. This tendency towards reduction of repetition in coordination – which we also noted at several other instances in TTnl and TTfr – can be seen in the light of the translation law of "growing standardization" proposed by Toury (1995, 267–274) and further discussed by Chesterman (2004). Together with the avoidance of "more difficult" syntactic constructions, which was particularly evident in the examples from TTnl, the avoidance of repetition has also been described as a typical feature in translation for children (O'Sullivan 2005, 88). While these tendencies could partly be related to a difference in linguistic norms between languages, they could also be interpreted as related to educational and didactic norms in translating for children, in other words reflecting expectations of what is deemed as suitable language in a text for children in a specific social and cultural context (see Van Meerbergen 2014). An interesting contrast to TTnl that can be noticed in TTfr is the active presence of rather complex stylistic verb structures used to depict simultaneous and ongoing action in the written text. This seems to be in line with translation norms noticed in previous studies about French translation of Swedish children's literature (Andersson et al. 2006; Lindgren et al. 2007; Renaud et al. 2007).

To conclude, this chapter has shown that while going global, the picture books about Pettson and Findus can certainly be described as 'glocal' artifacts, where globally spread images receive different meanings due to local choices made in the translations. We looked specifically at depictions of simultaneous action to illustrate this. Our conclusions come into sharper focus when seen from a social semiotic point of view. Translation, like all other forms of communication, is a social practice. Translators make motivated choices depending on the signs and resources that are culturally available within their social and situational context, be it through language, views on childhood or translation norms (see van Leeuwen 2005; Kress 2010). Furthermore, it is our hope that this contribution also adds to the understanding of picture book translation as a multimodal and a glocal text practice, where the visual and the verbal, but also the global and the local, intertwine in complex ways.

Bibliography

Andersson, Carina and Charlotte Lindgren. 2008. "Texte, image et désignateurs culturels: Réflexions sur la traduction et la réception de Pettson en France." *Moderna språk CII*, no. 2: 24–34.

Andersson, Carina, Charlotte Lindgren and Cathrine Renaud. 2006. "Vilken röra i kökssoffan. Att översätta barnböcker: ett svenskt-franskt perspektiv." *Barnboken* no. 2: 34–44.

Bernstein, Basil. 1996. *Pedagogy, Symbolic Control and Identity: Theory, Research, Critique*. London: Taylor & Francis.

Bezemer, Jeff and Gunther Kress. 2016. *Multimodality, Learning and Communication: A Social Semiotic Frame*. London: Routledge.

Borodo, Michał. 2017. *Translation, Globalization and Younger Audiences: The Situation in Poland*. Bern: Peter Lang.

Chesterman, Andrew. 2004. "Beyond the Particular." In *Translation Universals: Do They Exist?*, edited by Anna Mauranen and Pekka Kujamäki, 33–50. Amsterdam/Philadelphia: John Benjamins.

Coupland, Douglas. 2013. *The Handbook of Language and Globalization*. Chichester: Wiley Blackwell.

Davies, Máire Messenger. 2004. "Mickey and Mr Grumpy: The Global and the Universal in Children's Media." *European Journal of Cultural Studies* 7, no. 4: 425–440.

Díaz-Cintas, Jorge. 2004. "Subtitling: The Long Journey to Academic Acknowledgement." *The Journal of Specialised Translation*, no. 1: 50–68.

Dicerto, Sara. 2018. *Multimodal Pragmatics and Translation: A New Model for Source Text Analysis*. Basingstoke: Palgrave Macmillan.

Gossas, Carina, Marcus Axelsson, Ulf Norberg and Sara Van Meerbergen. 2015. "En katts resa: *Pettson och Findus* på norska, tyska, nederländska, franska och spanska." In *Översättning för en ny generation: Nordisk barn- och ungdomslitteratur på export*, edited by Valérie Alfvén, Hugues Engel and Charlotte Lindgren, 61–71. Falun: Högskolan Dalarna.

Halliday, M. A. K. and Christian M. I. Matthiessen. 2004. *An Introduction to Functional Grammar*. London: Routledge.

Hermans, Theo. 1999. *Translation in Systems: Descriptive and System-Oriented Approaches Explained*. Manchester: St. Jerome.

Källström, Lisa. 2011. *Berättelser om en röd stuga. Föreställningar om en idyll ur ett svenskdidaktiskt perspektiv*. Malmö Studies in Educational Sciences. Malmö: Malmö Högskola.

Kåreland, Lena. 1998. "1990-talets svenska bilderbok. Några exempel." In *Läs mig, sluka mig!*, edited by Kristin Hallberg, 277–295. Stockholm: Natur & Kultur.

Kortteinen, Pauli. 2005. *Les verbes suédois de position stå, sitta, ligga et leurs équivalents français: Étude constrastive*. Gothenburg: Göteborgs Universitet.

Kress, Gunther. 2003. *Literacy in the Age of New Media*. London: Psychology Press.

Kress, Gunther. 2010. *Multimodality: A Social Semiotic Approach to Contemporary Communication*. London/New York: Routledge.

Kress, Gunther and Theo van Leeuwen. 2006. *Reading Images: The Grammar of Visual Design*. London/New York: Routledge.

Kvist Darnell, Ulrika. 2008. *Pseudosamordningar i svenska: Särskilt sådana med verben sitta, ligga och stå*. Stockholm: Stockholms Universitet.

Lefevere, André. 1992. *Translation, Rewriting and the Manipulation of Literature*. London/New York: Routledge.

Lindgren, Charlotte. 2015. "Que reste-t-il du personnage de Findus dans les voix de Pettson et Picpus: étude d'une traduction du suédois au français." *Milli mála – Journal of Language and Culture* 7: 309–331.

Lindgren, Charlotte. 2016. "Identitet och gestaltning av en katt som är ett barn (eller tvärtom): Ett exempel från en modern svensk barnbok och dess översättning till franska." In *En profil i profilen: Vänbok till Bo G Jansson*, edited by Charlotte Lindgren, Catharina Nyström Höög and Wilde Sverre, 83–100. Falun: Högskolan Dalarna, Serie Kultur och lärande.

Lindgren, Charlotte, Carina Andersson and Catherine Renaud. 2007. "La traduction des livres pour enfants suédois en français: choix et transformation." *Revue des livres pour enfants*, no. 234: 87–93.

Machin, David and Theo van Leeuwen. 2007. *Global Media Discourse: A Critical Introduction*. London: Taylor & Francis.

McCloud, Scott. 1994. *Understanding Comics: The Invisible Art*. New York: William Morrow Paperbacks.

Moya, Jésus Guijarro and Maria Jésus Pinar Sanz. 2008. "Compositional Interpersonal and Representational Meanings in Children's Narrative: A Multimodal Discourse Analysis." *Journal of Pragmatics* 40: 1601–1619.

Nikolajeva, Maria. 2000. *Bilderbokens pusselbitar*. Lund: Studentlitteratur.

Nikolajeva, Maria and Carole Scott. 2001. *How Picturebooks Work*. New York/London: Garland Publishing.

Oittinen, Riitta, Anne Ketola and Melissa Garavini. 2017. *Translating Picturebooks: Revoicing the Verbal, the Visual and the Aural for a Child Audience*. London: Routledge.

O'Sullivan, Emer. 2005. *Comparative Children's Literature*. London: Routledge.
Painter, Clare, Jim Martin and Len Unsworth. 2013. *Reading Visual Narratives: Image Analysis of Children's Picture Books*. Sheffield: Equinox Publishing.
Rémi, Cornélia. 2011. "Reading as Playing: The Cognitive Challenge of the Wimmelbook." In *Emergent Literacy: Children's Books from 0 to 3*, edited by Bettina Kümmerling-Meibauer, 115–139. Amsterdam: John Benjamins.
Renaud, Catherine, Carina Andersson and Charlotte Lindgren. 2007. "L'image dans la traduction de livres pour enfants: défi ou soutien. Réflexions à partir de la traduction en français de quelques livres pour enfants suédois." *Revue des livres pour enfants*, no. 234: 94–101.
Ricento, Thomas. 2013. "Language Policy and Globalization." In *The Handbook of Language and Globalization*, edited by Thomas Coupland, 123–141. Chichester: Wiley Blackwell.
Robertson, Roland. 1995. "Glocalization: Time-space and Homogeneity-Heterogeneity." In *Global Modernities*, edited by Mike Featherstone, Scott Lash and Roland Robertson, 22–28. London: Sage.
Roudometof, Victor. 2016. *Glocalization: A Critical Introduction*. London: Routledge.
Sipe, Lawrence and Sylvia Pantaleo. 2010. *Postmodern Picturebooks*. London: Routledge.
Toury, Gideon. 1995. *Descriptive Translation Studies – and Beyond*. Amsterdam/Philadelphia: John Benjamins.
Unsworth, Len. 2005. *Children's Literature and Computer Based Teaching*. Maidenhead: Open University Press.
van Leeuwen, Theo. 2004. *Introducing Social Semiotics*. London: Routledge.
van Leeuwen, Theo and Usama Suleiman. 2013. "Globalizing the Local: The Case of an Egyptian Superhero Comic." In *The Handbook of Language and Globalization*, edited by Douglas Coupland, 232–254. Chichester: Wiley Blackwell.
Van Meerbergen, Sara. 2010. *Nederländska bilderböcker blir svenska: En multimodal översättningsanalys*. Stockholm: Stockholm University.
Van Meerbergen, Sara. 2012. "Play, Parody, Intertextuality and Interaction: Postmodern Flemish Picture Books as Semiotic Playgrounds." *Barnelitterært forskningstidsskrift* 3, no. 1: 1–13.
Van Meerbergen, Sara. 2014. "The Church as a Cream Pie: A Multimodal Translation Analysis of Changing Child Images in Picture Book Translation." In *True North: Literary Translation in the Nordic Countries*, edited by B. J. Epstein, 98–116. Newcastle upon Tyne: Cambridge Scholars Publishing.

Translating violence in children's picture books

A view from the former Yugoslavia

Marija Todorova

Abstract

This chapter examines the translation of violence in picture books through the example of *Hedgehog's Home* (2011), the English translation of the classic picture book *Ježeva kućica* (1949) by Branko Ćopić, one of the most enduring children's books from the former Yugoslavia. I focus specifically on the representations of direct, war-related violence in the original picture book and its translation. The analysis is multimodal and examines the text, paratext, and illustrations of each work. I also look at a musical stage adaptation. Written shortly after World War II, the picture book deals with the violent past of a threatened homeland. When translated and adapted, this reality is changed to fit the context of the target audience. The analysis shows that the English translation tones down the physical violence in the source text, erasing or muting most references to war and death. Simultaneously, it moves the story away from its original patriotic narrative by introducing a new narrative about the consequences of environmental violence and the need for protecting the natural habitat.

Introduction

The study of violence in children's literature is a question of considerable importance and has recently started gaining attention in scholarly debates. Violence in children's books is not a contemporary phenomenon but can in fact be traced back to the very first stories written for child audiences. Images of physical violence have been present for a long time in folklore and the fairy tale tradition. Violence can in fact be seen as an essential element of children's literature from Ancient Greece to the Middle Ages (Tomlinson 1995). Throughout the centuries, physical violence has been used as a didactic element in "stories in which the virtuous were rewarded and evildoers suffered retribution" (Nimon 1993, 29). If we look at the fairy tales of Charles Perrault and the Brothers Grimm, for instance, we are reminded that violence, as it is understood today, had in fact been a very common part of childhood and stories told to children from long ago, and in many places in the world. However, we can also observe that contemporary writers and publishers retelling fairy tales often decide to omit the grim parts to make them more "appropriate" for young readers (Tomlinson 1995, 39).

Traditionally produced for the youngest audience, picture books can nowadays be found for older readers as well, but the majority of them still target three- to seven-year-olds. Thus, there is a tendency for the translation of picture books to follow existing models of education and suitability for young children in the target culture (López 2006; Shavit 2006). Each culture has diverging expectations of child readers and faces its own ideological constraints. As Oittinen (2000, 6) points out, "much of the disagreement (...) in adaptation versus censorship reflects changes in culture and society, our child images and our views about translating."

Physical violence in picture books for children is not only present in the text, but also in the illustrations. Christina Moustakis asks the question "whether there can be a sound rationale for 're-doubling' the violence in children's literature by adding pictures to the text" (1982, 26). Thus, images of violence featured in picture books need to be addressed with special attention. Additionally, the analysis of translated picture books should extend beyond the translated texts and linguistic devices to encompass images and paratexts in order to explore the framing of translated texts. This is important because, in the case of picture books, the translation of words is inseparable from that of pictures.

The Oxford Dictionary defines violence as "behavior involving physical force intended to hurt, damage, or kill someone or something." Applying this to literary discourse, a violent text can be understood as a "text that depicts acts of injurious physical force; many commentators further see such depictions as causally connected to the violence of actual readers" (Reimer 1997, 102–104). When physical violence occurs, human beings are hurt somatically, to the point of killing (Galtung 1969). This type of violence is also known as direct violence and can be measured in numbers of deaths (Galtung and Höivik 1971, 73). This basic definition of violence has been further developed and redefined as a more complex human behavior. Beyond death and injuries, violence need not always be actual but can also be threatened. An example of the latter is a "psychological threat, which can equally cause harm" (Lee 2015, 201) in the form of psychological trauma. Furthermore, Galtung extends the concept of violence and identifies another form of violence, which he calls *structural* or indirect violence, referring to a condition where "violence is built into the structure and shows up as unequal power and consequently as unequal life chances" (Galtung 1969, 171). This type of violence does not affect people's lives immediately but over time: as resources are distributed unevenly, the average life expectancy of less well-off people decreases and these people are prevented from realizing their potential. This new shift in the definition of violence places importance on the intentionality of actions, irrespective of immediate direct violent outcomes, such as immediate death or physical injury. Structural violence is a comprehensive framework to explain how individuals suffer both physical and psychological deterioration due to poverty, class, racism, gender inequity, and environmental risk, all of which are being maintained by social structures.

In this context, it becomes relevant to bring into the debate the concept of ecological violence, that is, injury against the environment caused by pollution, deforestation and overexploitation (Kyrou 2007). Violence against the environment tends to be perpetrated over time and in multifarious ways, threatening nature, humans and livelihoods in the long term. In this way, it is similar to structural violence. Irreversible damage to the earth's environment threatens the very survival of humankind, making environmental violence a topic of great urgency (Lee 2015, 106).

My analysis of violence in translated picture books will focus on *Hedgehog's Home* (2011), an English translation of the classic picture book *Ježeva kućica* by Branko Ćopić (1949), one of the most enduring children's works from the former Yugoslavia, and one that is still read in Serbia, Montenegro, Croatia, and Bosnia and Herzegovina. First published in the late 1940s in Zagreb by Naša Djeca, and illustrated by Vilko Selan Gliha, the original language of the book can be identified as a dialect of Serbian. In terms of its genre, the narrative of *Ježeva kućica* can be classified as a fable. Following the structure of a fable, *Ježeva kućica* takes place in a wood in which the animals can talk, have their homes and spend time together, taking on human characteristics. Again, as a typical fable, the text ends with a strong moral about the importance of protecting one's home, no matter how humble it may be. The story is at first sight timeless and not located in a specific place. Nonetheless, as Sarah Godek notes, books for children are "a product of and respond to cultural and historical conditions" (2005, 90). We will look at this connection in more detail in the analysis below.

The selection of this work for translation into English was mainly based on personal interest and enthusiasm for the source text by the UK publisher Istros Books and its founder Susan Curtis, who is also the translator of *Ježeva kućica*. Istros Books is a growing publisher from London specialized in translating literature from the Balkans, and from Eastern Europe more broadly.

The English translation of the book was published with a new set of illustrations. Commissioning new illustrations is a long-established practice in translating and retranslating classics and fairy tales. However, "re-illustration may offer new insights or alter the tone of a book entirely" (Lathey 2016, 57). While the target language picture book has been illustrated by the Croatian illustrator Sanja Rašček, the new images follow and build on the narrative of placing the story in a British social context (Todorova 2018, 51), thus creating a completely new mood with a strong environmental focus that will be discussed in the analysis below. This newly introduced environmental framing of the translation is clearly present in the new paratext that accompanies the English translation. Although picture books rarely include dedications, the English translation of *Hedgehog's Home* is dedicated to Naomi Lewis, "lover of children's literature and defender of animals," foreshadowing the environmentalist refocusing of the translation. The environmental interpretation, or rather instruction to read this story in this way, is most prominent in another "less visible but equally powerful" (Pellatt, 2013, 2) paratext on the back cover of the translated book, where the blurb reads: "Hedgehog's House is a story about caring for your natural habitat. Set in the unspoilt environment of the forest, we find the wild creatures arguing about what home means…".

After the publication of the picture book in English, the story was adapted for the stage in the UK in two different settings. In 2012, Curtis commissioned the "Hedgehog's Home Opera," a professional production composed by Emily Leather and directed by Elinor Jane Moran, with sets designed by Andrew Miller. It was first workshopped with primary school pupils in Conway Hall. The director of the opera decided to have two characters, Hedgemond the Hedgehog and Ms. Fox, played by the professional actors Dario Dugandzic and Christina Gill, while the Wolf, the Bear and the Wild Boar were played by the Year 5 children of Fitzjohn's Primary School. Furthermore, a new character not present in the original book was introduced in the musical: the Teacher, played by Nicola Wydenbach. A year later, Istros Books joined forces with Honey-tongued Theatre Productions and reworked the musical adaptation with six professional actors featuring the five animals from the story and the newly introduced teacher. This was the first production of Honeybear Youth Theatre at the Tabernacle Theatre in London, shown in December 2013.

In previous research (Todorova 2018), I discussed the changes made in the English translation of this work, looking specifically at cultural markers and the representation of home. Here, I will specifically focus on the representations of violence, especially the direct violence of war, and the translation of direct violence. I use a multimodal analytical framework, combining analyses of the text and visual paratext of the original, the translation and the musical adaptation. As we will see, the English translation tones down the physical violence in the source text by erasing or muting most references to war and death. At the same time, it moves the story away from the original patriotic narrative, reframing it in terms of environmental violence and the need to protect the natural habitat.

Violence in children's books

Michelle Ann Abate's *Bloody Murder* (2013) studies the ways in which violence, and especially the most violent act of murder, appears in children's literature. She examines a range of books, from the most popular fairy tales intended for the youngest readers to contemporary bestsellers in the new genre of young adult fiction. In seven case studies, Abate shows how direct violence, crime and death "can be seen as acceptable and even necessary" for children (2013, 29). While violence may have been present in children's literature throughout its history, "[i]t is only in recent decades that the place of violence in children's books has been so vigorously questioned" (Nimon 1993, 31). And yet, today, as Vandergrigt points out, children spend their lives in a "culture of violence":

> Some of them actually dodge rocks and bullets in war-torn regions of the world; others are barricaded in comfortable homes where they bombard themselves with the sounds and images of guns, war, and violence on television and in the games they play. (Vandergrigt 2002, n.p.)

This is particularly relevant in a Western Balkan context, a region that has continuously been (re)presented and (re)invented across a variety of discourses as a result of armed conflicts. These discourses span the political, literary, journalistic and scientific. Throughout history, from the days of Ottoman Turkish rule to the communist regimes of the Cold War, "the Balkans has been traditionally portrayed as an alter-ego to Europe" (Dodovski 2008, 5), its dark side and its unconscious. Even today, more than two decades after the fall of the Berlin Wall, and with the prospect of integration into the European Union, the people of the Balkan region are still attributed the duality of being a part of Europe while also being outside of it. This "non-progressive narrative" is seen to have repeated images of barbarism and backwardness in the post-Cold War period (Hammond 2010, 11, 255) and was reactivated with the wars in ex-Yugoslavia during the 1990s.

In almost all countries that were created after the violent breakdown of Yugoslavia, the war and its consequences on the lives of children have become an important theme in literature for children. In her review of contemporary literature for children from south-east Europe, Mileva Blažić stresses that arguably the most "prominent genre that came about – owing to war and destruction – was the genre of the journal and diary, suggesting the need for imaginary states and locations of peace through memory" (2011, n.p.). Some of the authors of these new books (diaries and journals) were children themselves, or adults who had experienced the war during their childhoods. Examples of this new non-fictional genre include Zlata Filipović's *Zlata's Diary* (1994) and Nadja Halilbegovich's *My Childhood Under Fire* (2006), both translations into English. Another similarly realistic book, which uses almost photographic illustration to present the war in Sarajevo, is Alija Duboćanin's *Pas pismonoša* [The Postdog]. Blažić identifies many other books for children in Bosnia and Herzegovina which have the war as a topic, such as Duraković's *Još jedna bajka o ruži* [Yet Another Fairy Tale about Rose], *Mikijeva abeceda* [Mickey's Alphabet], and *Najnovije vijesti iz Sarajeva* [Latest News from Sarajevo]; Željko Ivanković's novel *Tko je upalio mrak? Sarajevski pojmovnik* [Who Switched on Darkness? Sarajevo's Dictionary]; and Advan Hozić's short stories *Na kraju placa* [At the End of the Lot]. Similar to the situation in Bosnia and Herzegovina, Croatian children's literature has seen a considerable change since the war (1992–1995) and books about children's experiences of war are appearing in Croatia with increasing regularity. Books selected for translation into English from these countries tended to foreground the experiences of children, which "serve the Western perspective about the sides of the war and intensify wartime deprivation" (Todorova 2017, 20).

Violence in the translated text

Like many of the recently translated books for children from the Western Balkans, physical violence is noticeably present in Branko Ćopić's classic picture book *Ježeva kućica*. Written shortly after World War II, the picture book's narrative refers to the real past of a homeland threatened by the violence of war. Ćopić's own life was also marked by war: he took an active part in World War II, having been involved in the Yugoslav resistance from the very beginning in 1941 to the end in 1945. The experience of these war years featured prominently in his postwar writings both for adults and for children.

Violence is present from the very beginning of *Ježeva kućica*, when we are introduced to the main character, the Hedgehog. While he comes across as a very friendly animal, he is also described as a hunter with three hundred spikes who is feared by all the other wild animals in the wood. There is also the portending of a coming battle:

Pred njim dan hoda, širi se strava,
njegovim tragom putuje slava
(Ćopić 1949)

Backtranslation:
The day walks in front of him, terror is spreading,
glory travels on his trail.[1]

Ako bi usput došlo do boja,
nek bude spremna obrana moja
(Ćopić 1949)

Backtranslation:
If there will be a battle along the way,
let my defense be ready.

zategnu trbuh k'o bubanj ratni.
(Ćopić 1949)

Backtranslation:
stomach as tight as a war drum.

A sova huknu svoj ratni zov:
– Drž'te se, ptice, počinje lov!
(Ćopić 1949)

Backtranslation:
The owl hooted its war cry:
Hold on birds, the hunt has begun!

In the English translation, Hedgemond does preserve some of the Hedgehog's warlike characteristics: he calls him a "fearsome defender" who "looks over his spikes and sharpens each one." Most references to war in the translation have, however, been erased or toned down: for example, "battle" is translated as "fight" and "war drum" becomes just "drum," while the "owl's war cry" is transformed into a mere "hoot." The same happens with the reference to death in the final song, "The Ending," where the "enemy" threatening the sanctity of the home gets the ultimate punishment. The end met by the three

---

1 The backtranslations are mine unless otherwise noted.

negative characters is harsh: they pay for their vices with their lives. The wolf is killed by the villagers, the boar is killed by hunters, and the bear is stung to death by bees. The child reader, Culley (1991) suggests, is implicitly already familiar with the conservative pattern of such narratives where good triumphs over evil, and wicked characters are punished with death; therefore it should not come as a big surprise when the three "bad" animals get their "deserved" punishment:

> Krvnika vuka, jadna mu majka
> umlati brzo seljačka hajka.
> Trapavog medu, oh, kuku, lele,
> do same smrti izbole pčele
> I divlja svinja pade k'o kruška,
> smače je zimus lovačka puška
> (Ćopić 1949)

> Backtranslation (my emphasis):
> The bloodthirsty wolf, his poor mother,
> was quickly *battered* by peasant chase.
> The slothful/sluggish bear, oh, poor him
> was stung *to death* by bees.
> And the boar fell down like a pear,
> stricken by a hunter's gun in winter.

> Ježurka često zdravicu diže:
> u zdravlje lije i njene kuće,
> za pogibiju lovčeva Žuće.
> (Ćopić 1949)

> Backtranslation (my emphasis):
> Ježurka frequently raises his glass:
> To the health of the fox, and her house,
> and for the *untimely death* of hunter's dog Žućo.

We notice that in the published English translation of the story the word 'death' is not mentioned.

> The greedy old wolf, just up to no good
> Was chased by farmers, right out of the wood
> And slovenly bear with great honeyed paw

Was beaten by bees till he was no more
And even the boar, that horrid grunter
Fell into the trap set by the hunter
(Ćopić 2011)

"And regular toasts from the honored guest:
'To fox and her home, may good luck abound
And to swift demise of hunter's fierce hound!'"
(Ćopić 2011, "At Fox's House")

While death is implied in the English translation, the word itself is eschewed in favor of a higher register: "stung to death" becomes "was no more," and "untimely death" becomes "swift demise." Although the antagonists are punished for their unacceptable behavior, their punishment is milder and does not explicitly involve death.

Violence in the image

This erasure of direct violence is further reflected in the new illustrations produced for the English translation of the book. Comparing the illustrations of the source text and the re-illustrated target text, we immediately see a difference in style: where the source text depicts the animals more realistically, the target illustrations are more cartoon-like, rendered with much rounder lines. Animals are portrayed in close-ups, accentuating child-like features. The illustrator of the source text, Vilko Gliha Selan, colored the 'bad' animals in black or very dark colors, thus marking them visually as 'negative' and anticipating emotions of emptiness, gloom or sadness. Furthermore, in the original illustrations, the forest, as a setting for the plot, is represented as a dark and threatening place. In most of the illustrations, the 'bad' animals do not wear clothes. This serves to accentuate their animalistic (and non-human) nature. It should be noted that the text itself makes no mention of any clothes apart from the Hedgehog's hat, which he uses to bow to his hostess. On the other hand, in the newly illustrated target text, the Wolf, Boar and Bear are all dressed like human children, in bright colors and striking patterns, making them likable and relatable. Although they do use very harsh words in their speech, and make angry expressions during the pursuit, at the end of the verbal exchange they are illustrated as scared, child-like creatures who seem to have regretted their actions. The visual direct violence represented by the angry faces of the animals in the original illustrations has been replaced in the target illustrations with a visual logic that instead draws attention to environmental violence, that is, the destruction of forests and animals' natural habitats at the hands of humans.

This new emphasis on the natural environment in the target text is accentuated by the green color that dominates the target illustrations. In Ražček's account, the publisher had quite a few comments about the first color artwork she produced and seems to have wanted a more naturalistic overall look, while still emphasizing the aggressiveness of the Hedgehog. She insisted that he remain "the 'fierce hunter and proud defender,' so he should have one arm raised in the air, and his spikes should stick out a bit more threateningly" (personal communication, March 24, 2014). However, taken together, the translation presents a new representation of reality suited to a new audience. The environmental focus is further present throughout the visual paratexts of *Hedgehog's Home*. The endpapers – the "pages glued inside the front and back covers of a book, [which] are thus the first parts of the interior of the book to be seen when the book is opened, as well as the last to be seen after the story has been read and the book is about to be closed" (Sipe and McGuire 2006, 291) – replicate a wallpaper-like pattern featuring big green tree leaves. The same pattern can be found in the homes of four of the book's characters. As Nikolajeva and Scott emphasize, "endpapers are not merely a decoration, but convey important additional information" (2001, 248).

In summary, the new illustrations used in the translation transform the threat of war and aggression into a threat to nature and natural habitats. It also changes formerly threatening and chilling representations into more visually pleasing and non-threatening ones. This contrasts with the severity of the damage to the environment and natural habitats that threatens the very survival of humanity and other species.

The musical stage adaptation of the text seems to present a variation on this theme of ecological violence. It characterizes the story's animals as being harmed and the natural English countryside as being under attack. This is reflected in the costume design and the choice of music rhythms in the musical, which are inspired by English society in the 1920s. The fox, for example, is dressed in traditional red foxhunting attire, marking him as controversial for contemporary audiences, which see foxhunting as both classist and cruel. Drawing on the feudal history connected to ownership of land and the animals living on it, hunting can thus be interpreted as a tool of asserting dominance and social superiority over the poorer rural population, peasant livelihoods, and the environment. The bearer of this class violence is the Hedgehog, who is costumed to represent the British peasant. His part is sung in English folk music tempo, thus representing the English countryside, whereas the other four 'bad' animals are represented with the more urban and 'foreign' sounds of boogie-woogie, Charleston and tango. The musical adaptation of *Hedgehog's Home* shows yet again how the original narrative of Ćopić's picture book has been retooled to represent new forms of (in this case, class) violence.

Conclusion

In wartime, there is always the threat of direct and indirect violence "insofar as insight and resources are channeled away from constructive efforts to bring the actual closer to the potential" (Galtung 1969, 169). War has been ever-present in the world since the origins of humanity, thus making it important for children to learn how to "construct both a personal and a social identity in an unstable and war-torn world" (Miller 2009, 274). In her introduction to a special issue of *The Lion and the Unicorn* (2000) dedicated to "the complex ways violence and war have been written and interpreted for young readers since the Great War," guest editor Elizabeth Goodenough suggests that in contemporary society, where "connections between childhood, injury, and death headline concerns about living in a culture spinning out of control," it is very important to have examples of survival strategies that will provide "secret spaces for the young to frame, interpret, and relieve atrocious anxieties related to bombings, hiding out, exile, persecution…" (*ibid.*, vi).

Branko Ćopić's *Ježeva kućica* is a narrative for children written in a postwar period when memories of the violence were still very fresh in the minds of both adults and children, as reflected in the war-infused language used by the author. For this reason, we would expect a focus on personal violence in after-war periods (lest they should become inter-war periods). If the periods protract sufficiently for the major outburst of personal violence to be partly forgotten, we would expect a concentration on structural violence, provided the societies are dynamic enough to make any stability stand out as somehow unnatural (Galtung 1969, 174).

As demonstrated above, the English translation of this picture book, produced more than sixty years after the original, significantly changes the war-filled language used, erasing the mention of war and death from the text. The selection of the book for translation and the translation strategies that have been used can be seen as building on the prominence of the hedgehog as a symbol for environmental activism throughout Europe in the 1970s and 1980s (Todorova 2018, 51). The translation moves the narrative away from the original message of physical violence and fighting against the invader and introduces it in a new, environmentally conscious narrative raising awareness about environmental violence as a psychological threat, as we saw in the discussion of the translation's illustrations and the paratext. Consequently, in the English translation the text has been framed within this modern take on the image of the hedgehog, diverting it away from the patriotic narrative upon which the source text is built, so that the dark forest is not so dark anymore. The war in former Yugoslavia in the 1990s is also an important element in the introduction to the opera adaptation of *Hedgehog's Home*. However, the costumes and music of the stage translation make yet another transformation, replacing the direct violence of war in the Western Balkans with class violence of 1920s Britain, which is also linked to environmental themes like land ownership and stewardship and the treatment of rural workers. These works twice remove the story from its original geographical and historical context by removing references to physical violence and war. At the same time, they arguably offer target readers a more complex and nuanced understanding of the issue of violence and its psychological and structural manifestations.

Bibliography

Abate, Michelle Ann. 2013. *Bloody Murder: The Homicide Tradition in Children's Literature*. Baltimore: Johns Hopkins University Press.

Alcantud Diaz, Maria. 2010. "Cruelty and Violence in the Brothers Grimm's Fairy Tales Collection: A Corpus-Based Approach." *Revista Alicantina de Estudios Ingleses*, 23: 173–185.

Blažić, Milena Mileva. 2011. "Children's Literature in South-East Europe." *CLCWeb: Comparative Literature and Culture* 13.1: Article 10. http://dx.doi.org/10.7771/1481-4374.1714.

Ćopić, Branko. 1949. *Ježeva kučica*. Zagreb/Belgrade: Novo pokolenje. [Ћопић, Бранко. Јежева кућа. Београд, Загреб: Ново поколење].

Ćopić, Branko. 2011. *Hedgehog's Home*. Translated by Susan Curtis. London: Istros Books.

Culley, Jonathon. 1991. "Roald Dahl – 'It's about children and it's for children' – But Is It Suitable?" *Children's Literature in Education* 22, no. 1: 59–73.

Dewan, Pauline. 2004. *The House as Setting, Symbol and Structural Motif in Children's Literature*. Lewinston: The Edwin Mellen Press.

Dodovski, Ivan. 2008. "Imagining the West: Representations of Europe and America in Contemporary Balkan Drama." *CERC Working Papers Series*, no. 2. Victoria: University of Melbourne.

Filipović, Zlata. 1994. *Zlata's Diary: A Child's Life in Wartime Sarajevo.* Translated by Christina Pribićević-Zorić. New York: Penguin Books.

Haase, Donald, ed. 2008. *The Greenwood Encyclopedia of Folktales and Fairy Tales.* Westport, CT: Greenwood Press.

Halilbegovich, Nadja. 2006. *My Childhood Under Fire: A Sarajevo Diary.* Toronto: Kids Can Press.

Hammond, Andrew. 2010. *British Literature and the Balkans: Themes and Contexts.* Amsterdam: Rodopi.

Galtung, Johan. 1969. "Violence, Peace, and Peace Research." *Journal of Peace Research* 6, no. 3: 167–191.

Galtung, Johan and Tord Höivik. 1971. "Structural and Direct Violence: A Note on Operationalization." *Journal of Peace Research* 8, no. 1: 73–76.

Godek, Sarah. 2005. "Fantasy – Postwar, Postmodern, Postcolonial: Houses in Postwar Fantasy." In *Modern Children's Literature: An Introduction,* edited by Kimberly Reynolds, 89–107. New York: Palgrave Macmillan.

Goodenough, Elizabeth. 2000. "Introduction." *The Lion and the Unicorn* 24, no. 3: v–ix.

Kyrou, Christos. 2007. "Peace Ecology: An Emerging Paradigm in Peace Studies." *International Journal of Peace Studies,* 12, no. 1: 73–92.

Lee, X. Bandy. 2015. "Causes and Cures I: Towards a New Definition." *Aggression and Violent Behavior* 25: 199–203.

Lee, X. Bandy. 2016. "Causes and Cures VIII: Environmental Violence." *Aggression and Violent Behavior* 30: 105–109.

López, Fernández Marisa. 2006. "Translation Studies in Contemporary Children's Literature: A Comparison of Intercultural Ideological Factors." In *The Translation of Children's Literature: A Reader,* edited by Gillian Lathey, 41–53. Clevendon: Multilingual Matters.

Miller, Kristine. 2009. "Ghosts, Gremlins, and 'the War on Terror' in Children's Blitz Fiction." *Children's Literature Association Quarterly* 34, no. 3: 272–284.

Moustakis, Christina. 1982. "A Plea for Heads: Illustrating Violence in Fairy Tales." *Children's Literature Association Quarterly* 7, no. 2: 26–30.

Myers, Mitzi. 2000. "Storying War: A Capsule Overview." *The Lion and the Unicorn* 24, no. 3: 327–336.

Nikolajeva, Maria and Carole Scott. 2001. *How Picturebooks Work.* London: Garland.

Nimon, Maureen. 1993. "Violence in Children's Literature Today." In *Selected Papers from the Annual Conference of the International Association of School Librarianship, Adelaide, Australia, 27–30 September 1993,* 29–33. Washington, D.C.: Eric Clearinghouse.

Nurse, Angus. 2013. *Animal Harm: Perspectives on Why People Harm and Kill Animals.* New York: Routledge.

Oittinen, Riitta. 2000. *Translating for Children*. New York: Garland.
Pellatt, Valerie. 2013. "Introduction." In *Text, Extratext, Metatext and Paratext in Translation*, edited by Valerie Pellatt, 1–6. Newcastle upon Tyne: Cambridge Scholars Publishing.
Reimer, Mavis. 1997. "Introduction: Violence and Violent Children's Texts." *Children's Literature Association Quarterly* 22, no. 3: 102–104.
Shavit, Zohar. 2006. "Translation of Children's Literature." In *The Translation of Children's Literature: A Reader*, edited by Gillian Lathey, 25–40. Clevedon: Multilingual Matters.
Sipe, Lawrence and Caroline E. McGuire. 2006. "Picturebook Endpapers: Resources for Literary and Aesthetic Interpretation." *Children's Literature in Education* 37, no. 4: 291–304.
Tatar, Maria. 1992. *Off With Their Heads!: Fairy Tales and the Culture of Childhood*. Princeton, NJ: Princeton University Press.
Tatar, Maria. 2004. *Secrets Beyond the Door: A Story of Blubeard and his Wives*. Princeton, NJ: Princeton University Press.
Todorova, Marija. 2017. "Children's Voices from War Zones: Muted by Adult Mediation." *Bookbird: A Journal of International Children's Literature* 55, no. 2: 20–27.
Todorova, Marija. 2018. "Into the Dark Woods: A Cross-Cultural Reimagination of Home." *Bookbird: A Journal of International Children's Literature* 56, no. 4: 46–52.
Tomlinson, Carl. 1995. "Justifying Violence in Children's Literature." In *Battling Dragons: Issues and Controversy in Children's Literature*, edited by Susan Lehr, 39–50. Portsmouth, NH: Heinemann.
Vandergrigt, Key E. 2014. "The Culture of Violence and Picture Books." Accessed July 27, 2014. http://comminfo.rutgers.edu/professional-development/childlit/911/childwar.html.

Defying norms through unprovoked violence

The translation and reception of two Swedish young adult novels in France

Valérie Alfvén

Abstract

This chapter examines the translation and reception of two Swedish young adult novels – *Spelar död* [Play Dead] and *När tågen går förbi* [When the Trains Pass By] – published in France in the 2000s. Both books use unprovoked violence in a realistic genre for adolescents, something no French author had dared to do previously. The two novels ignited a moral panic in France that led to heated debates in the French literary field. This chapter retraces the stormy reception of these novels in France and analyzes the constraints to which translations of unprovoked violence are often subject, especially when translated from a source culture whose norms are more liberal than the target culture. Linking translation strategies with reception, this chapter uses Even-Zohar's polysystem theory to determine how the two novels became 'innovative' (in Even-Zohar's sense of the term) in the French literary field in the 2000s.

Introduction

– Nu brinner han! garvar Någon.
– Det var fan på tiden.
– Pissa på'n då annars brinner han upp.
– Det gör väl fan ingenting.
Jag känner hur elden fräser till. Det stänker i ansiktet. När jag öppnar ögonen ser jag Någons kraftiga lem ovanför mig. Den riktas mot mig. Pisset skvalar. Det träffar ömsom min kropp, ömsom mitt ansikte. (Casta 1999, 118).

Backtranslation:[1]
– Now he burns! says Someone laughing.
– Finally, it was not fucking too early.
– Piss on him, otherwise he will burn up.
– Well, that fucking doesn't matter.
I feel how the fire frizzles and I feel drops on my face. When I open my eyes, I see Someone's vigorous male organ above me. It is directed at me. The piss squeals. It hits my body, sometimes my face.

Although this example is extreme, violence has become a common theme in contemporary young adult and adolescent literature. As Mary Owen (2013, 12) points out,

[i]n today's YAL [young adult literature] there is virtually no topic that is off-limits. Readers can vicariously explore gay love, AIDS, rape, teen parenting, depression, violent acts (physical and psychological), passionate vampires and fairies, suicide, incest, murder, political choice and belief and concerns about money, society, the environment and the future.

But just how explicit can an author be in describing violence? Even while YAL authors today have greater freedom to include violence in their books, some types remain taboo. When are graphic depictions *too* graphic? How do such works transcend national boundaries? How are they translated? This chapter applies these questions to the case of the reception and translation of two Swedish novels for adolescents translated into French in the 2000s. The goal is to better understand how the French literary field dealt with such a sensitive topic at the turn of the century.

Swedish literature for adolescents is one of the most open-minded literatures in the world, particularly with regard to sensitive topics (Delbrassine 2006; Christensen 2011; Kokko 2011; Svenbro 2011).[2] Swedish young adult and children's literature often highlights dark and difficult themes that may be considered taboo or sensitive in other countries. Unprovoked violence is one such theme. In a way, violence feels less shocking or is comprehensible or even acceptable when it happens in a fantasy world. The same can be said of stories that take place during another period or in an environment with serious social problems that can explain the violence (such as in some 'hard

---

1   All backtranslations and glosses are by the author unless otherwise noted.
2   Sensitive topics include, for example, sexuality, homosexuality, suicide, violence, rape, religion and depression.

suburbs' with deep social inequalities). In these cases, adolescents are violent because they are victims and must defend themselves against adolescent bullies, disorderly adults or an unjust society. But it is still rare for realistic novels to depict adolescents engaging in violence against other adolescents *for no apparent reason*.

Even today, it is difficult to translate novels describing unprovoked violence from Swedish, Danish or Norwegian into other languages because of reticence regarding the topic and the age of the intended readers of these works. Such topics broach notions of norms, ethics, and morals, which differ from one country to another. More and more Swedish authors highlight unprovoked violence in their realistic novels for young adults, and it is not inaccurate to speak of a tradition within Swedish literature. Already by the end of the 1990s, the Swedish researcher Sonja Svensson had coined the term *idyllophobia* (Svensson 1995, 1999) to classify Swedish teen novels of the period. This term emphasizes the desire of Swedish authors to avoid writing idylls (which typically have happy endings) and to write instead on dark and heavy topics in realistic genres. Many contemporary novels for adolescents continue this tradition and have attained a high status in the Swedish literary system. In fact, violence in young adult literature in Sweden is so common that it is no longer considered controversial. In 2015, *När hundarna kommer* [When the Dogs Arrive], a dark, realistic novel depicting a typical adolescent engaging in unprovoked lethal violence, won the prestigious Swedish Literary August Prize. But despite its accolades, the novel has so far only been translated into Danish and Finnish.

Two Swedish novels in a realistic genre

In the 2000s, two Swedish novels for adolescents, *Spelar död* [Play Dead][3] by Stefan Casta and *När tågen går förbi* [When the Trains Pass By][4] by Malin Lindroth, crossed borders and were published in France. Both novels broach the sensitive topic of unprovoked violence, which was not being explored by French writers at that time (Alfvén 2016, 168–173).

---

3   *Spelar död* has not been translated into English. I use the Swedish or the French title in this chapter.
4   *När tågen går förbi* has been translated and published in English with the title *Train Wreck* (Annick Press, 2010). However, an English word-for-word translation of the title would be "When the Trains Pass By," as I have indicated in the gloss.

Spelar död was written in 1999 by a well-established Swedish author, Stefan Casta, and that year won the August Prize, one of the most prestigious literary prizes in Sweden. It was translated into French in 2004 by Agneta Ségol, a well-established Swedish-French translator, with the title *Faire le mort*. The story revolves around an event in which Kim, the protagonist (who is also the primary narrator), is beaten up and left for dead in the middle of the forest by his own teenage friends. The rest of the book is Kim's reflections on this act and his attempt to try to understand how this unprovoked and incomprehensible violence occurred. As Kim says:

Jag försöker hitta en förklaring. Jag ställer frågor. Jag har så manga frågor. (Casta 1999, 8)

Backtranslation:
I try to find an explanation. I'm wondering. I have so many questions.

När tågen går förbi was translated into French as *Quand les trains passent*. It was originally a Swedish play from 2005, shifting to another literary genre when it was translated and published as a young adult novel in French in 2007. The novel depicts an act of unprovoked violence told from the perspective of the tormentor. It centers around the rape of a character named Suzy P. by a group of male teenagers from her class. It tells how the female narrator was present at the violent event and simply observed it, possibly even encouraging it, without ever trying to stop it. The rape is the result of a bullying incident that escalates and has no apparent motive.

The only thing that angers the narrator during this event is when she discovers that the boys have put her own blue boots on Susie: "*Ni har knullat henne och gett bort mina bästa stövletter! As!*" (Lindroth 2005, 25–26); "Have you screwed her and given her my best boots! You asshole!" (Lindroth 2010, 40, trans. Marshall). This reinforces the revolting nature of the situation through an absurd and selfish reply.

In these two situations, the ferocity of the violence used by the teenagers is intensified by the fact that the adolescents could be defined as 'normal' or 'average.' The characters are from a middle-class background with few financial or social problems. They also live in quiet areas of the city and not, for example, in poor suburbs where poverty could be a motive for the violence. Their language is colloquial but is not marked by a unique dialect that would indicate a restricted social class or environment. Their violence makes no political, social or religious demands. In other words, they could be considered typical, normal teenagers, passing from kind to monstrous, from innocent to nasty.

A stormy French reception

The books evoked strong reactions from different actors in the French literary field. In the daily paper *Le Monde* in 2007, Marion Faure accused the novels of being too 'dark' and 'wicked' for teenagers to read and said they might even be dangerous. She highlighted *Quand les trains passent* in particular. Likewise, *Faire le mort* was considered by critics to be unnecessarily dark literature for adolescents because reading it creates a "malaise. A big one" (*Citrouille* 2004, 31). When its literary qualities *were* recognized, protestations were not far behind. In the same *Citrouille* review, Gégène describes the book as a "wintry novel, dark, violent, too much for some, nevertheless deeply human. Only Jan Guillou's book, *Ondskan*,[5] (…) has impressed me as much" (Gégène, 2010).

Fauvre's article set off a moral panic, leading to a virulent debate among publishers, editors, authors and illustrators (see *Liberation* 2007; Tanguy 2009; *La Liberté* 2007; Joubert 2008; Combet 2007). Various translators such as Blandine Longre (2007) and authors such as Simon Roguet (2007) were compelled to defend their practices and their choices (Barnabé 2012). The following year, a clinical psychologist, Annie Rolland, analyzed this controversy in her book *Qui a peur de la littérature ado?* [Who's Afraid of Teen Literature?] (2008). A wide-ranging media debate began in which the editor, Thierry Magnier, had to defend his editorial choices (France Culture 2007). Along with Magnier, the editors François Martin, Jeanne Benameur and Claire David responded to the criticism in *Le Monde* by arguing that young readers were "intelligent" and had the right to read literary works, being, as they were, "capable of knowing the difference between being a voyeur (…) and being a reader" (*Le Monde des livres* 2007).[6] But other editors, such as those at Bayard Publishing House, disagreed and admitted that there were "taboo topics" and that "not everything is publishable, even if it is very well written" (*ibid.*).[7]

Additionally, Magnier was even the target of censorship pressure from the government's special commission tasked with monitoring publications for children and young adults (*Commission de surveillance et de contrôle*

---

5   *Ondskan* (Norstedts, 1990) by Jan Guillou, translated into French as *La fabrique de violence* (Agone Editions, 1990), is the story of a male adolescent at a boarding school who is severely and violently bullied.

6   In French: "Nous croyons aussi que les jeunes filles et les jeunes gens sont intelligents et qu'ils ont droit à la littérature. Ils savent faire la différence entre la place de voyeur qui leur est largement offerte dans les médias et celle de lecteur" (*Le Monde* 2007, 12–20).

7   In French: "Oui, les sujets tabous existent (…) tout n'est pas publiable, même un texte très bien écrit" (*Le Monde* 2007, 12–20).

des publications destinées à l'enfance et à l'adolescence), created in 1949. The commission sent Magnier a letter in November 2007 in which it strongly recommended reducing the size of the font in *Quand les trains passent* to make the text look less attractive or less affordable to younger readers. It also recommended adding a label on the cover warning potential readers of the book's violent themes and indicating an appropriate reading age – which the commission suggested should be fifteen years old (Delbrassine 2008, 10).

The debate shifted to the classic (and maybe endless) questioning of what is moral or amoral to talk about in children's literature. The moral panic crystallized a social fear and was a way to react against a deep, ongoing societal change. *Faire le mort* and *Quand les trains passent* were received as 'deviant' novels compared to other, non-translated literary works in French. Because they present sensitive topics, the works are associated with something violent and "become defined as a threat to societal values and interests" (Cohen 2011, 1). As literature for adolescents and children has long been seen as a literature with primarily pedagogical aims (Nières-Chevrel 2009), fears arise when this literature goes beyond doxa or social morals and begins addressing taboo and dark topics. At any rate, the French reception of these two novels reveals the reaction of the French literary system to be similar to what played out in Sweden in the 1970s, when Swedish young adult literature was changing, thanks to the introduction of new, controversial topics, including violence (Poslaniec 1997; Thaler and Jean-Bart 2002, 155; Delbrassine 2006, 51; Escarpit 2008; Perrin 2009). This reaction also clarifies the differences in standards and norms between the French and Swedish systems, where the former rejects dark topics and the latter wishes to discuss them. In France, talking about nasty adolescents may feel like a threat for an (adult?) reader because unprovoked violence not only rejects lawfulness, it also seeks to destroy it. And once the absence of laws has been posited, violence can repeat itself indefinitely (Kriegel 2002, 23–24).

Translation of violence into French

In a French context of strong pedagogical norms and reticence about dark and difficult topics, the risk that the Swedish texts would undergo restrictions in the translation was high. An analysis of the translation of violent passages provides a good indication of the current standards and norms in the French system. Perhaps surprisingly, I found that the changes were minimal and that the translators chose to translate close to Swedish norms, in the Touryian sense (see Toury 1995). Violence takes places in different ways in the texts.

The most evident is physical violence, such as the rape of Suzy P. or when the adolescents batter Kim. But there is another form of violence in the stories which operates on the level of register and lexical choice, particularly in the use of swearwords and insults.[8] Choosing milder words or even suppressing them could be a way to reduce this violence.

Lexical choices: Swearwords and insults

According to the translator Agneta Ségol (interview with Agneta Ségol 2014), Swedish uses more swearwords than French, and given the pedagogical nature of children's literature, there is a strong tradition in French not to use swearwords in literary texts, especially literary texts for children. But in the context of violence, swearwords and insults play a reinforcing role. The French translation of *När tågen går förbi* (*Quand les trains passent*) by Jacques Robnard is very close to the original and uses the same register:

> Jag ville bara slå henne. **Ett käftslag**. Det var nära. (Lindroth 2005, 21)

> Je voulais la gifler. **Lui foutre un coup sur la gueule**. C'était pas loin. (Lindroth 2007, 42, trans. Robnard)

> Backtranslation:
> I just wanted to smack her. **To punch her in the jaw**. It was close.

In comparing the Swedish text with the published English text (*Train Wreck*) and French text (*Quand les trains passent*), the English version seems to include more indirect judgements that are not in the source text, as shown in the example below. The narrator, who is a female adolescent, enters the classroom and discovers her boyfriend and some of his friends raping Suzy P. The word 'rape' is never employed in the source text; rather, the word *knullat* [fucked] is used. It is translated into French as *baisée*, whereas the English version uses the vague expression "something horrible" (this is why I use backtranslation throughout this article):

> Det luktade helvete därinne. Fylla, spya…
> Jag, här, hon där… Sussi P. för helvete… du får liksom… resa dig…

---

8   We focus here on the comparison between the French and Swedish texts. I provide glosses in English.

Dom var fyra. Han och hans kompisar. Jag förstod att dom…**varit på henne. Knullat henne…typ**…Man förstod det för hon var helt naken. Eller nästan då…Så när som på ett par mocka stövletter…mina mocka stövletter, dom blå… (Lindroth 2005, 25)

Ça puait là-dedans. L'alcool, la pisse, le vomi…
Moi ici, elle là… Suzy P. bordel… tu devrais… relève-toi…
Ils étaient quatre. Lui et ses copains. J'ai compris qu'ils avaient…**été sur elle. Qu'ils l'avaient baisée**…On comprend pourquoi elle était complètement à poil. Ou presque. Elle n'avait qu'une paire de bottines en daim…mes bottines en daim, les bleues… (Lindroth 2007, 51–52, trans. Robnard)

Backtranslation:
It stank in there. Booze, vomit…
I, here, her there… Suzy P., damn… you should… get up…
There were four. He and his friends. I understood that **they… were on her. Fucked her… kind of**… you understood that because she was completely naked. Or almost so… except for a pair of suede boots… my suede boots, the blue ones…

It smelled awful in that room. Alcohol, vomit… Still I stood there. And she – Susie P., for chrissake! You should…get up. There were four of them. Him and his friends. I knew right away **they had done something horrible**. Because she was completely naked. Or almost. Right down to a pair of suede boots. My suede boots, the electric-blue ones. (Lindroth 2010, 39, trans. Marshall)

Jacques Robnard chose to translate swearwords using equivalents in French even if some of the insults are a bit outdated. For example, the Swedish text uses the word *mesig* (Lindroth 2005, 3), which means 'wimpish,' to characterize Susie P. Robnard translates it as *bouchée à l'émeri* (Lindroth 2007, 7),[9] a familiar but outdated expression for an adolescent today.

Agneta Ségol chose to keep some of the swearwords as well (as in Example 1 below) and to select which swearwords she considered significant for the force of the text. She cleared from the text those swearwords she judged to be unnecessary (Example 2 and 3) and sometimes went even further; while

---

9   The word-for-word translation is 'sealed with emery,' which means 'to be dumb.' It is an old expression referring to a process for hermetic sealing of bottles with a dark, abrasive granular rock.

omitting the swearword, she sometimes used a complex phrase structure (as in Example 3), suppressing its orality and raising the register:

(1) **Käften** nu då! tjatar Criz. (Casta 1999, 19)
Shut up now! nags Criz. (Backtranslation)

Vos gueules! crie Criz. (Casta 2004, 28, trans. Ségol)
Shut up! screams Criz. (Backtranslation)

(2) Äh, **vad fan**, säger Many. Det kunde du väl ha sagt (Casta 1999, 19)
Oh **what the hell**, says Many. Well, you could have said that before. (Backtranslation)

T'avais qu'à le dire avant. (Casta 2004, 29, trans. Ségol)
You should have said that before. (Backtranslation)

(3) **Fan** *vad jag är glad att ni dök upp* alltså, säger hon. Jag höll på att dö när jag märkte att ni inte var vid vägen. (Casta 1999, 106)
Damn I'm so glad you showed up, she says. I thought I was going to die when I noticed you were not on the path. (Backtranslation)

Vous pouvez pas vous imaginer *comme j'ai été heureuse quand je vous ai vus*, dit-elle. J'ai cru mourir quand vous n'étiez pas au rendez-vous. (Casta 2004, 139, trans. Ségol).
You can't imagine *how glad I was when I saw you*, she says. I thought I was dying when you were not at the rendezvous. (Backtranslation)

But even if the French translation of *Spelar död* has been polished a bit more to be closer to French norms and to keep the literary aspect of the text, in general the text is adequate in terms of Swedish norms. After an experiment with Swedish native speakers who also speak French fluently and French native speakers who speak Swedish fluently, it appears that readers who read the Swedish text and the French one perceived more violence on a scale of 0 to 5 in the Swedish text (an average of 5) than in the French one (an average of 4). However, if only the French text was read by only French-speaking people, the violence is felt to be identical to that of the original text (average of 5) (Alfvén and Engel 2015).

The role of the translators and editors

By choosing to remain faithful to the source text and to Swedish norms, the translators and editors attached to *Faire le mort* and *Quand les trains passent* played pivotal roles in how the books traveled from Sweden to France. The French translator of *När tågen går förbi*, Jacques Robnard, is not part of the children's literature system. Robnard used to translate plays for adults. During the 1950s, he worked in Sweden at the Royal Opera in Stockholm, learning Swedish in the process. He then worked for different French cultural institutions around the world before retiring. Translating is an activity he does 'on the side.' When Tiina Kaartama, a Finnish stage director, proposed that he translate Malin Lindroth's play, he accepted. Reflecting back a few years later, he said of the project: "I had never translated a work for children or young adults before Lindroth (...) and when I translated it, I never considered it as children's literature" (interview with Jacques Robnard, 2014). He translated it as a play, and it was then, when talking with an editor at Actes Sud Junior, that he began to take out the stage directions and transform the text into a work of prose. Robnard's purpose was to produce a translation as close as possible to the original text. He was not particularly aware of the norms of the French (or Swedish) children's literature system.

The French translator of *Spelar död*, Agneta Ségol, is Swedish, but has lived in France since the 1970s. She became interested in children's literature early on in life. During the 1990s, she worked at the famous publishing house Père Castor Flammarion, where she met, among others, Soazig Le Bail, who later become editor at Thierry Magnier and agreed to publish *Faire le mort*. Ségol has translated many novels and picture books from Swedish to French, including works by Astrid Lindgren, Henning Mankell and Annika Thor. She has attained a very well-established and respected position that has given her legitimacy and the opportunity to introduce new work. She "hope[s] not to be conscious of the norms in children's literature and think[s] first of the force of the text" (interview with Agneta Ségol, 2014). For her, the literary aspect of the text is most important.

A translator's position in the literary field plays a role in the translation process and has bearing on the final text. Robnard approached his translation from outside the field of children's literature and is thus free from its norms, while Ségol was inside the system, where she enjoys a high and respected status. This position, and her close relation to Soazig Le Bail, editor at Thierry Magnier and commissioning editor at that time, made it possible for *Faire le mort* to be published. Likewise, the positions of the publishing house and editor were pivotal in shaping the import and distribution of the two works.

Actes Sud Junior and Thierry Magnier are not the largest publishing houses in terms of distribution and economic capital (compared to Gallimard or Hachette),[10] but they have strong symbolic capital in the Bourdieusian sense (1992) and are well respected by other actors in the field. On the surface, these are two different publishing houses, but in fact they are quite homologous. Indeed, Thierry Magnier merged with Actes Sud Junior in 2006. Although they remain two distinct publishing houses, the same man, Thierry Magnier, an editor and publisher with strong standing in the field, heads both houses. His clout facilitated the importation and then the distribution of the two novels. The presence of *Faire le mort* and *Quand les trains passent* owe their existence in the French system to the role of their translators and the will of their editors. This combination was crucial to the introduction of the topic of unprovoked violence in France, which in turn made it possible for French authors to adopt the Swedish model.

Transforming norms?

I argue that the Swedish novels discussed in this chapter are *innovative* in Even-Zohar's sense of the term (1990). According to his polysystem theory, the position of a translated work in a literary (poly)system may become significant and play an active role in "shaping the center of the polysystem" (Even-Zohar 1990, 46), where high literature and literary models reside. Translation can introduce new models into a literary system, particularly at a time when older models no longer correspond to the needs of a new generation. To determine the position of *Faire le mort* and *Quand les trains passent* in the French system, it is necessary to identify whether they are connected to *innovatory* ("primary") or *conservatory* ("secondary") repertoires" (*ibid.*) Even-Zohar distinguishes three situations where this can happen:

> (a) when a polysystem has not yet been crystallized, that is to say, when a literature is "young," in the process of being established; (b) when a literature is either "peripheral" (within a large group of correlated literatures) or "weak," or both; and (c) when there are turning points, crises, or literary vacuums in a literature. (Even-Zohar 1990b, 48)

---

10   Thierry Magnier publishes more Scandinavian novels for adolescents than any other French publisher (Alfvén 2016, 166). Actes Sud Junior is also interested in literary and sometimes cheeky texts.

Measured by these criteria, it seems that *Faire le mort* and *Quand les trains passent* arrived in France at a historical moment where old models and norms were no longer tenable, as illustrated by the moral panic that ensued (Alfvén 2016, 145–148). Both are literary and consecrated novels that won literary prizes and are recognized by critics, underlining the literary quality of the texts. The translation of the works adheres to Swedish norms and introduces a topic rarely exploited until now by French authors in a realistic genre. Only Guillaume Guéraud, with *Je mourrai pas gibier* (2006), dared to write on unprovoked violence, but he did so by focusing on a specific, gory style with lots of bloody scenes. Later works, such as Julia Kino's *Adieu la chair* (2007) and Clémentine Beauvais's *La pouilleuse* (2012), can be said to be French children's novels that follow the Swedish example. The transfer of the two Swedish novels addressed here also shows the pivotal role of both the editor and translators. Their positions inside or outside the system, and the strong symbolic capital of the editor and one translator were important factors that made their publication in France possible at the time.

The translation and reception of *Faire le mort* and *Quand les trains passent* highlight a deep and durable change in the norms of the French system. By introducing and shaping unprovoked violence in a realistic genre, these works filled a vacuum in the French system and injected it with a new dynamic. They made possible the introduction of new models and created openings for topics that had previously been taboo. Since their publication, some French authors have even dared to write about unprovoked violence themselves (Alfvén 2016, 168–173). The cases examined here suggest that the significance of Swedish literature for adolescents is far greater than the modest numbers of translated titles suggests. Indeed, *Spelar död* and *När tågen går förbi* can be seen as early markers of an evolution in young adult literature playing out not only in Sweden and France, but in (poly)systems around the globe.

Bibliography

Alfvén, Valérie. 2016. *Violence gratuite et adolescents-bourreaux: Réception, traduction et enjeux de deux romans suédois pour adolescents, en France, au début des années 2000*. Doctoral diss., Stockholms Universitet.

Alfvén, Valérie and Hugues Engel. 2015. "Hur översätts oprovocerat våld i ungdomslitteratur från svenska till franska?" In *Översättning för en ny generation: nordisk barn- och ungdomslitteratur på export*, edited by Valérie Alfvén, Hugues Engel and Charlotte Lindgren, 31–41. Falun: Högskolan Dalarna. http://urn.kb.se/resolve?urn=urn:nbn:se:su:diva-118393

Barnabé, Fanny. 2012. "Les polémiques autour de la littérature jeunesse, ou la quête sans cesse rejouée de la légitimité." *COnTEXTES* [online] 10. https://doi.org/10.4000/contextes.5020.

Bourdieu, Pierre. 1992. *Les règles de l'art: Genèse et structure du champ littéraire*. Paris: Éditions du Seuil.

Casta, Stefan. 1999. *Spelar död*. Bromma: Opal förlag.

Casta, Stefan. 2004. *Faire le mort*. Translated by Agneta Ségol. Paris: Éditions Thierry Magnier.

Christensen, Nina. 2011. "Les tout-petits et leurs albums: Une perspective scandinave." *La Revue des livres pour enfants* 257, February: 83–88. Special issue on "Les pays nordiques."

Citrouille. 2004. "Romans ados, Sélection, Librairies des sorcières." *Le magazine des libraires* 39, November: 30–31.

Cohen, Stanley. 2011. *Folk Devils and Moral Panics: The Creation of the Mods and Rockers*. Abingdon: Routledge.

Combet, Claude. 2007. "Sous surveillance." *Livres Hebdo* 0714, December 14, 2007.

Delbrassine, Daniel. 2006. *Le Roman pour adolescents aujourd'hui: Ecriture, thématiques et réception*. Créteil: SCÉRÉN-CRDP & La Joie par les livres.

Delbrassine, Daniel. 2008. "Censure et autocensure dans le roman pour la Jeunesse." *Paroles* 2: 8–11.

Escarpit, Denise. 2008. *La Littérature de jeunesse: Itinéraires d'hier à aujourd'hui*. Paris: Magnard.

Even-Zohar, Itamar. 1990a. "Polysystem Theory." *Poetics Today* 11, no. 1: 9–26.

Even-Zohar, Itamar. 1990b. "The Position of Translated Literature within the Literary Polysystem." *Poetics Today* 11, no. 1: 45–51.

Faure, Marion. 2007. "Un âge vraiment pas tendre." *Le Monde des livres*, November 29, 2007. Accessed April 14, 2020. https://www.lemonde.fr/livres/article/2007/11/29/un-age-vraiment-pas-tendre_983787_3260.html.

France Culture. 2007. *Du grain à moudre*. Radio broadcast. December 21, 2007.

Gégène. 2010. "Ce roman a pris trois ans de ma vie." *Citrouille* 55, March: 45–47.

Joubert, Bernard. 2008. "Des recommandations mais pas de loi." *Livres Hebdo* 0716, January 11, 2018.

Kokko, Mirja. 2011. "Un souvenir ne finit jamais: Face à la mort, des pistes de consolation dans la littérature pour enfants nordique." *La Revue des livres pour enfants* 257, February: 111–118.

Kriegel, Blandine. 2002. *La Violence à la télévision: Rapport de la Mission d'évaluation d'analyse et de propositions relatives aux représentations violentes à la télévision*. Paris: Ministère de la culture et de la communication.

Lindroth, Malin. 2005. *När tågen går förbi*. Stockholm: Dramaten förlag.

Lindroth, Malin. 2007. *Quand les trains passent*. Translated by Jacques Robnard. Arles: Actes Sud Junior.

Lindroth, Malin. 2010. *Train Wreck*. Translated by Julia Marshall. Toronto: Annick Press.

Longres, Blandine. 2017. "'Un livre doit être un danger', disait Cioran…" *Littérature, traduction*, December 13, 2007. http://blongre.hautetfort.com/archive/2007/12/11/litterature-pour-ados.html.

Nières-Chevrel, Isabelle. 2009. *Introduction à la littérature de jeunesse*. Paris: Didier Jeunesse.

Noiville, Florence. 2007. "La noirceur contestée des livres de jeunesse, des éditeurs répondent à notre enquête." December 20, 2007. Accessed April 14, 2020. https://www.lemonde.fr/livres/article/2007/12/20/la-noirceur-contestee-des-livres-de-jeunesse_991706_3260.html.

Owen, Mary. 2003. "Developing a Love of Reading: Why Young Adult Literature Is Important." *Orana* 39, no. 1: 11–17.

Poslaniec, Christian. 1997. *L'Évolution de la littérature de jeunesse de 1850 à nos jours au travers de l'instance narrative*. Doctoral diss., Université Paris-Nord: Presses universitaires du septentrion.

Robnard, Jacques. Interview by Valérie Alfvén. 2014, Paris.

Roguet, Simon. 2007. "Littérature malsaine, vraiment?" *Libération*, December 21, 2007. Accessed April 14, 2020. http://livres.blogs.liberation.fr/2007/12/21/littrature-mals/.

Rolland, Annie. 2008. *Qui a peur de la littérature ado?* Paris: Éditions Thierry Magnier.

Ségol, Agneta. Interview by Valérie Alfvén. 2014, Caen.

Svenbro, Anna. 2011. "Quelques repères historiques et culturels." *La Revue des livres pour enfants* 257, February: 83–88.

Svensson, Sonja. 1995. "Tankar kring några tendenser i 90-talets ungdomsbok." *Abrakadabra*, October: 18–26.

Svensson, Sonja. 1999. "Dödspolare, skuggmän och förlorade fäder. Idyllfobin i 1990-talet ungdomsbok." In *Föränkring och förnyelse. Nordiska ungdomsromaner inemot år 2000*, edited by Eli Flatekval, 107–121. Oslo: Cappelen Akademisk Förlag/LNU.

Tanguy, Jean. 2009. *Chroniques de littérature pour la jeunesse*. August 19, 2009. http://www.livres-jeunesse.net/Ouvrages/lindroth.htm.

Thaler, Danielle and Jean-Bart, Alain. 2002. *Les Enjeux du roman pour adolescents. Roman historique, roman miroir, roman d'aventures*. Paris/Budapest/Turin: L'Harmattan.

Toury, Gideon. 1995. *Descriptive Translations Studies – and Beyond*. Amsterdam/Philadelphia: John Benjamins.

Index

acceptability/adequacy 13, 18, 34, 46, 134, 139, 149, 151, 188, 234, 235, 253, 264, 271
adaptation 17, 18, 21, 22, 27, 75, 84, 85, 114, 117, 126, 138, 144, 147, 149, 160, 164, 167, 170, 172, 192, 197, 198, 204, 207, 212, 249, 250, 252, 258
    cultural adaptation 29, 62, 141, 142, 146, 151, 179, 181, 184
agency 164, 217
agent 15, 24, 26, 28, 56, 57, 58, 73, 75, 82, 88, 94, 100, 139, 198, 203, 210
Alice's Adventures in Wonderland 30, 62, 117, 146, 159
Andersen, Hans Christian 114, 147, 149, 175, 201
Anglophone market 24, 25, 29, 42, 55, 64, 98, 104, 120, 142, 143, 150, 151, 251
asymmetry 11, 22, 26, 98, 218
Baker, Mona 12, 222
Bassnett, Susan 14, 164
book market 15, 21, 23, 24, 27, 30, 44, 47, 49, 59, 64, 93, 98, 104, 115, 119, 120, 142, 151, 200, 234
Bourdieu, Pierre 15, 76, 93, 273
Brazil 27, 31, 111, 199
Brothers Grimm, the 114, 170, 199, 201, 250
canon 21, 85, 112, 143, 161, 180, 202
Carroll, Lewis 30, 62, 160
censorship 19, 118, 211, 250, 267
child image 19, 22, 29, 30, 32, 141, 144, 146, 147, 151, 159, 162, 170, 174, 216, 217, 219, 226, 250
co-edition 27
co-editions 26, 94
colonization 14, 115, 165, 232
commercialization 29, 68, 100, 118, 143, 203
co-productions 94, 149, 235
crossover 161, 165, 172, 174, 215, 217, 219, 226
cultural capital 15, 85
cultural studies 14, 18
cultural translation 26, 75

culture-specific items 17, 23, 31, 126, 127, 145, 146, 151, 180, 182, 185
Descriptive Translation Studies 31, 112, 198, 233
digital books 29, 150
discourse analysis 12, 21
diversity 29, 49, 59, 141, 142, 149, 232
domestication/foreignization 14, 19, 45, 51, 62, 66, 117, 125, 137, 144, 151, 160, 164, 167, 180, 193
dual audience 22, 88, 126, 127, 148, 161, 215
editor 21, 28, 33, 41, 97, 115, 126
    text editor 28, 134
equivalence 117, 181
ethics 14, 181, 265
Even-Zohar, Itamar 13, 26, 75, 105, 112, 273
fable 114, 204, 251
fairy tale 18, 116, 147, 165, 198, 219, 249
field 15, 27, 51, 74, 93, 235, 264
frame 14, 137, 149, 170, 250, 259
France 26, 33, 42, 94, 210, 234, 265
function 13, 18, 73, 142, 162, 181, 200, 218, 233
globalization 29, 43, 141, 143, 231
glocalization 51
habitus 15, 76
Harry Potter 17, 43, 47, 51, 59, 146
Hebrew 57, 84, 86
Heilbron, Johan 15, 42, 93, 98, 106
Hermans, Theo 15, 217, 233
Hungary 31, 166
ideology 20, 21, 145
institution 14, 49, 94, 118, 198, 272
intertextuality 142, 215, 236
Ireland 24, 47, 55
Jewish society 26, 74, 179
Katan, David 14
Kruger, Haidee 22, 52, 144, 182
Lathey, Gillian 19, 68, 182, 222
Lefevere, André 14, 198, 233
literary system 13, 112, 198, 265
localization 17, 151, 232
Low Countries, the 142, 235

marketing 22, 44, 49, 66, 121, 143, 151, 184, 234
mediation 17, 44, 74, 134, 138, 175, 216, 218, 219
moral 31, 42, 168, 198, 200, 210, 251, 267
multimodality 22, 215, 233, 252
Munday, Jeremy 17
names, translation of 19, 46, 62, 132, 137, 145, 165, 184, 202, 235
national literature 16, 19, 27, 57, 94, 104, 111, 199
nonsense 30, 160, 161
non-standard language 106, 118, 126, 187, 192, 266
Nord, Christiane 13, 18
norms 13, 18, 34, 76, 113, 125, 137, 138, 145, 171, 233, 244, 268, 272
Oittinen, Riitta 19, 46, 162, 181, 217
orality 63, 170, 200, 202, 205, 210, 216, 271
O'Sullivan, Emer 19, 144, 217
patronage 20, 31, 57, 198
Perrault, Charles 31, 114, 198, 201, 249
picture book 28, 32, 48, 58, 94, 126, 145, 174, 215, 232, 250
plurilingualism 50, 63, 101, 150
Poland 52, 78, 183
polysystem 13, 17, 27, 105, 112, 126, 273
power 14, 22, 28, 42, 93, 106, 133, 144, 160, 250
pragmatics 12
prizes 15, 25, 47, 118, 265, 274
production 15, 23, 43, 58, 94, 112, 113, 231, 234
reader 11, 14, 27, 43, 46, 141, 144, 180
  adult reader 49, 127, 148
  aloud reader 127, 148, 218, 219

child reader 17, 18, 19, 22, 30, 46, 49, 61, 160, 162, 168, 170, 175, 250
  implied reader 30, 32, 162, 163, 170, 175, 218
reception 18, 43, 68, 112, 145, 204, 267
retranslation 20, 30, 32, 62, 149, 219, 226
rewriting 20, 31, 112, 164, 197, 198, 207
Sapiro, Gisèle 15, 93, 106, 143
Shavit, Zohar 17, 126, 216
simplification 33, 136, 139, 172
Skopos theory 13, 18
Slovenia 125
sociology 14, 26, 93
Spain 26, 94
spoken language 87, 129
stylistic changes 136, 167, 205, 257
subsidies 25, 49, 55, 63, 67, 102, 128
Sweden 142, 265
symbolic capital 93, 107, 273, 274
taboo 29, 127, 149, 264, 267, 268
Toury, Gideon 13, 17, 20, 26, 34, 75, 233, 235, 244, 268
translation flows 15, 42, 51, 93, 106, 141, 151
translation policy 59, 66, 142
translation strategies 13, 30, 62, 141, 162, 204, 216, 217
United Kingdom 24, 42, 59, 97, 251
untranslatability 161
Van Coillie, Jan 11, 175, 219
Venuti, Lawrence 14, 43, 62, 151, 180
Vermeer, Hans 13
violence 33, 249, 264
Wolf, Michaela 14
young adult 33, 47, 61, 74, 126, 143, 253, 264
Yugoslavia 251
Zipes, Jack 162, 198

www.ingramcontent.com/pod-product-compliance
Lightning Source LLC
Chambersburg PA
CBHW051050230426
43666CB00012B/2634